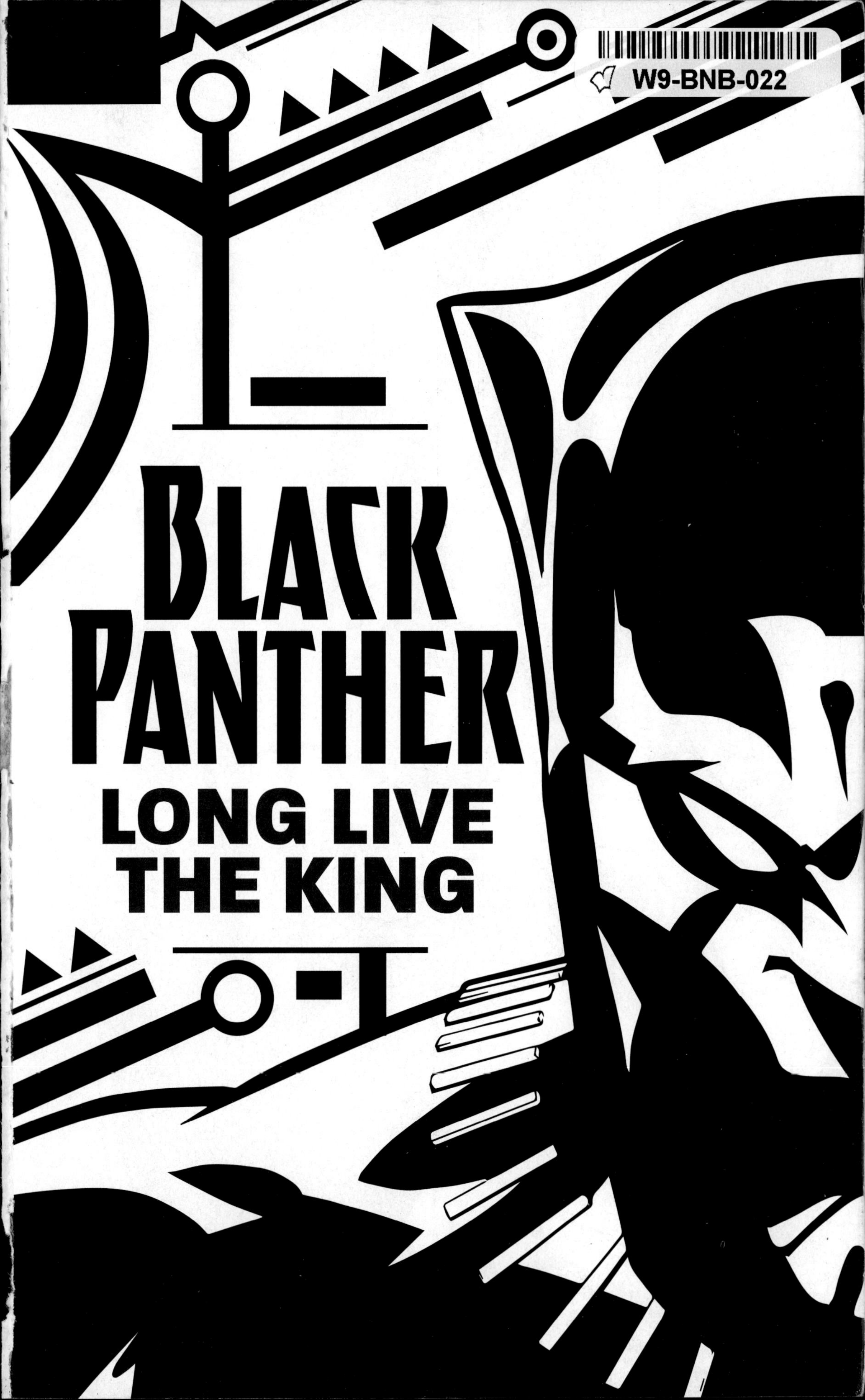
BLACK
PANTHER
LONG LIVE
THE KING

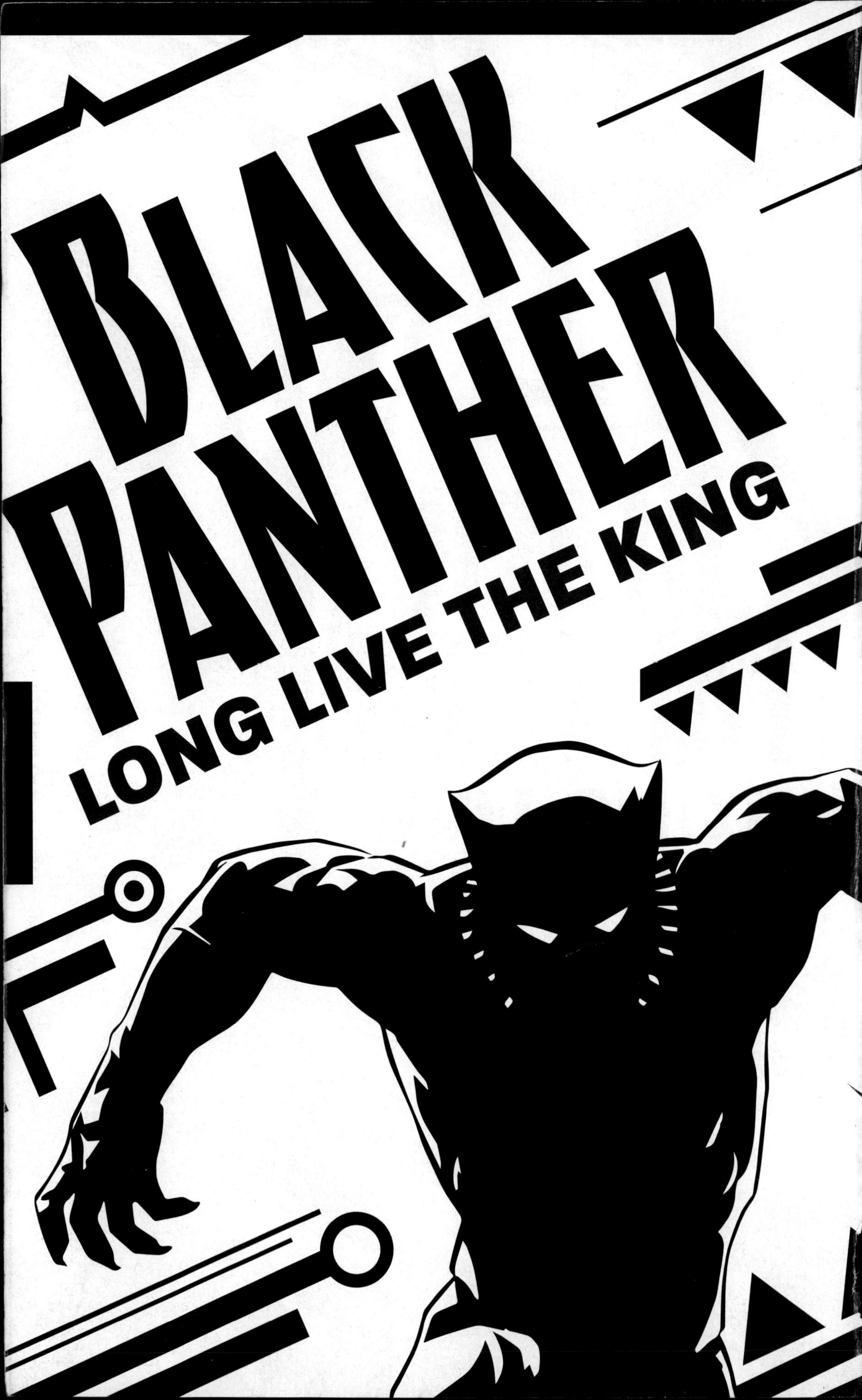
BLACK PANTHER
LONG LIVE THE KING

"BLACKOUT," "THE SACRIFICE" & "OBINNA'S FOLLY"
writer **NNEDI OKORAFOR**
artist **ANDRÉ LIMA ARAÚJO**
color artist **CHRIS O'HALLORAN**

"KEEP YOUR FRIENDS CLOSE"
writer **AARON COVINGTON**
artist **MARIO DEL PENNINO**
color artist **CHRIS O'HALLORAN**

"UNDER THE BRIDGE"
writer **NNEDI OKORAFOR**
penciler **TANA FORD**
inkers **TANA FORD, TERRY PALLOT & SCOTT HANNA**
color artists **IAN HERRING & IRMA KNIIVILA**

letterer **COMICRAFT'S JIMMY BETANCOURT**
cover artists **ANDRÉ LIMA ARAÚJO & CHRIS O'HALLORAN** (#1-2, #5),
KHARY RANDOLPH & EMILIO LOPEZ (#3-4) and **DAVID WILLIAMS & CHRIS O'HALLORAN** (#6)
assistant editors **TOM GRONEMAN & ALLISON STOCK**
editor **DEVIN LEWIS**

Black Panther created by **STAN LEE & JACK KIRBY**

collection editor **MARK D. BEAZLEY**
assistant editor **CAITLIN O'CONNELL**
associate managing editor **KATERI WOODY**
senior editor, special projects **JENNIFER GRÜNWALD**
vp production & special projects **JEFF YOUNGQUIST**
svp print, sales & marketing **DAVID GABRIEL**
book designer **JAY BOWEN** with **MANNY MEDEROS**
logo **RIAN HUGHES**

editor in chief **C.B. CEBULSKI**
chief creative officer **JOE QUESADA**
president **DAN BUCKLEY**
executive producer **ALAN FINE**

BLACK PANTHER: LONG LIVE THE KING. First printing 2018. ISBN 978-1-302-90538-5. Published by MARVEL WORLDWIDE, INC., a subsidiary of MARVEL ENTERTAINMENT, LLC. OFFICE OF PUBLICATION: 135 West 50th Street, New York, NY 10020. Copyright © 2018 MARVEL No similarity between any of the names, characters, persons, and/or institutions in this magazine with those of any living or dead person or institution is intended, and any such similarity which may exist is purely coincidental. **Printed in Canada.** DAN BUCKLEY, President, Marvel Entertainment; JOHN NEE, Publisher; JOE QUESADA, Chief Creative Officer; TOM BREVOORT, SVP of Publishing; DAVID BOGART, SVP of Business Affairs & Operations, Publishing & Partnership; DAVID GABRIEL, SVP of Sales & Marketing, Publishing; JEFF YOUNGQUIST, VP of Production & Special Projects; DAN CARR, Executive Director of Publishing Technology; ALEX MORALES, Director of Publishing Operations; DAN EDINGTON, Managing Editor; SUSAN CRESPI, Production Manager; STAN LEE, Chairman Emeritus. For information regarding advertising in Marvel Comics or on Marvel.com, please contact Vit DeBellis, Custom Solutions & Integrated Advertising Manager, at vdebellis@marvel.com. For Marvel subscription inquiries, please call 888-511-5480. **Manufactured between 3/30/2018 and 5/1/2018 by SOLISCO PRINTERS, SCOTT, QC, CANADA.**

10 9 8 7 6 5 4 3 2 1

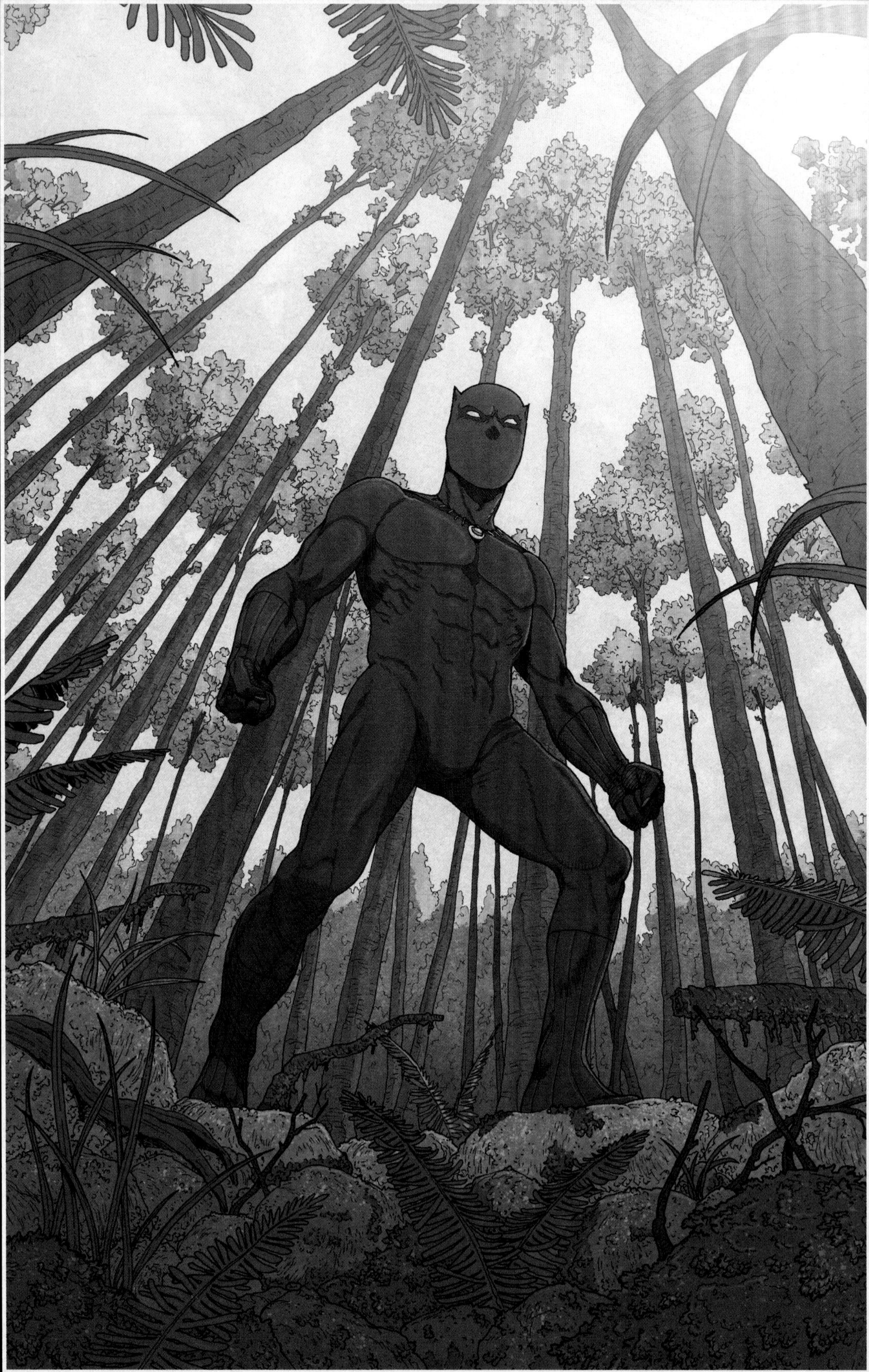

BLACKOUT

PREVIOUSLY

BLACK PANTHER is the ancestral ceremonial title of **T'CHALLA**, the king of Wakanda. T'Challa splits his time between defending his kingdom and helping protect the entire world, as a member of super hero teams such as the Avengers and the Ultimates.

The African nation of **WAKANDA** is the most technologically advanced society on the globe – thanks in great part to its large deposit of an extremely rare natural resource called **VIBRANIUM**. The Vibranium's unique properties can sometimes have powerful and interesting effects on the country.

Recent events such as a biblical flood that killed thousands, an invasion by the villain Thanos and a rebellion to overthrow the dynasty have humbled the kingdom. T'Challa and his allies struggle to find a new way forward for their nation and people.

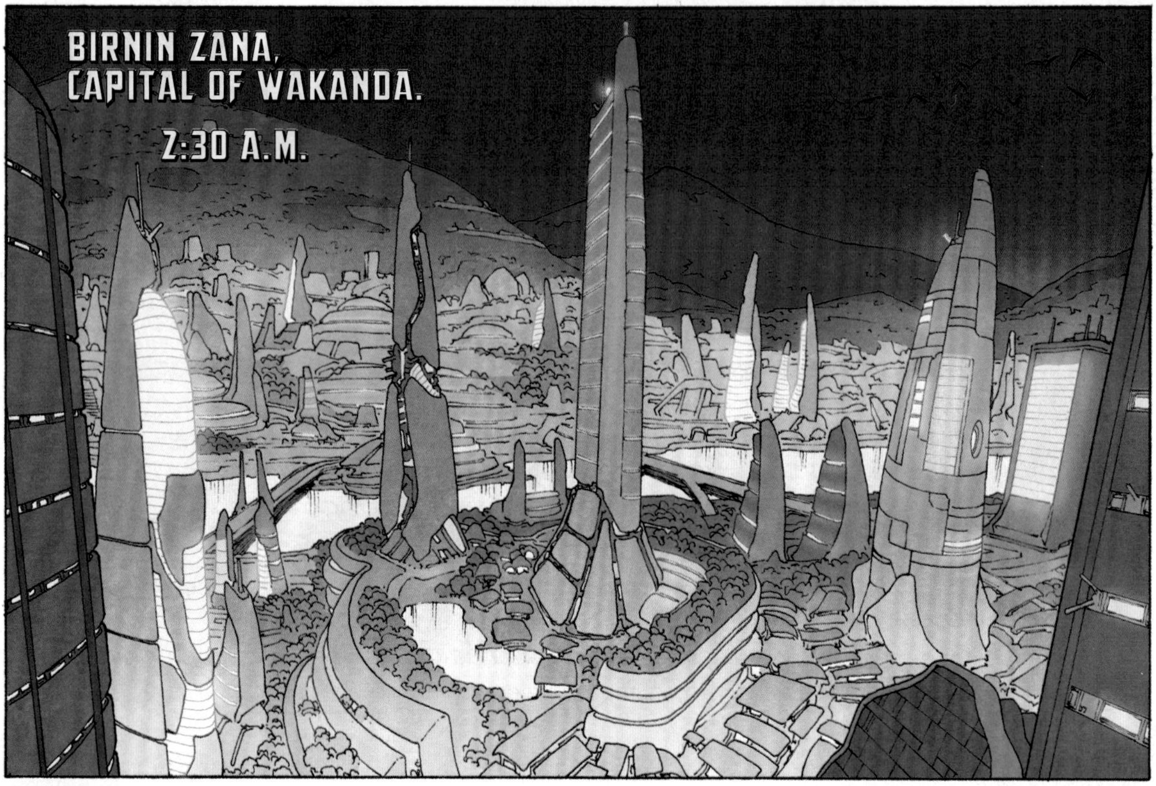
BIRNIN ZANA,
CAPITAL OF WAKANDA.
2:30 A.M.

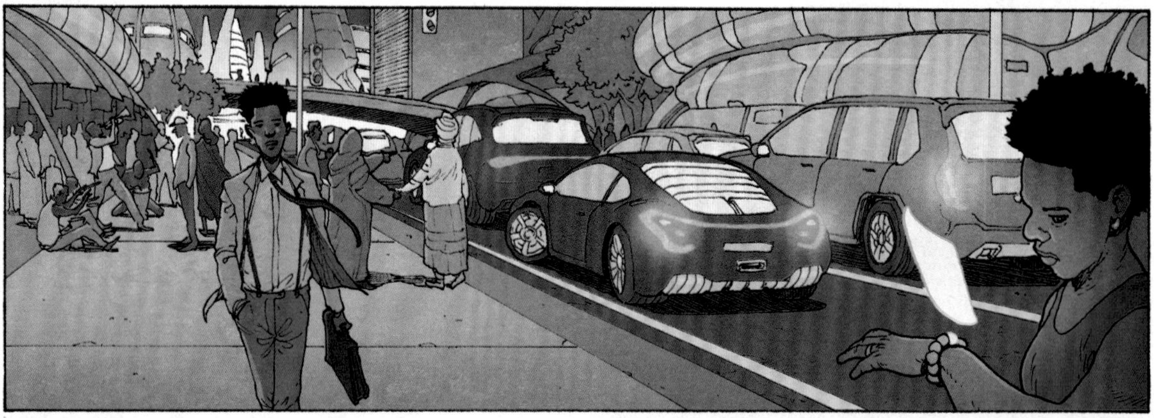

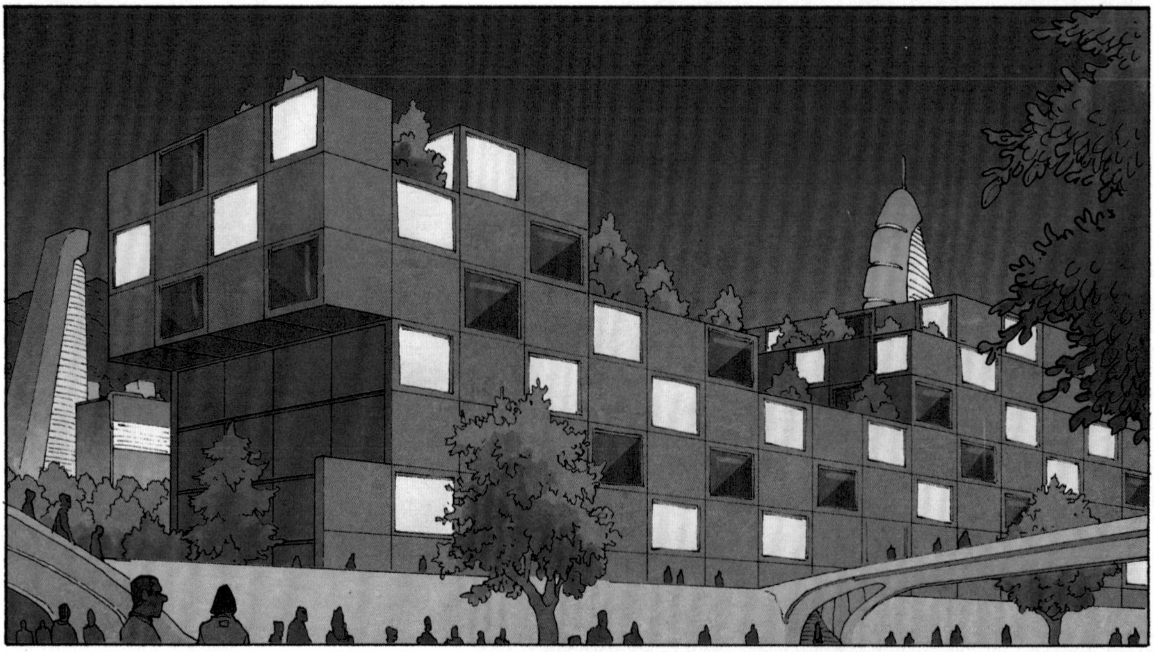

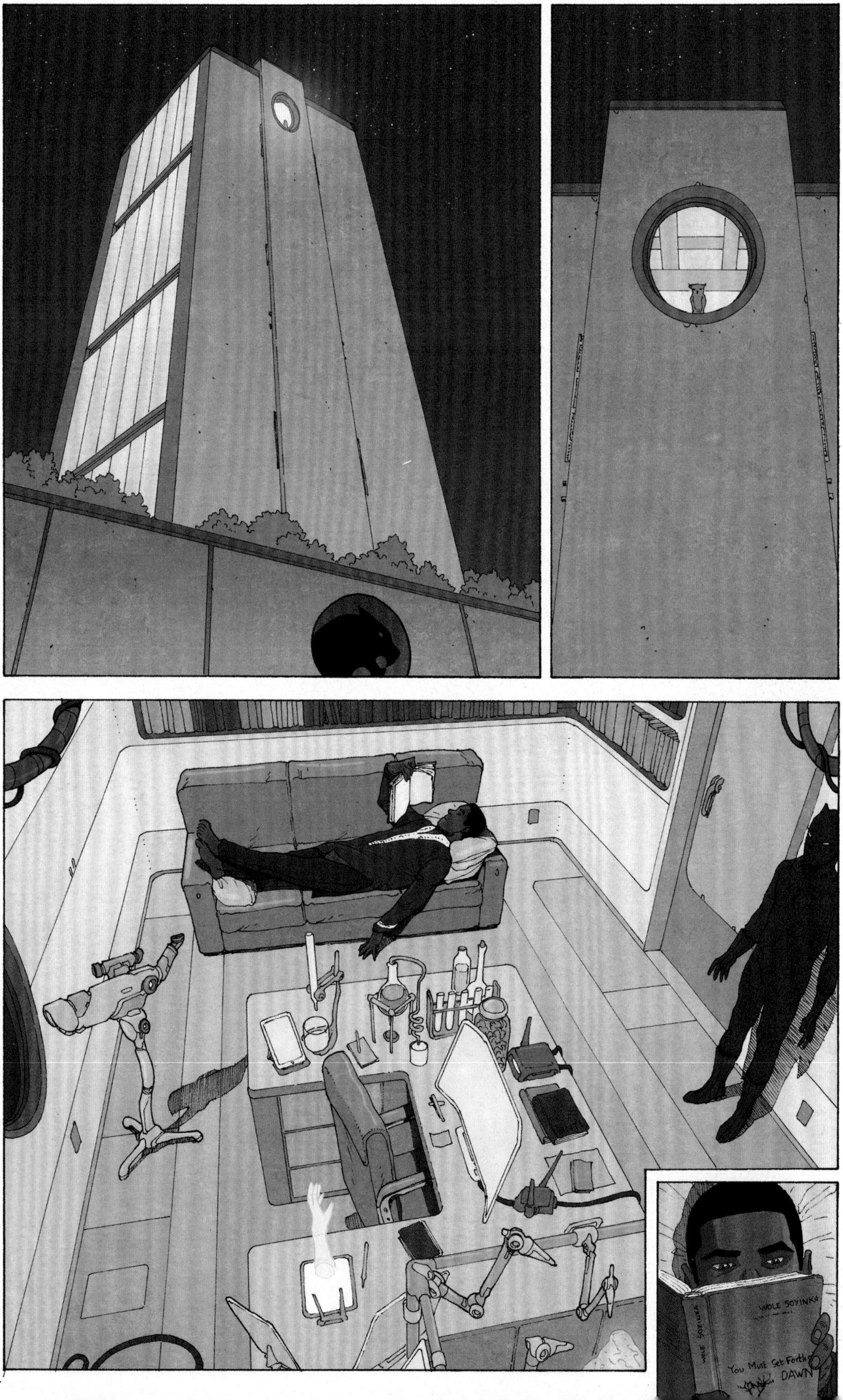
WOLE SOYINKA
WOLE SOYINKA
You Must Set Forth
DAWN

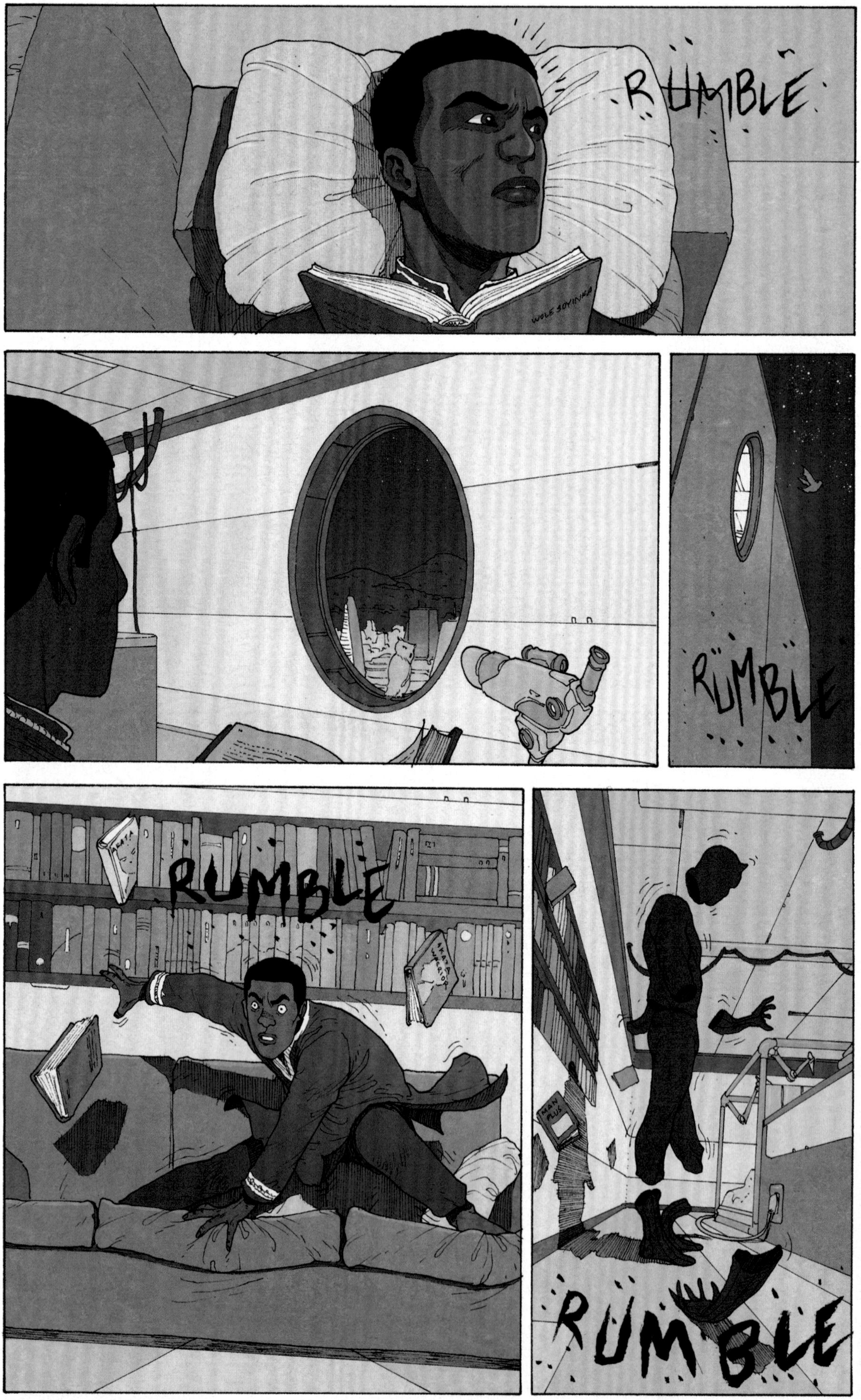
RUMBLE
WOLE SOYINKA
RUMBLE
RUMBLE
AKATA WARRIOR
MAN PLUS
RUMBLE

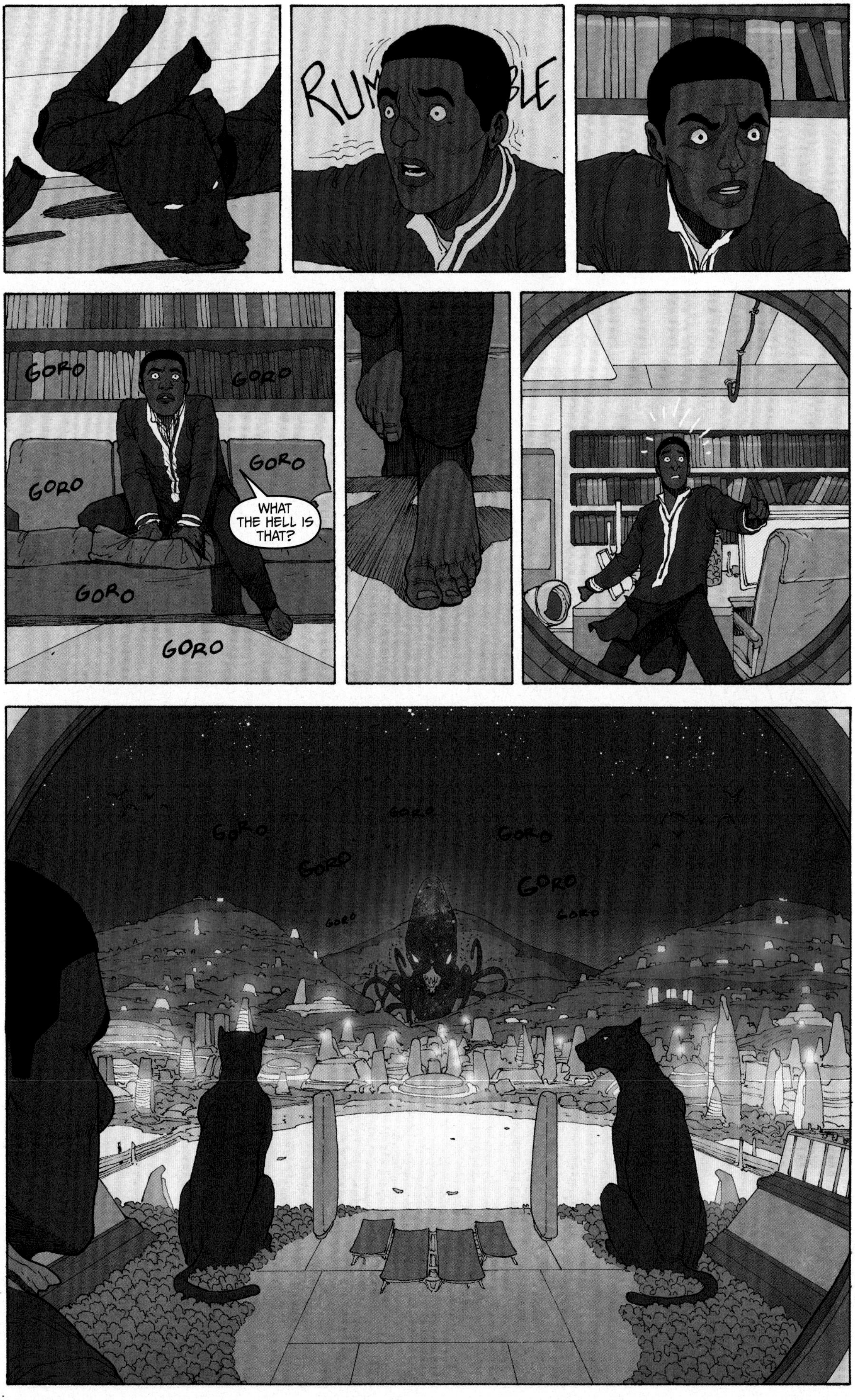
RUM
BLE
GORO
GORO
GORO
GORO
WHAT THE HELL IS THAT?
GORO
GORO
GORO
GORO
GORO
GORO
GORO
GORO
GORO

GORO

GORO

GORO

GORO

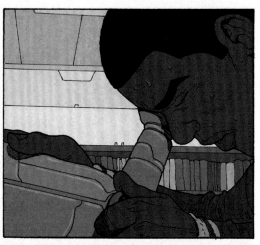

HOOOOOOOMM MMMMMMMMMMMM

MMMMM MMM

MMMMMMMMMMMMM

TH-THAT *NOISE!*

LIKE IT'S--NNGH-- CRACKING MY SKULL!

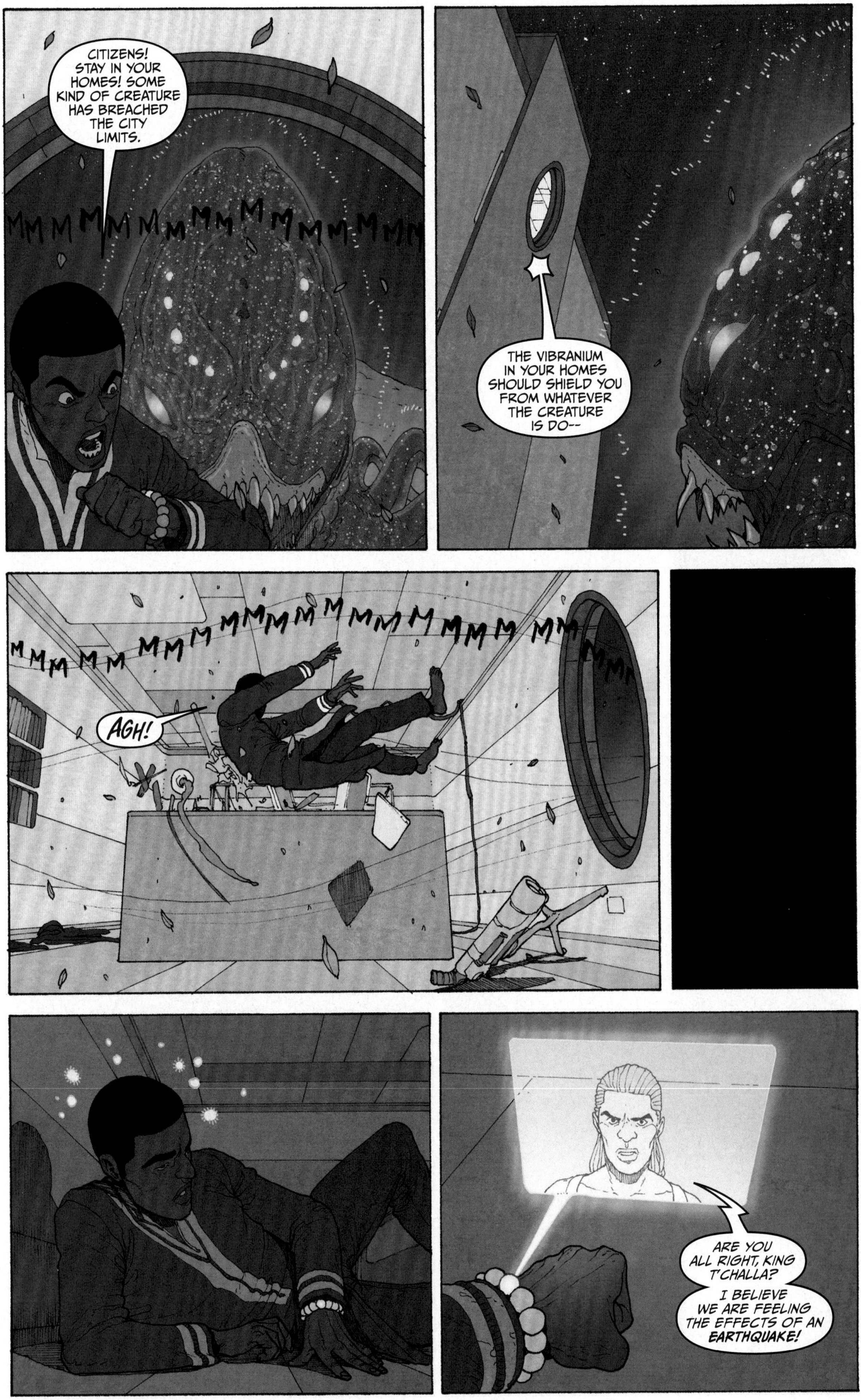
CITIZENS! STAY IN YOUR HOMES! SOME KIND OF CREATURE HAS BREACHED THE CITY LIMITS.
THE VIBRANIUM IN YOUR HOMES SHOULD SHIELD YOU FROM WHATEVER THE CREATURE IS DO--
AGH!
ARE YOU ALL RIGHT, KING T'CHALLA?
I BELIEVE WE ARE FEELING THE EFFECTS OF AN EARTHQUAKE!

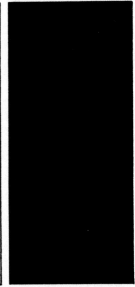

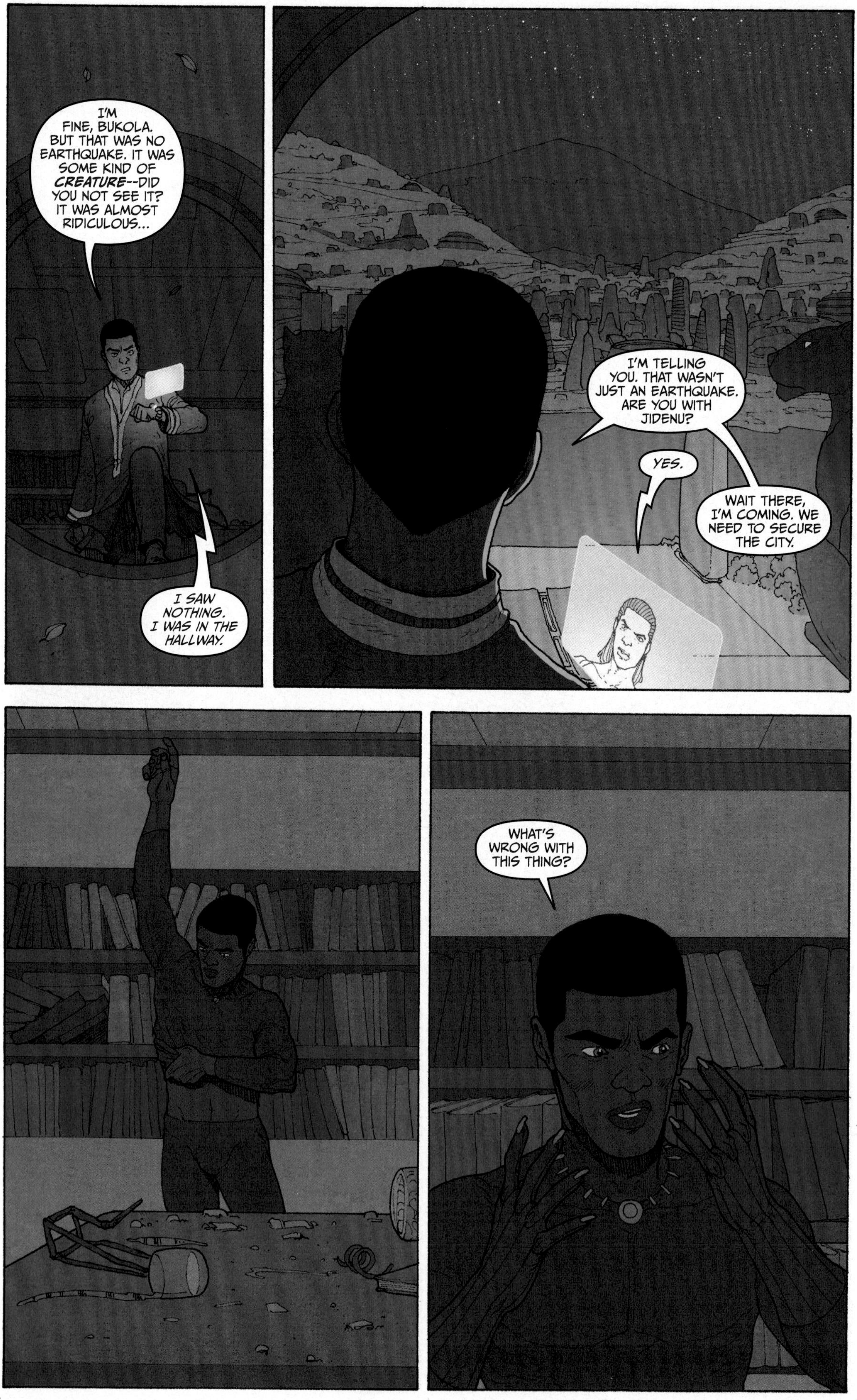
I'M FINE, BUKOLA. BUT THAT WAS NO EARTHQUAKE. IT WAS SOME KIND OF *CREATURE*--DID YOU NOT SEE IT? IT WAS ALMOST RIDICULOUS...
I SAW NOTHING. I WAS IN THE HALLWAY.
I'M TELLING YOU. THAT WASN'T JUST AN EARTHQUAKE. ARE YOU WITH JIDENU?
YES.
WAIT THERE, I'M COMING. WE NEED TO SECURE THE CITY.
WHAT'S WRONG WITH THIS THING?

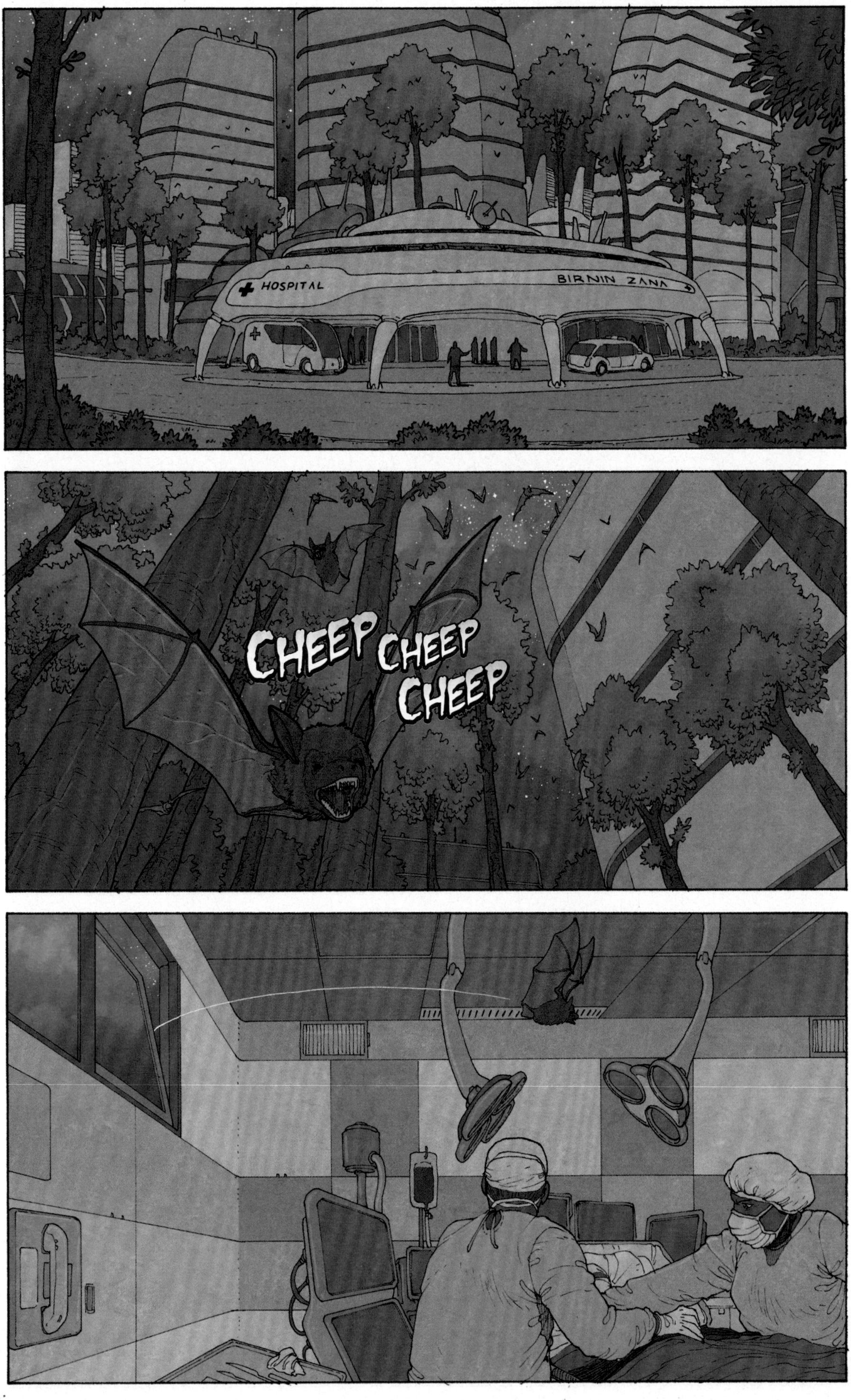
HOSPITAL
BIRNIN ZANA
CHEEP CHEEP
CHEEP

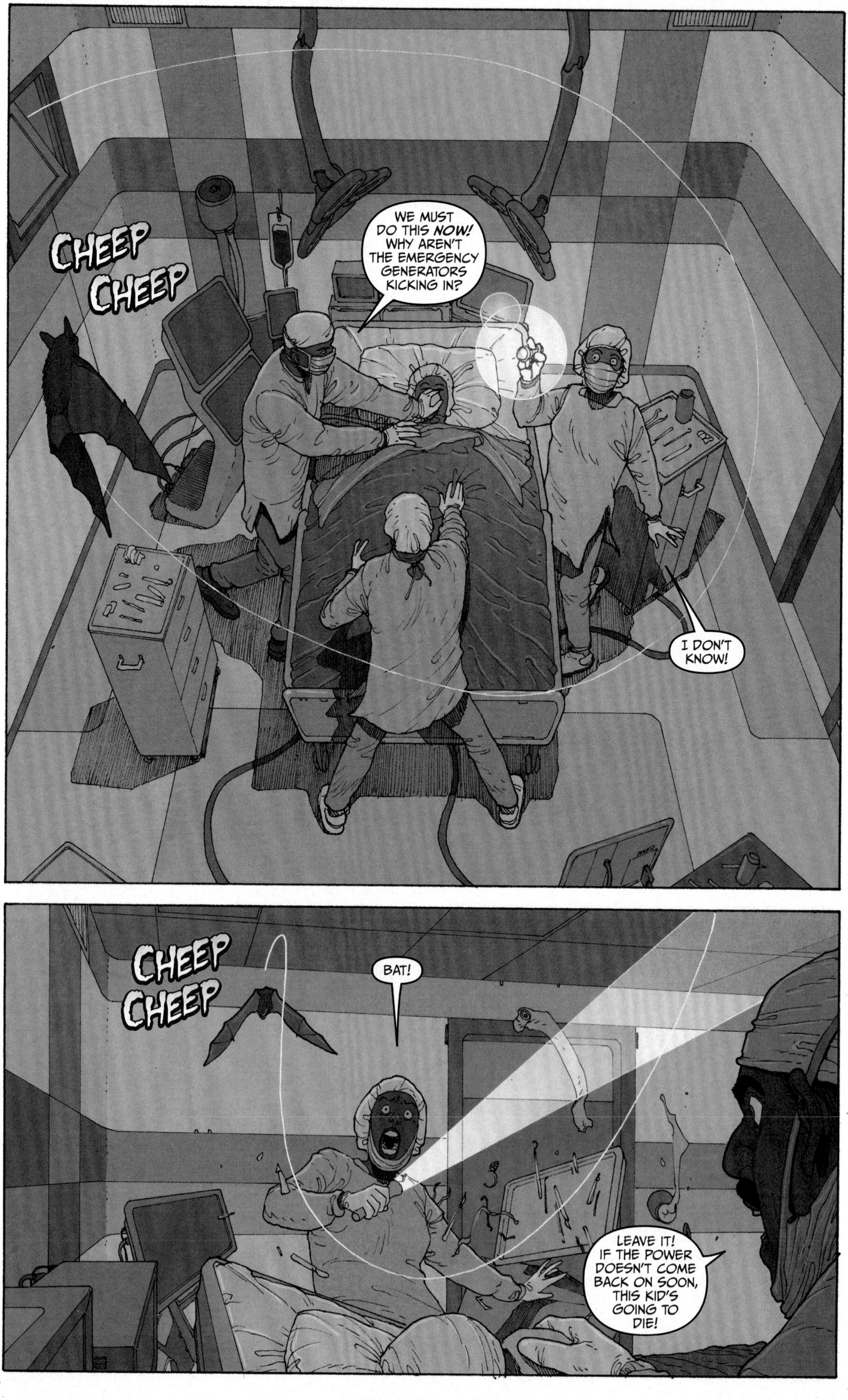
CHEEP CHEEP
WE MUST DO THIS NOW! WHY AREN'T THE EMERGENCY GENERATORS KICKING IN?
I DON'T KNOW!
CHEEP CHEEP
BAT!
LEAVE IT! IF THE POWER DOESN'T COME BACK ON SOON, THIS KID'S GOING TO DIE!

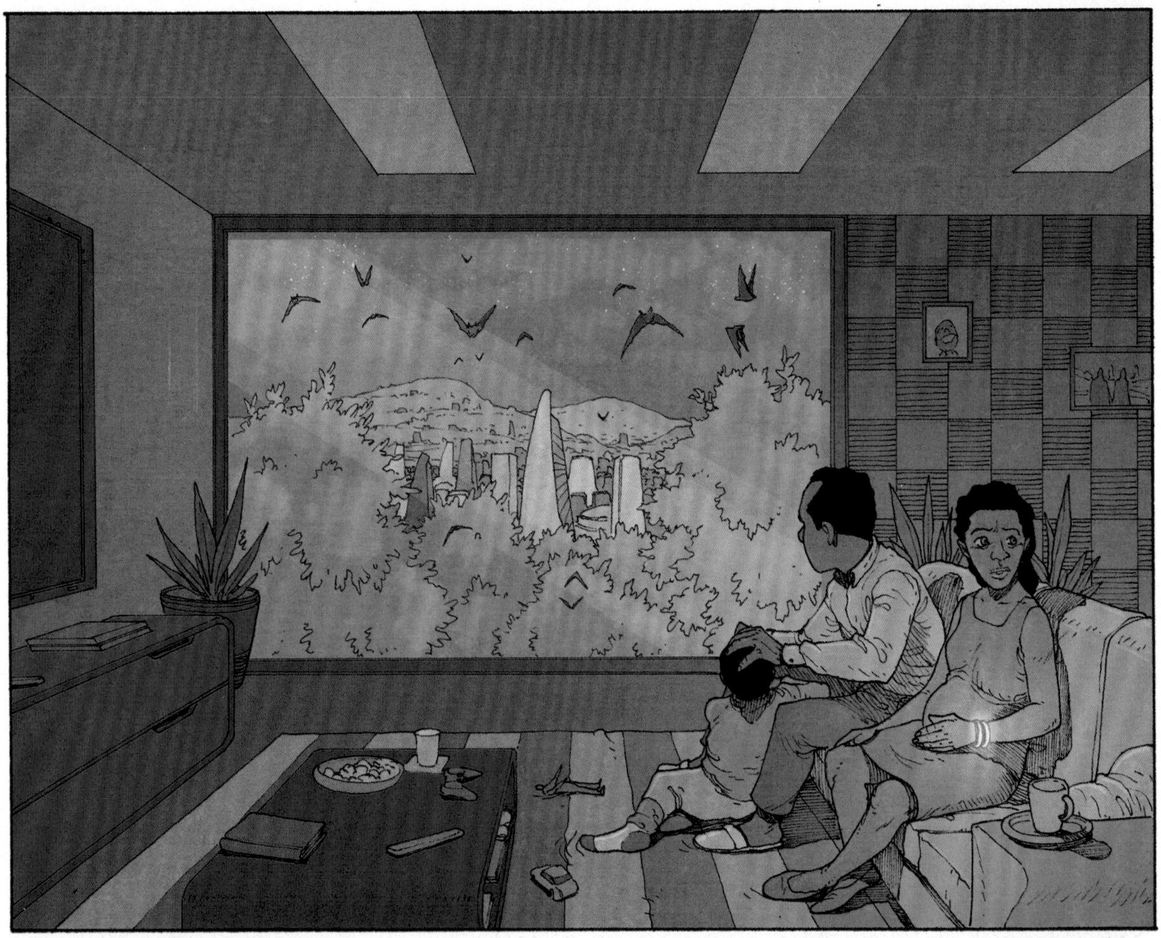

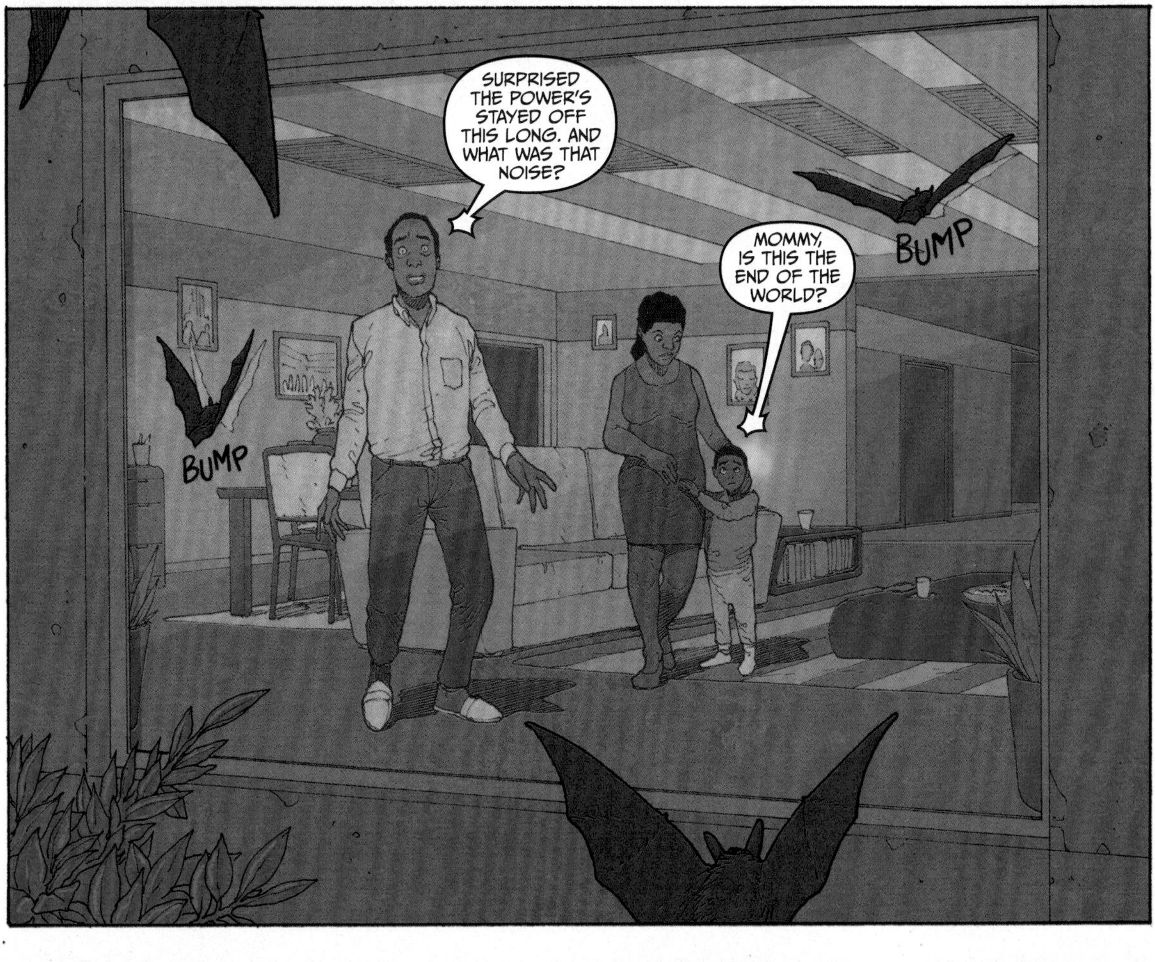
SURPRISED THE POWER'S STAYED OFF THIS LONG. AND WHAT WAS THAT NOISE?
BUMP
MOMMY, IS THIS THE END OF THE WORLD?
BUMP

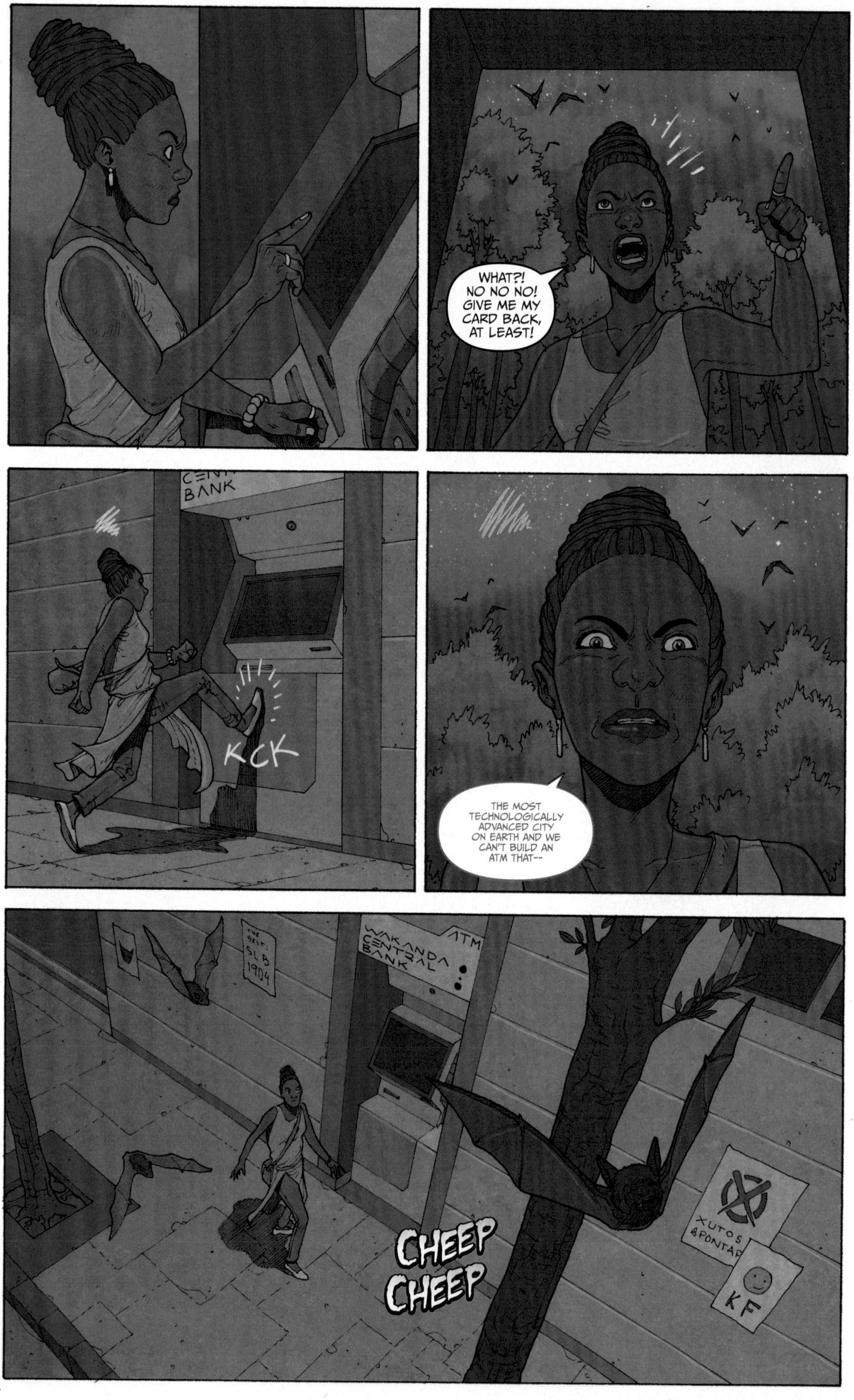
WHAT?! NO NO NO! GIVE ME MY CARD BACK, AT LEAST!
KCK
THE MOST TECHNOLOGICALLY ADVANCED CITY ON EARTH AND WE CAN'T BUILD AN ATM THAT--
WAKANDA CENTRAL BANK
ATM
SLB 1904
KF
CHEEP
CHEEP

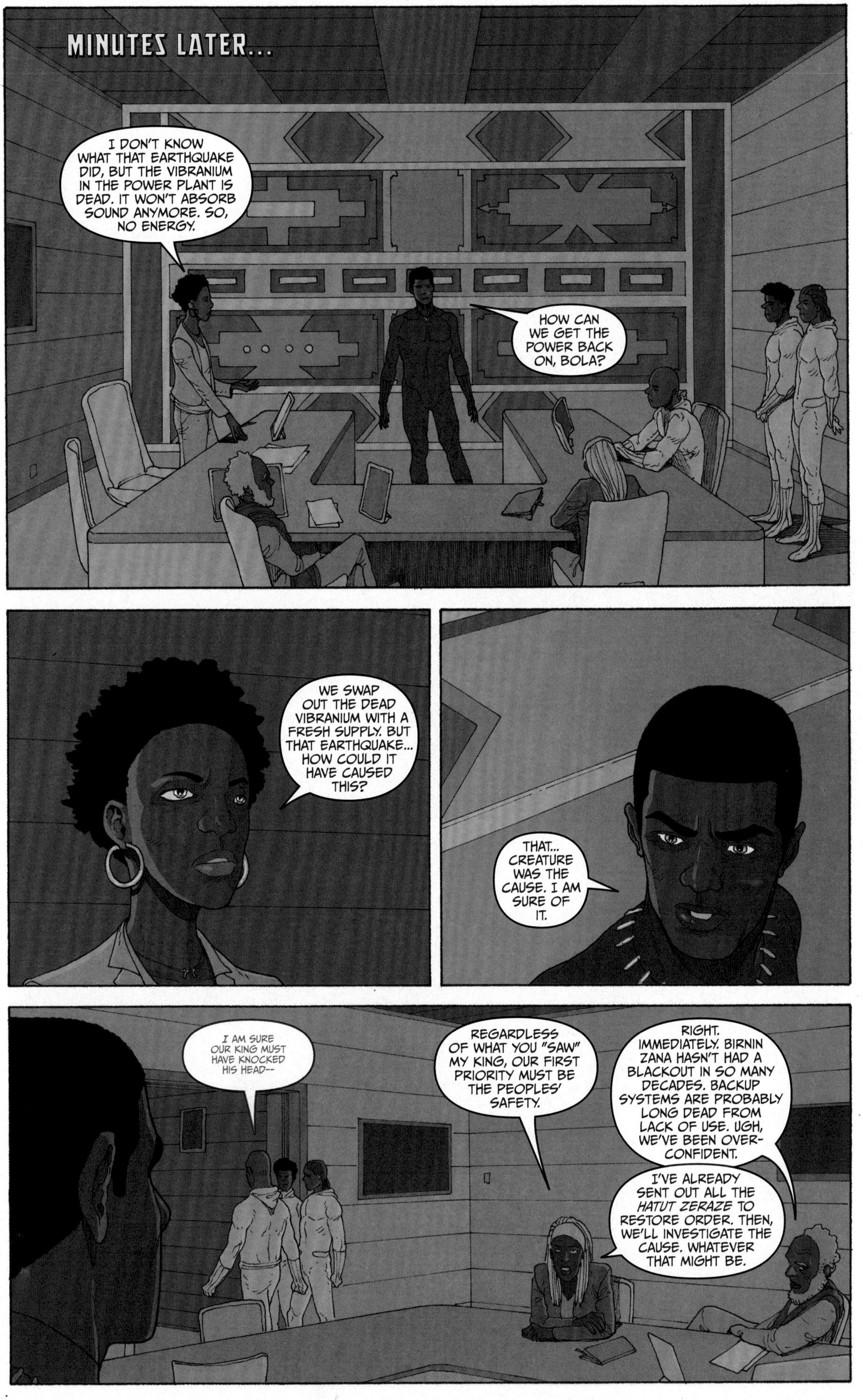
MINUTES LATER...
I DON'T KNOW WHAT THAT EARTHQUAKE DID, BUT THE VIBRANIUM IN THE POWER PLANT IS DEAD. IT WON'T ABSORB SOUND ANYMORE. SO, NO ENERGY.
HOW CAN WE GET THE POWER BACK ON, BOLA?
WE SWAP OUT THE DEAD VIBRANIUM WITH A FRESH SUPPLY. BUT THAT EARTHQUAKE... HOW COULD IT HAVE CAUSED THIS?
THAT... CREATURE WAS THE CAUSE. I AM SURE OF IT.
I AM SURE OUR KING MUST HAVE KNOCKED HIS HEAD--
REGARDLESS OF WHAT YOU "SAW" MY KING, OUR FIRST PRIORITY MUST BE THE PEOPLES' SAFETY.
RIGHT. IMMEDIATELY. BIRNIN ZANA HASN'T HAD A BLACKOUT IN SO MANY DECADES. BACKUP SYSTEMS ARE PROBABLY LONG DEAD FROM LACK OF USE. UGH, WE'VE BEEN OVER-CONFIDENT.
I'VE ALREADY SENT OUT ALL THE *HATUT ZERAZE* TO RESTORE ORDER. THEN, WE'LL INVESTIGATE THE CAUSE. WHATEVER THAT MIGHT BE.

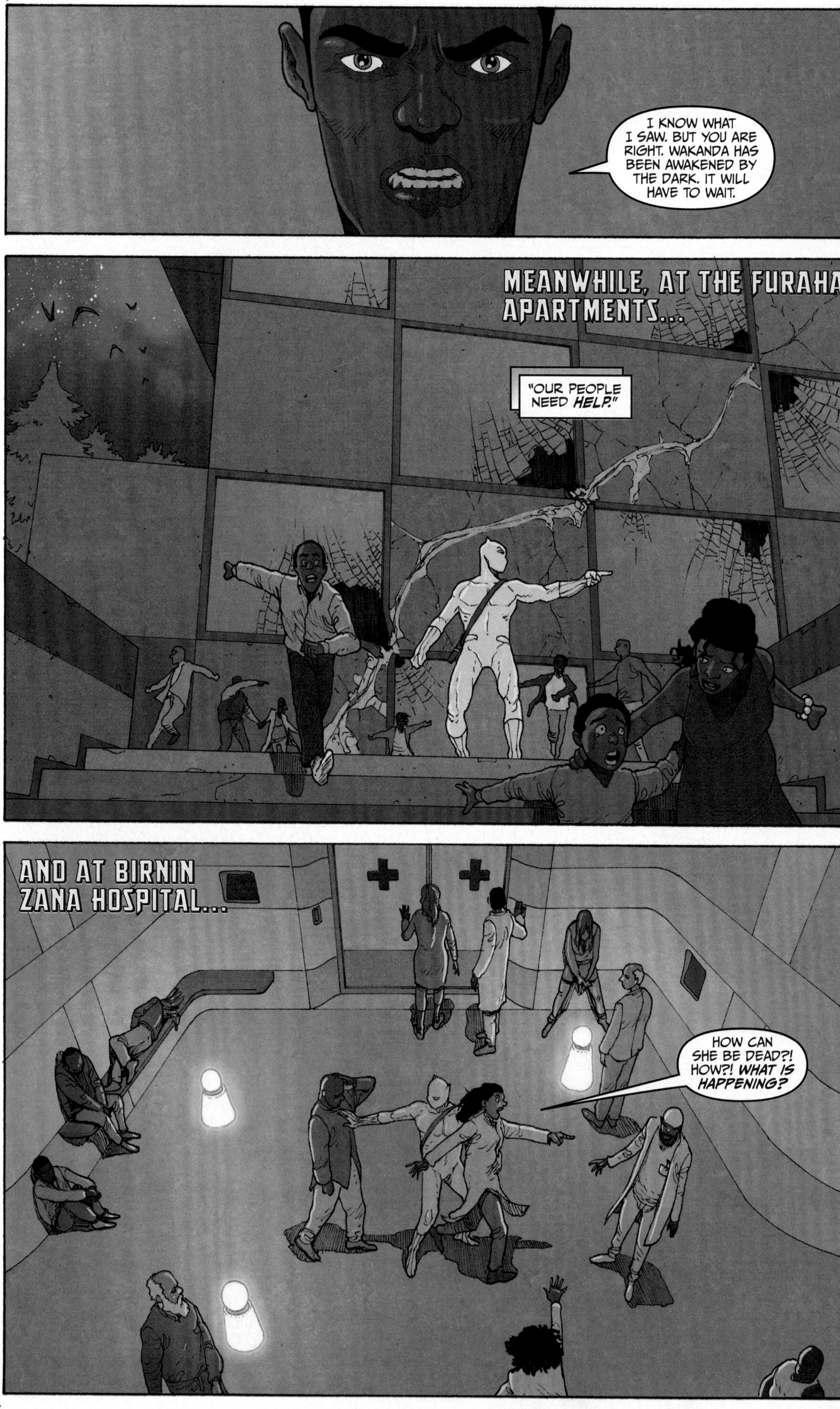
I KNOW WHAT I SAW. BUT YOU ARE RIGHT. WAKANDA HAS BEEN AWAKENED BY THE DARK. IT WILL HAVE TO WAIT.
MEANWHILE, AT THE FURAHA APARTMENTS...
"OUR PEOPLE NEED HELP."
AND AT BIRNIN ZANA HOSPITAL...
HOW CAN SHE BE DEAD?! HOW?! WHAT IS HAPPENING?

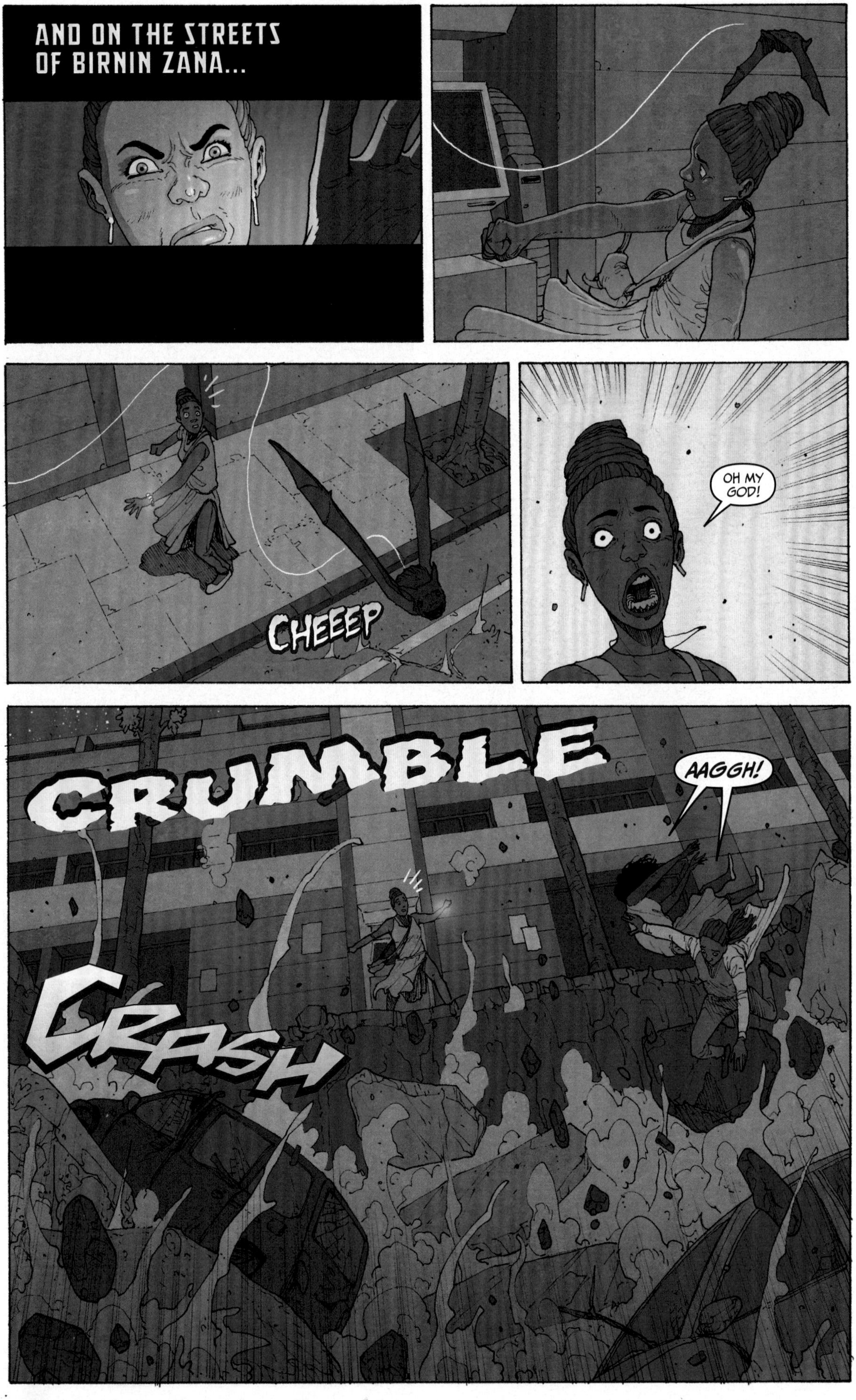
AND ON THE STREETS OF BIRNIN ZANA...
CHEEEP
OH MY GOD!
CRUMBLE
AAGGH!
CRASH

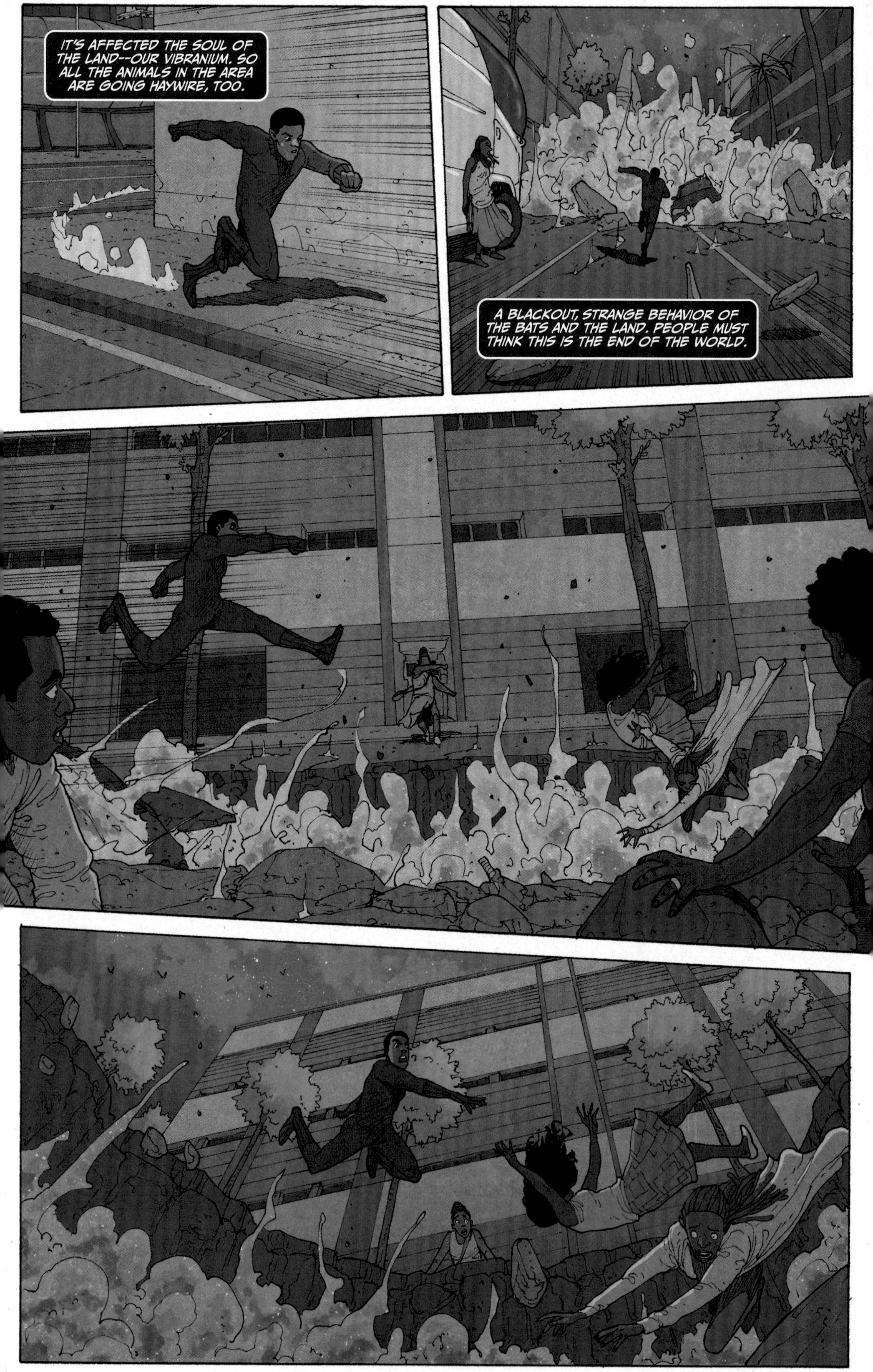
IT'S AFFECTED THE SOUL OF THE LAND--OUR VIBRANIUM. SO ALL THE ANIMALS IN THE AREA ARE GOING HAYWIRE, TOO.
A BLACKOUT, STRANGE BEHAVIOR OF THE BATS AND THE LAND. PEOPLE MUST THINK THIS IS THE END OF THE WORLD.

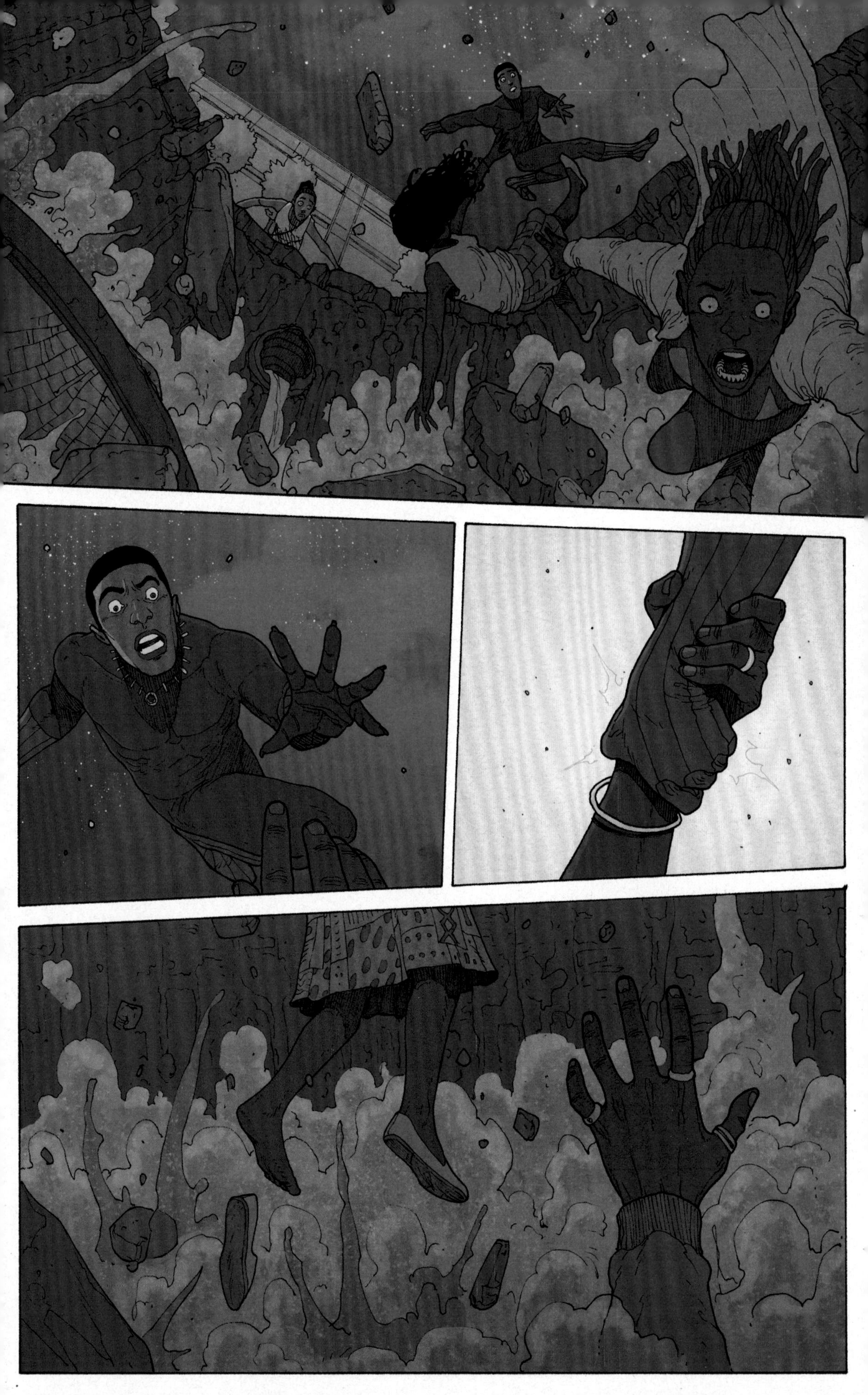

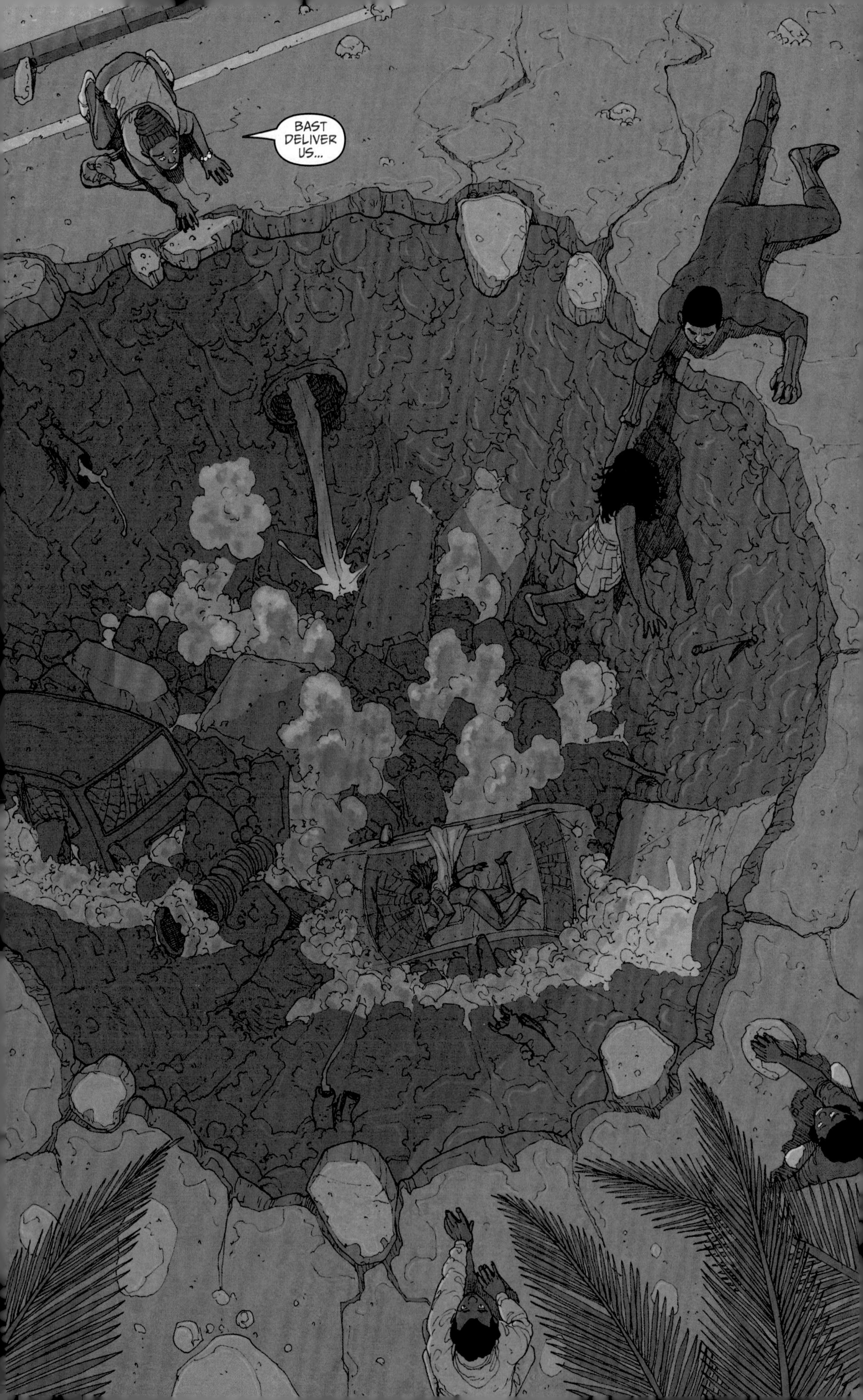
BAST
DELIVER
US...

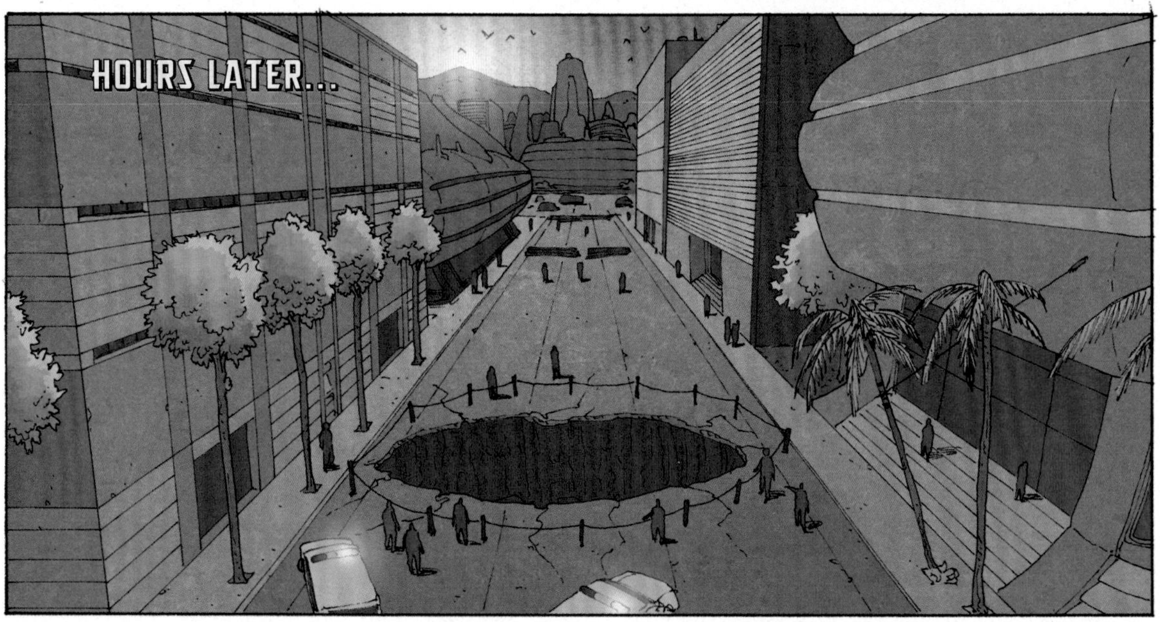
HOURS LATER...

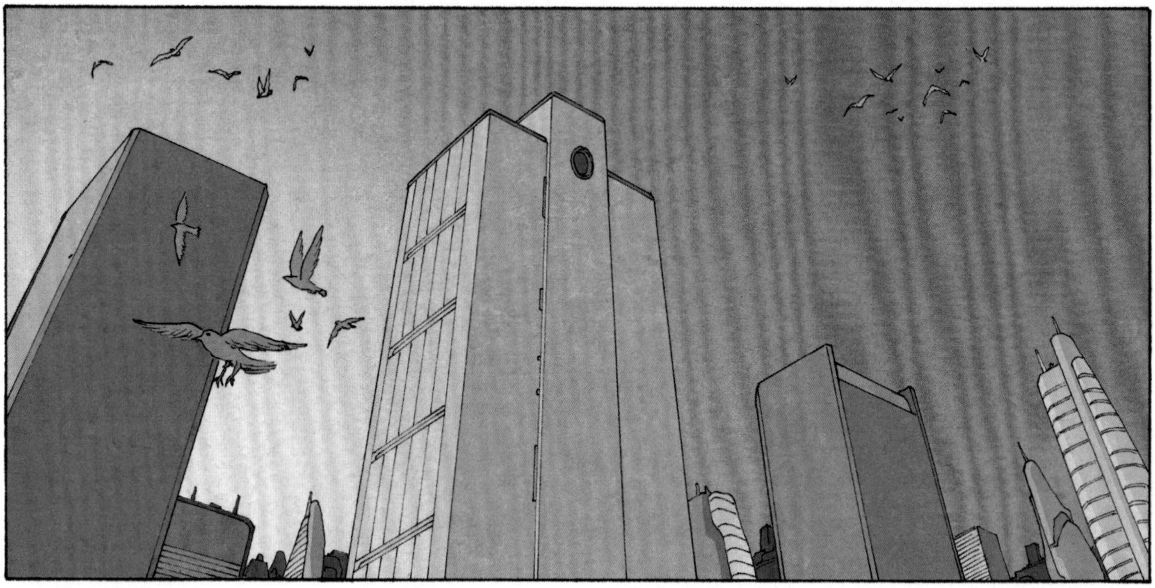

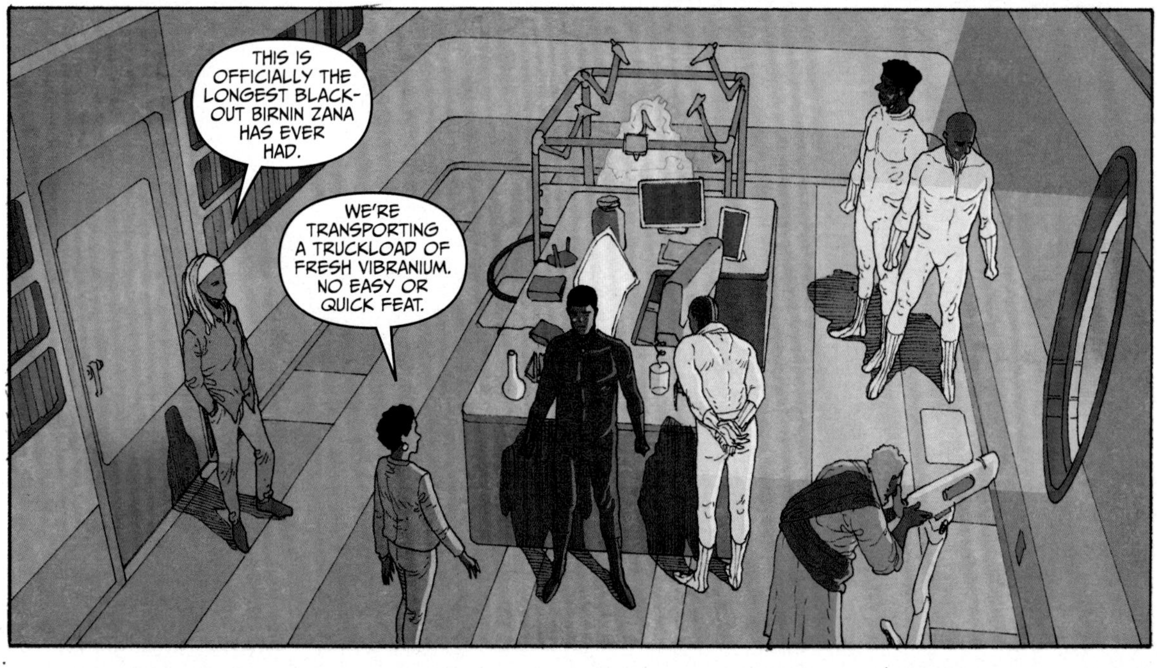
THIS IS OFFICIALLY THE LONGEST BLACK-OUT BIRNIN ZANA HAS EVER HAD.
WE'RE TRANSPORTING A TRUCKLOAD OF FRESH VIBRANIUM. NO EASY OR QUICK FEAT.

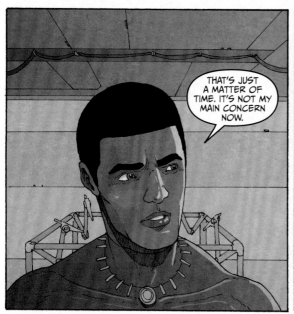

THAT'S JUST A MATTER OF TIME. IT'S NOT MY MAIN CONCERN NOW.

I'D HOPE IT'S YOUR CONCERN. TEN PEOPLE WERE KILLED LAST NIGHT, MY KING.

I KNOW THE NUMBER OF DEAD. I MEANT THAT THE CITY IS UNDER CONTROL. NOW WE MUST FOCUS ON THE CAUSE SO IT DOESN'T HAPPEN AGAIN.

THE EARTHQUAKE ORIGINATED FROM ONE OF THE MUTE ZONES. IF IT WEREN'T FOR THE VIBRANIUM IN THAT HILL ABSORBING SO MUCH OF THE EARTHQUAKE, THE DAMAGE WOULD HAVE BEEN MUCH WORSE.

SEND A GROUP OF *HATUT ZERAZE* TO INVESTIGATE IT, T'CHALLA.

NO. I'LL GO. I WANT TO SEE THIS THING UP CLOSE.

COME ON, T'CHALLA. MUTE ZONERS LIKE TO BE LEFT ALONE. THAT'S WHY THEY HACK THEMSELVES OFF THE GRID. THEY'RE NOT GOING TO LIKE A MEMBER OF THE ROYAL FAMILY WALKING INTO THEIR VILLAGE.

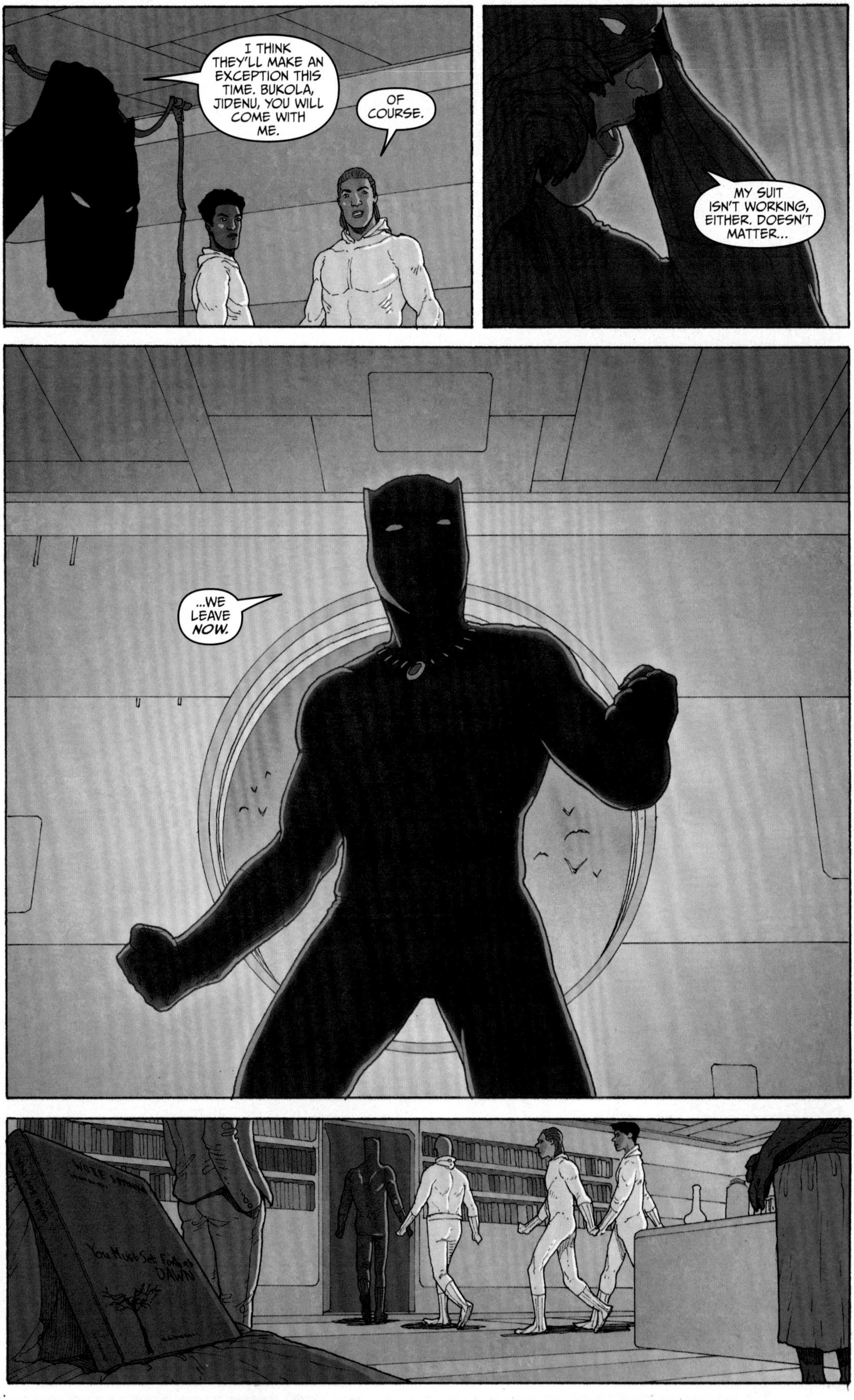
I THINK THEY'LL MAKE AN EXCEPTION THIS TIME. BUKOLA, JIDENU, YOU WILL COME WITH ME.
OF COURSE.
MY SUIT ISN'T WORKING, EITHER. DOESN'T MATTER...
...WE LEAVE *NOW.*
You Must Set Forth at DAWN

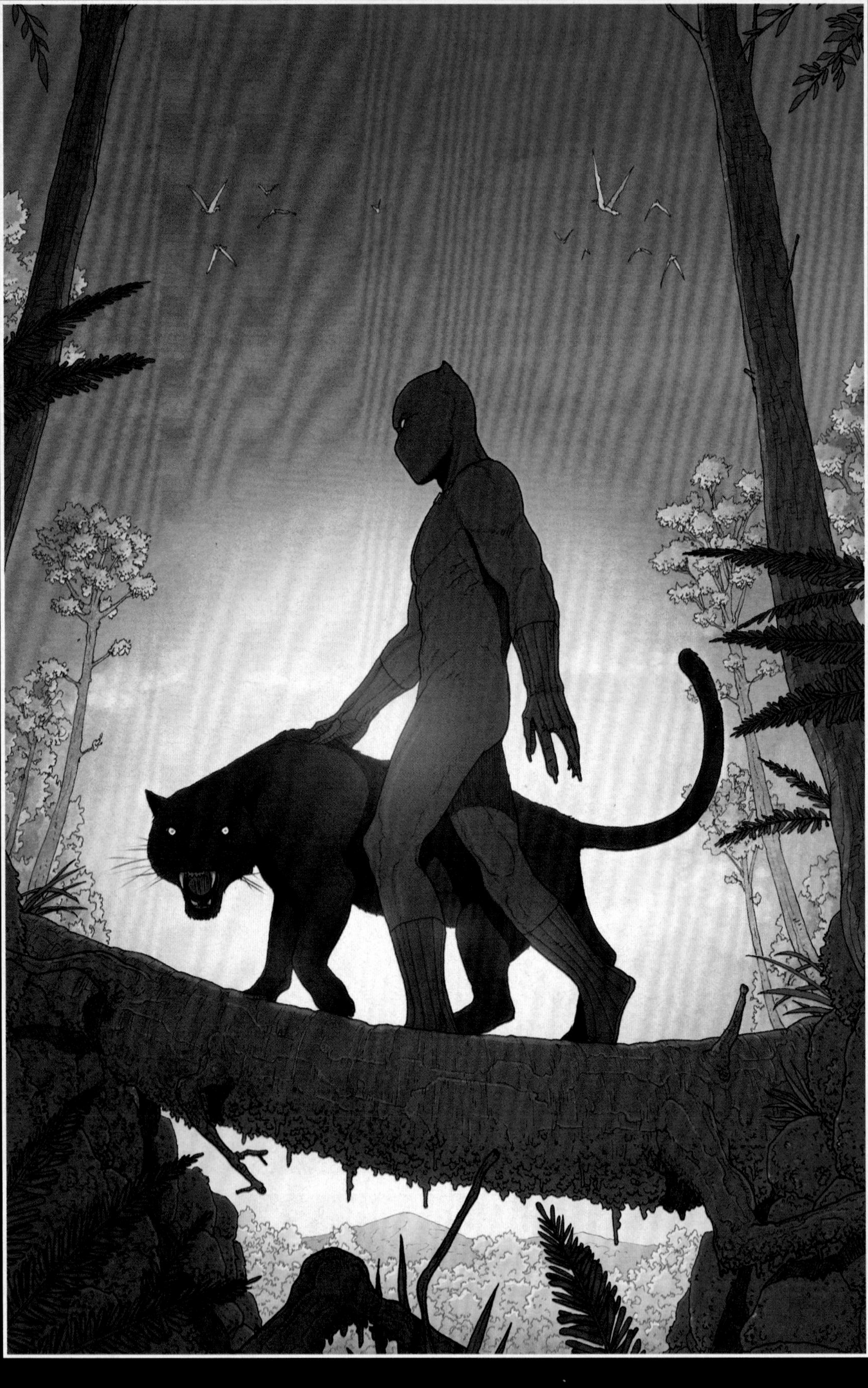

THE SACRIFICE

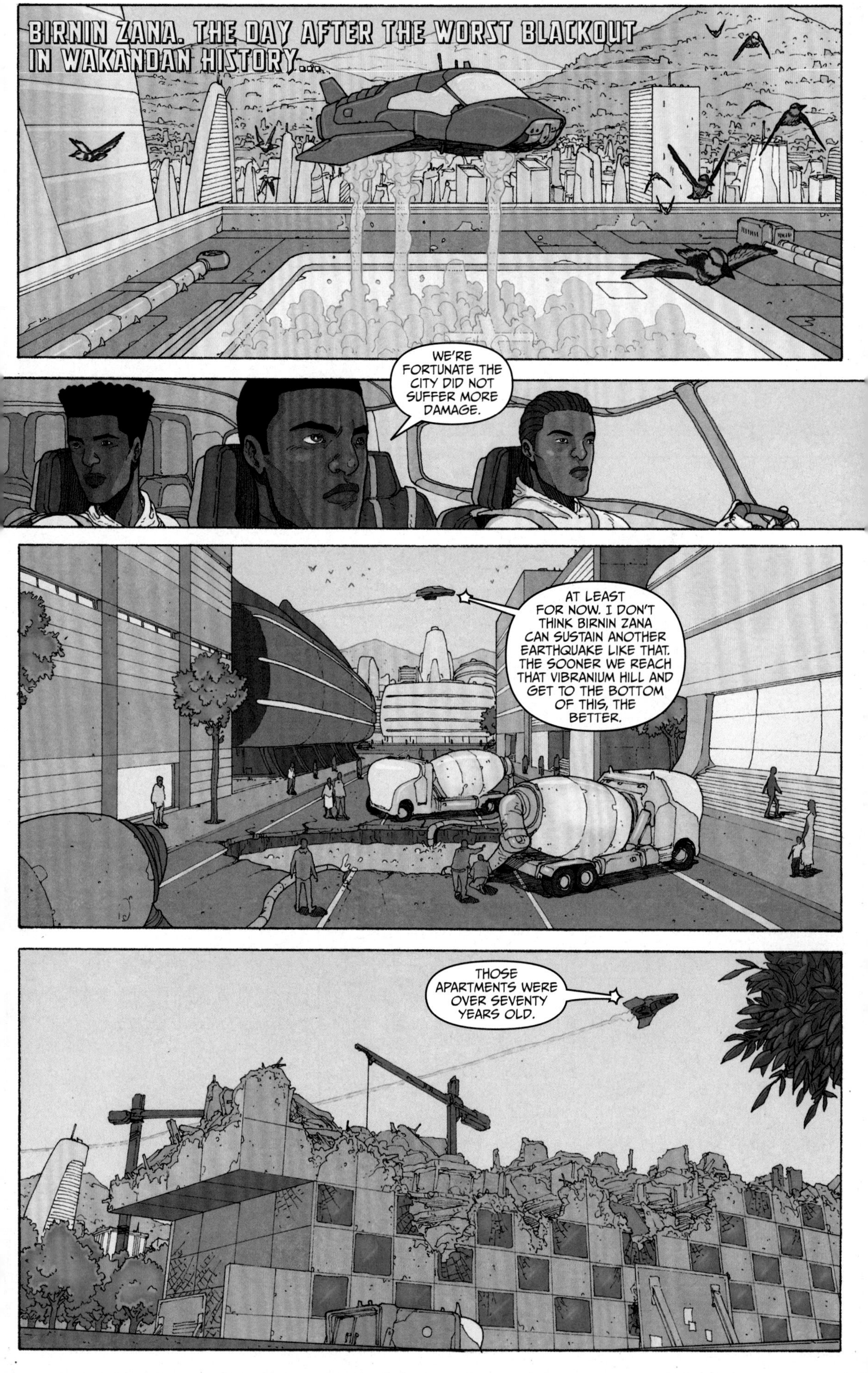
BIRNIN ZANA. THE DAY AFTER THE WORST BLACKOUT IN WAKANDAN HISTORY...
WE'RE FORTUNATE THE CITY DID NOT SUFFER MORE DAMAGE.
AT LEAST FOR NOW. I DON'T THINK BIRNIN ZANA CAN SUSTAIN ANOTHER EARTHQUAKE LIKE THAT. THE SOONER WE REACH THAT VIBRANIUM HILL AND GET TO THE BOTTOM OF THIS, THE BETTER.
THOSE APARTMENTS WERE OVER SEVENTY YEARS OLD.

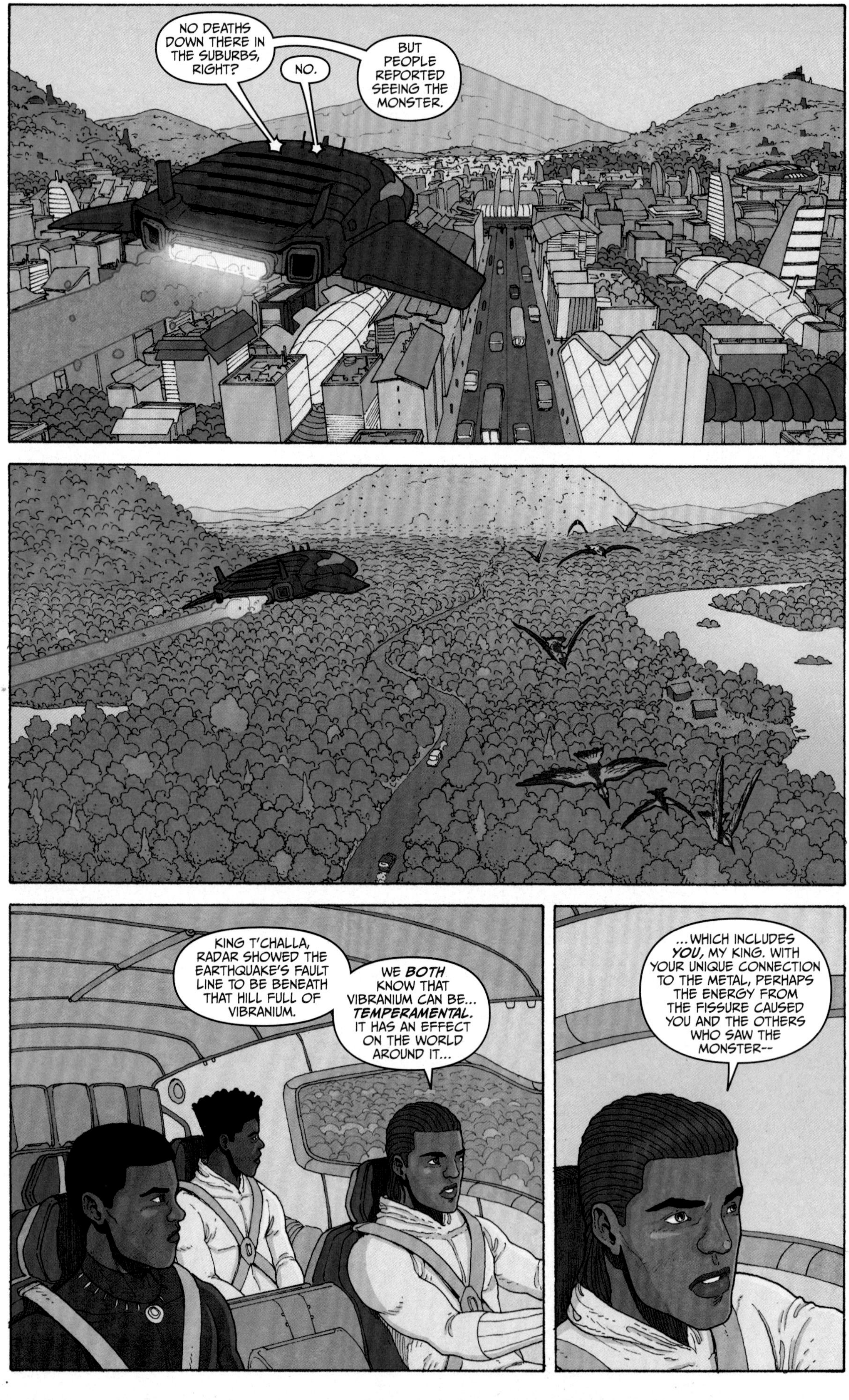
NO DEATHS DOWN THERE IN THE SUBURBS, RIGHT?
NO.
BUT PEOPLE REPORTED SEEING THE MONSTER.
KING T'CHALLA, RADAR SHOWED THE EARTHQUAKE'S FAULT LINE TO BE BENEATH THAT HILL FULL OF VIBRANIUM.
WE BOTH KNOW THAT VIBRANIUM CAN BE... TEMPERAMENTAL. IT HAS AN EFFECT ON THE WORLD AROUND IT...
...WHICH INCLUDES YOU, MY KING. WITH YOUR UNIQUE CONNECTION TO THE METAL, PERHAPS THE ENERGY FROM THE FISSURE CAUSED YOU AND THE OTHERS WHO SAW THE MONSTER--

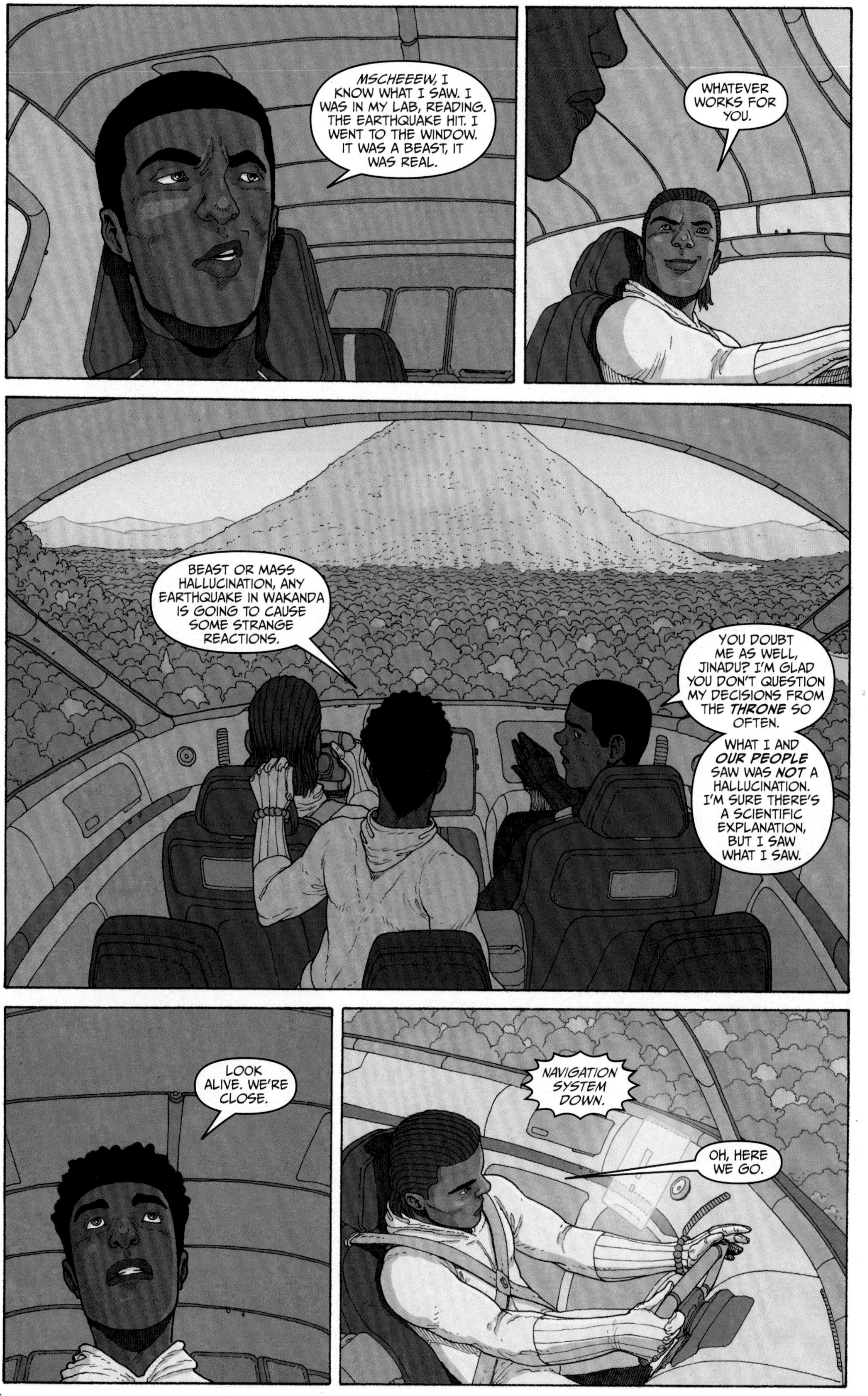
MSCHEEEW, I KNOW WHAT I SAW. I WAS IN MY LAB, READING. THE EARTHQUAKE HIT. I WENT TO THE WINDOW. IT WAS A BEAST, IT WAS REAL.
WHATEVER WORKS FOR YOU.
BEAST OR MASS HALLUCINATION, ANY EARTHQUAKE IN WAKANDA IS GOING TO CAUSE SOME STRANGE REACTIONS.
YOU DOUBT ME AS WELL, JINADU? I'M GLAD YOU DON'T QUESTION MY DECISIONS FROM THE THRONE SO OFTEN.
WHAT I AND OUR PEOPLE SAW WAS NOT A HALLUCINATION. I'M SURE THERE'S A SCIENTIFIC EXPLANATION, BUT I SAW WHAT I SAW.
LOOK ALIVE. WE'RE CLOSE.
NAVIGATION SYSTEM DOWN.
OH, HERE WE GO.

NAVIGATION SYSTEM DOWN. REBOOT AND RECONNECT.

ARE YOU KIDDING? THEY HACK THEMSELVES OFF OUR GRID, THEN SET UP A FULL FIREWALL!

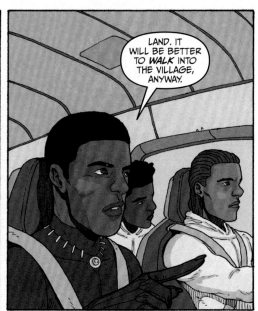

LAND. IT WILL BE BETTER TO *WALK* INTO THE VILLAGE, ANYWAY.

DISCONNECTED GPS, SATELLITES, TRAFFIC CAMS, INTERNET. THEY DON'T EVEN USE KIMOYO BRACELETS. IF THE KING OF WAKANDA'S GOING TO ENTER A MUTE ZONE, BEST BE ON FOOT. ARRIVING WITH RESPECT WILL GET US FASTER RESULTS.

EASE ON DOWN THE RO--

DON'T EVEN.

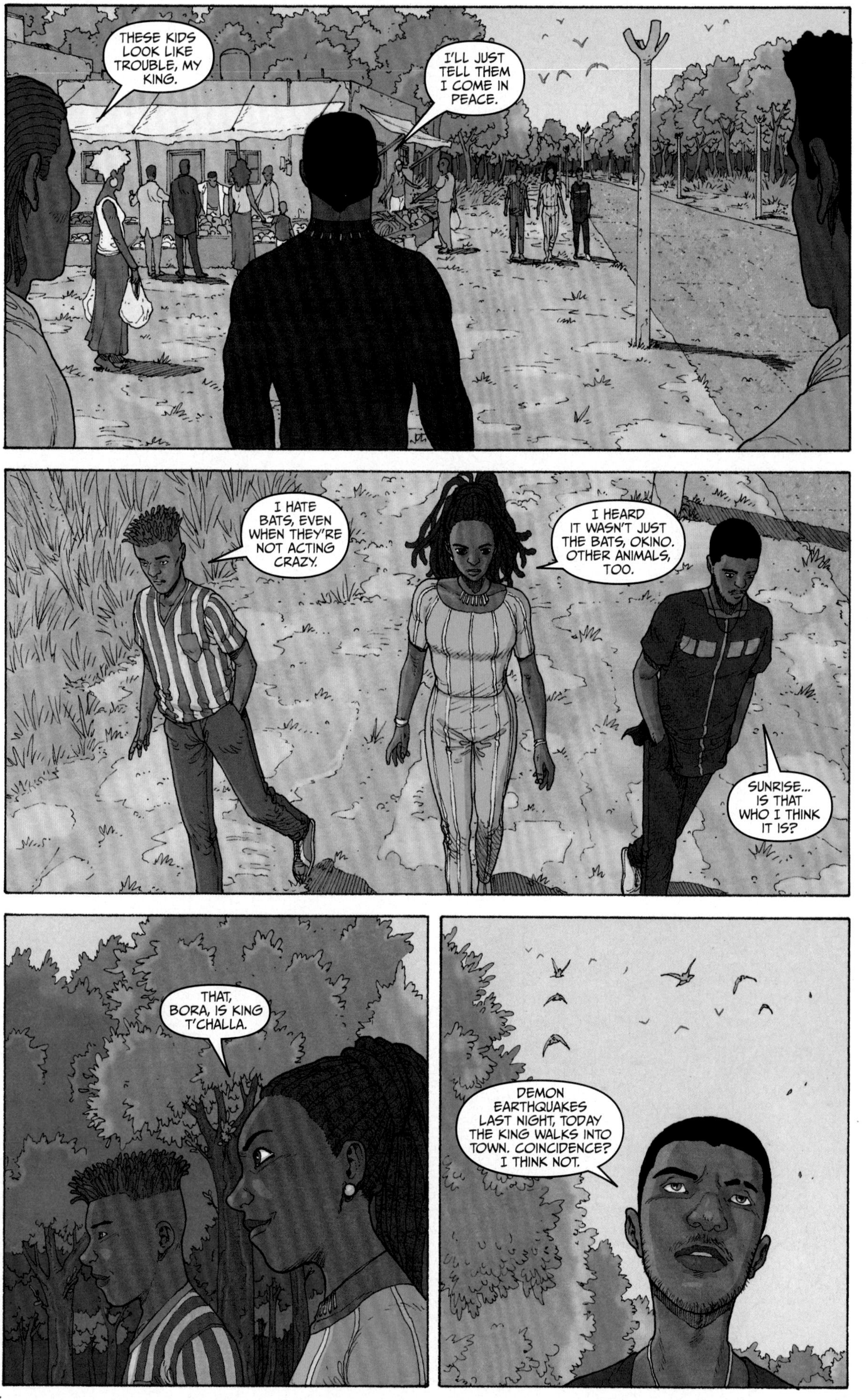
THESE KIDS LOOK LIKE TROUBLE, MY KING.
I'LL JUST TELL THEM I COME IN PEACE.
I HATE BATS, EVEN WHEN THEY'RE NOT ACTING CRAZY.
I HEARD IT WASN'T JUST THE BATS, OKINO. OTHER ANIMALS, TOO.
SUNRISE... IS THAT WHO I THINK IT IS?
THAT, BORA, IS KING T'CHALLA.
DEMON EARTHQUAKES LAST NIGHT, TODAY THE KING WALKS INTO TOWN. COINCIDENCE? I THINK NOT.

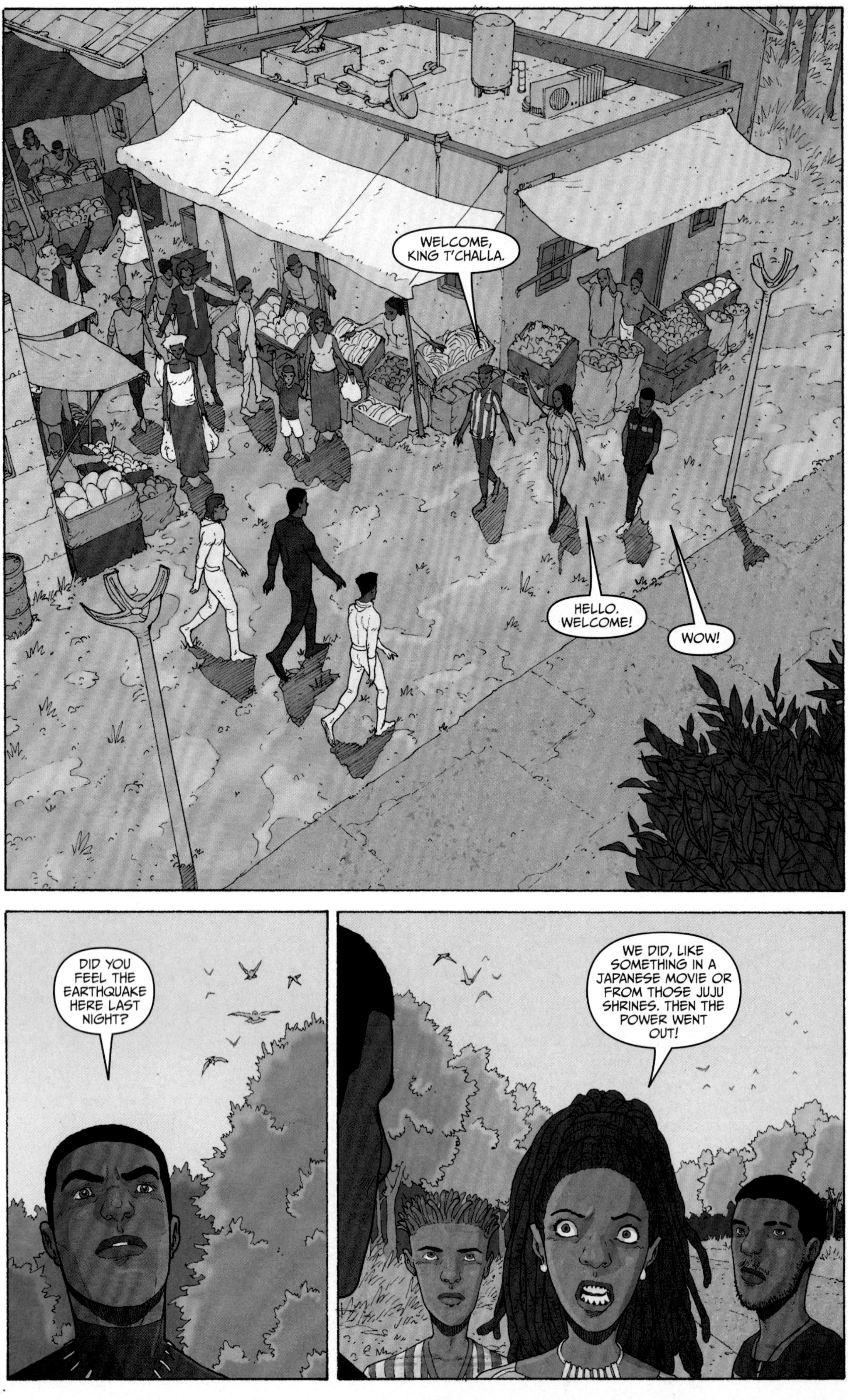
WELCOME, KING T'CHALLA.
HELLO. WELCOME!
WOW!
DID YOU FEEL THE EARTHQUAKE HERE LAST NIGHT?
WE DID, LIKE SOMETHING IN A JAPANESE MOVIE OR FROM THOSE JUJU SHRINES. THEN THE POWER WENT OUT!

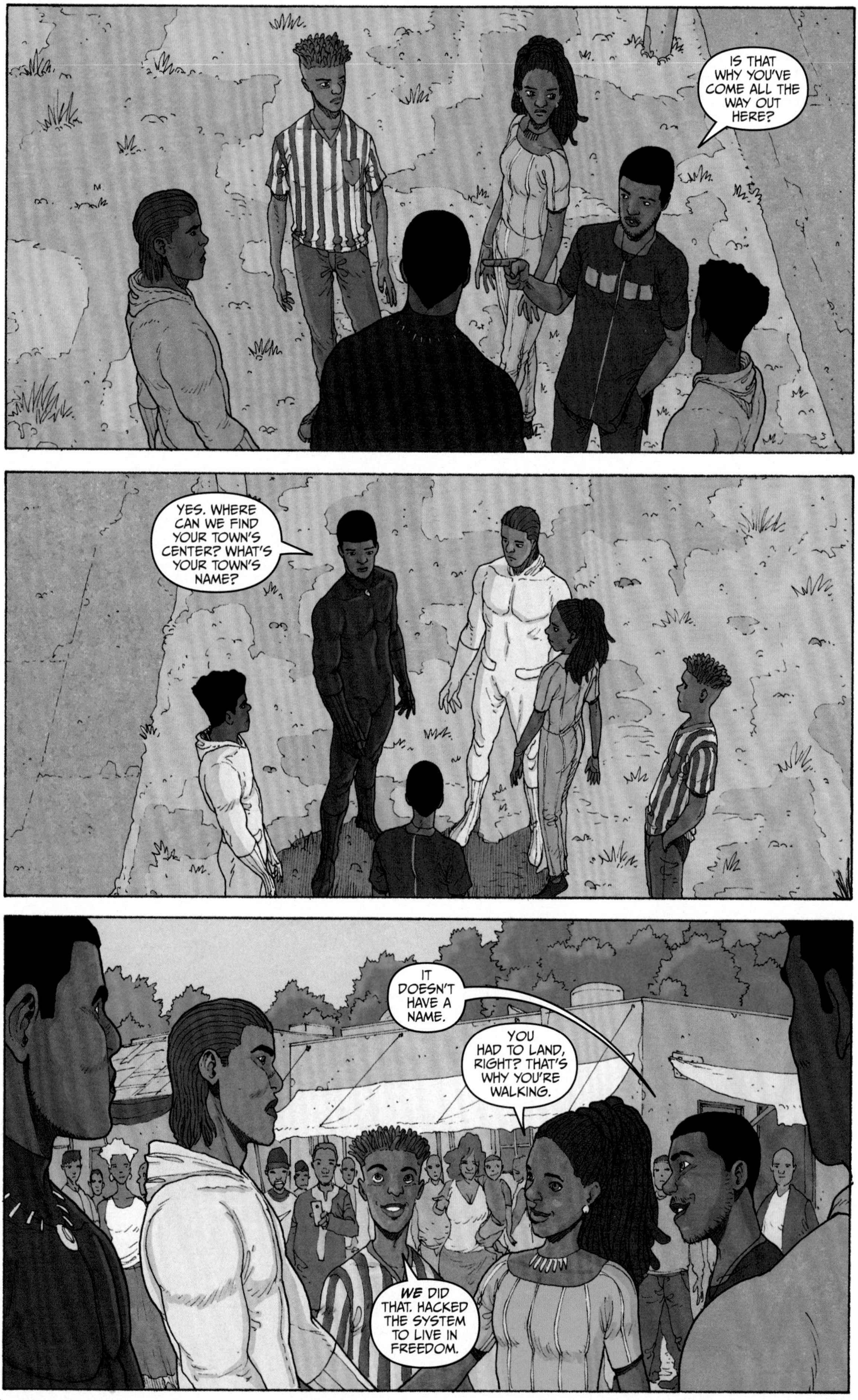
IS THAT WHY YOU'VE COME ALL THE WAY OUT HERE?
YES. WHERE CAN WE FIND YOUR TOWN'S CENTER? WHAT'S YOUR TOWN'S NAME?
IT DOESN'T HAVE A NAME.
YOU HAD TO LAND, RIGHT? THAT'S WHY YOU'RE WALKING.
WE DID THAT. HACKED THE SYSTEM TO LIVE IN FREEDOM.

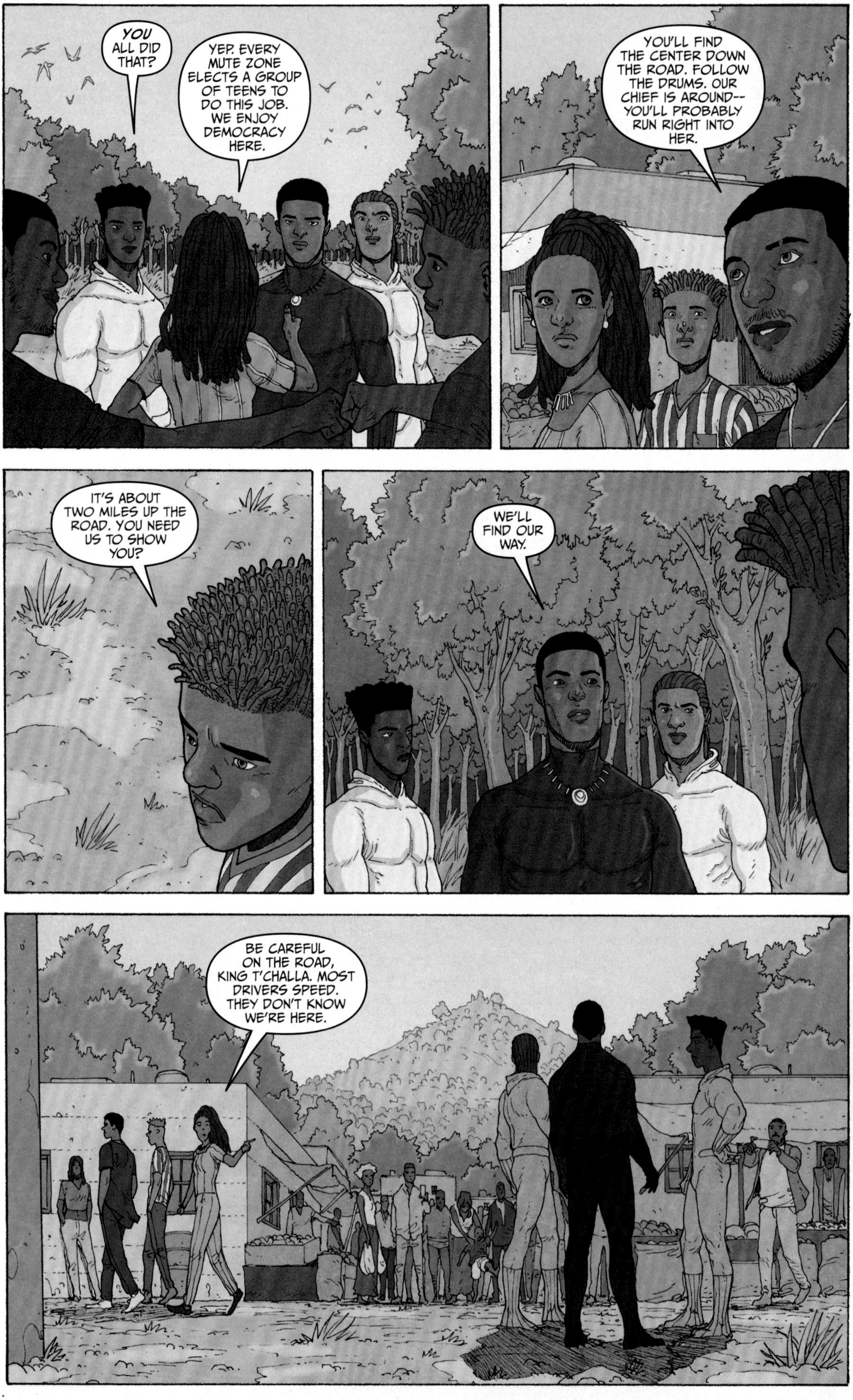
YOU ALL DID THAT?
YEP. EVERY MUTE ZONE ELECTS A GROUP OF TEENS TO DO THIS JOB. WE ENJOY DEMOCRACY HERE.
YOU'LL FIND THE CENTER DOWN THE ROAD. FOLLOW THE DRUMS. OUR CHIEF IS AROUND-- YOU'LL PROBABLY RUN RIGHT INTO HER.
IT'S ABOUT TWO MILES UP THE ROAD. YOU NEED US TO SHOW YOU?
WE'LL FIND OUR WAY.
BE CAREFUL ON THE ROAD, KING T'CHALLA. MOST DRIVERS SPEED. THEY DON'T KNOW WE'RE HERE.

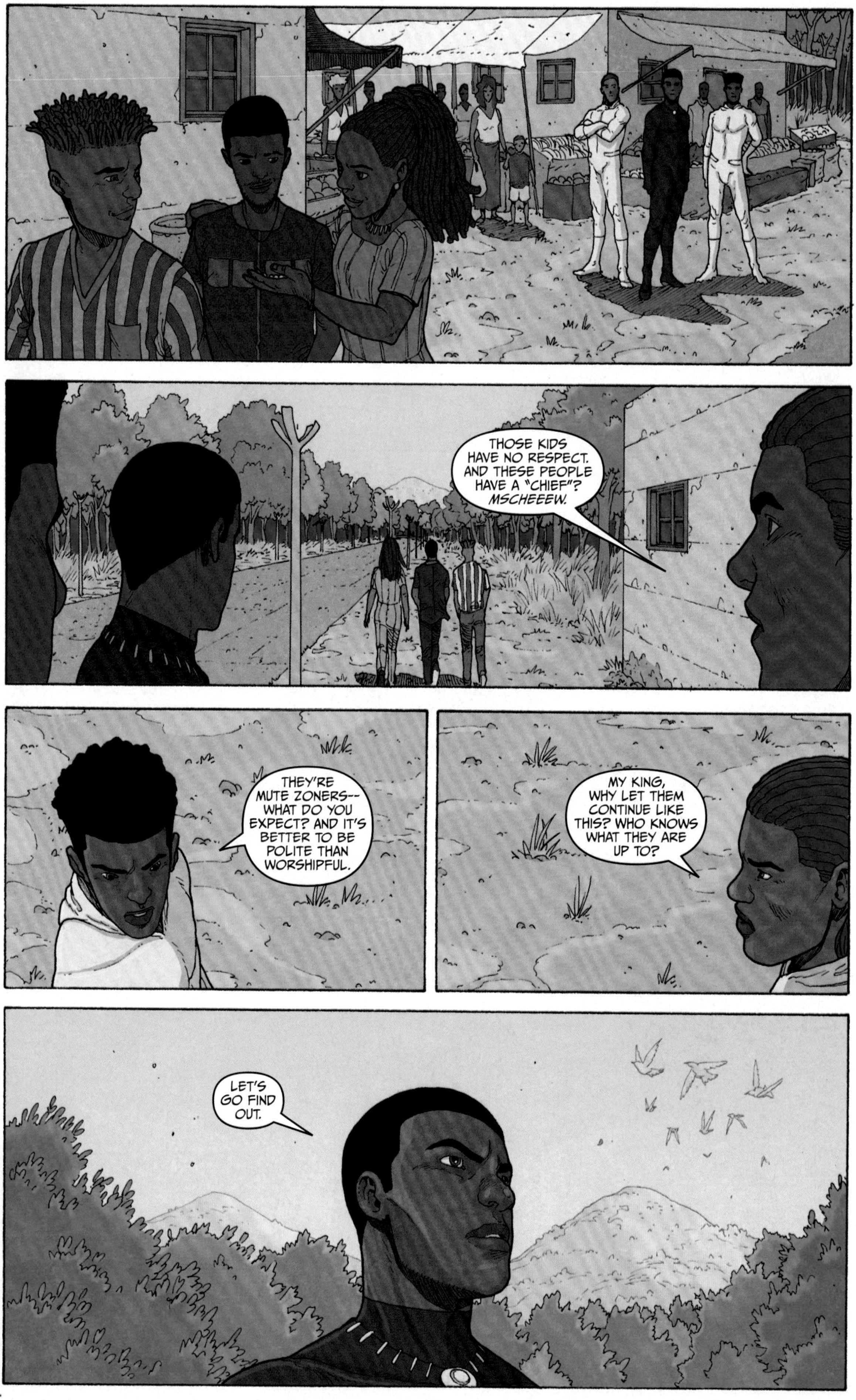
THOSE KIDS HAVE NO RESPECT. AND THESE PEOPLE HAVE A "CHIEF"? *MSCHEEEW.*
THEY'RE MUTE ZONERS-- WHAT DO YOU EXPECT? AND IT'S BETTER TO BE POLITE THAN WORSHIPFUL.
MY KING, WHY LET THEM CONTINUE LIKE THIS? WHO KNOWS WHAT THEY ARE UP TO?
LET'S GO FIND OUT.

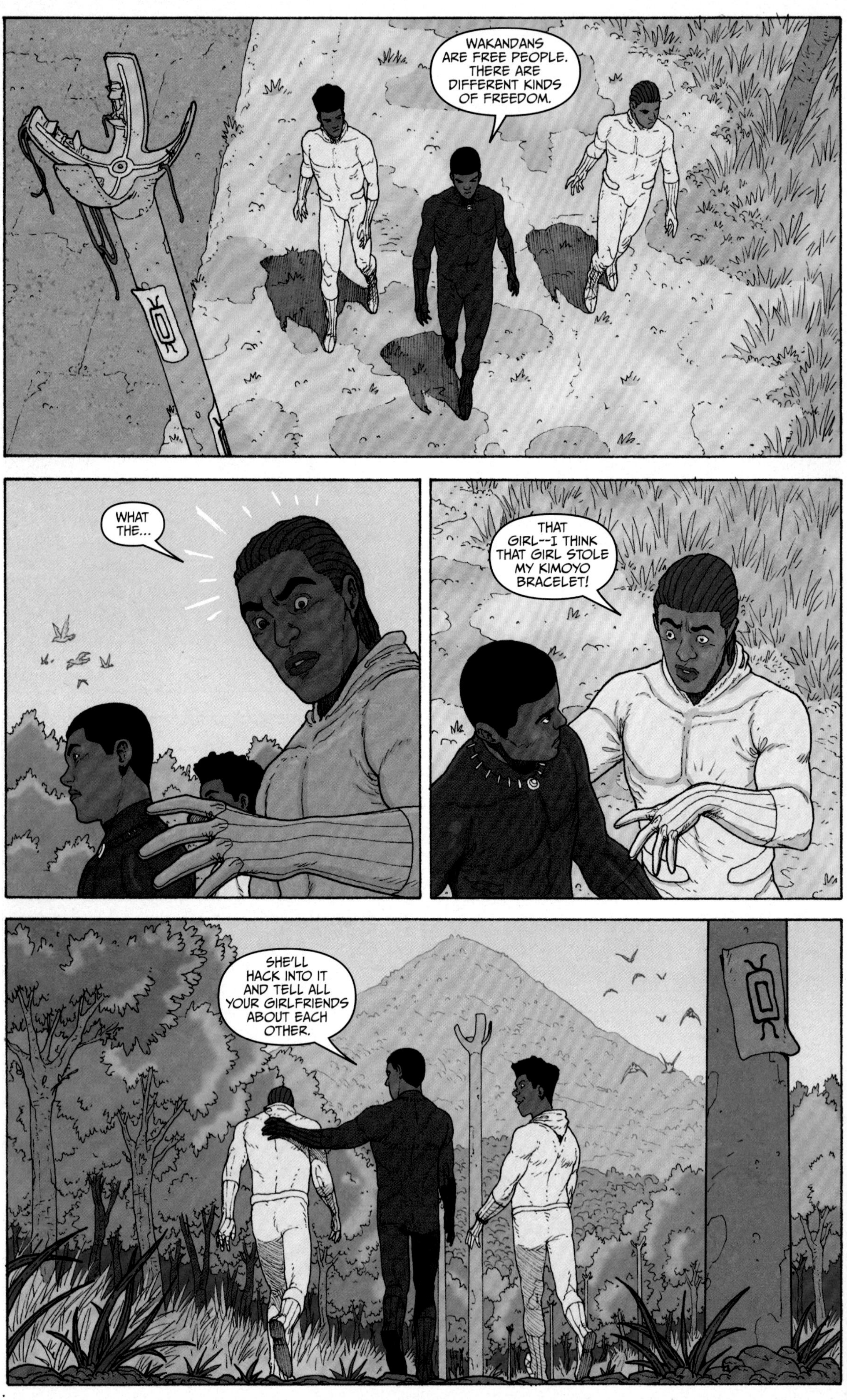
WAKANDANS ARE FREE PEOPLE. THERE ARE DIFFERENT KINDS OF FREEDOM.
WHAT THE...
THAT GIRL--I THINK THAT GIRL STOLE MY KIMOYO BRACELET!
SHE'LL HACK INTO IT AND TELL ALL YOUR GIRLFRIENDS ABOUT EACH OTHER.

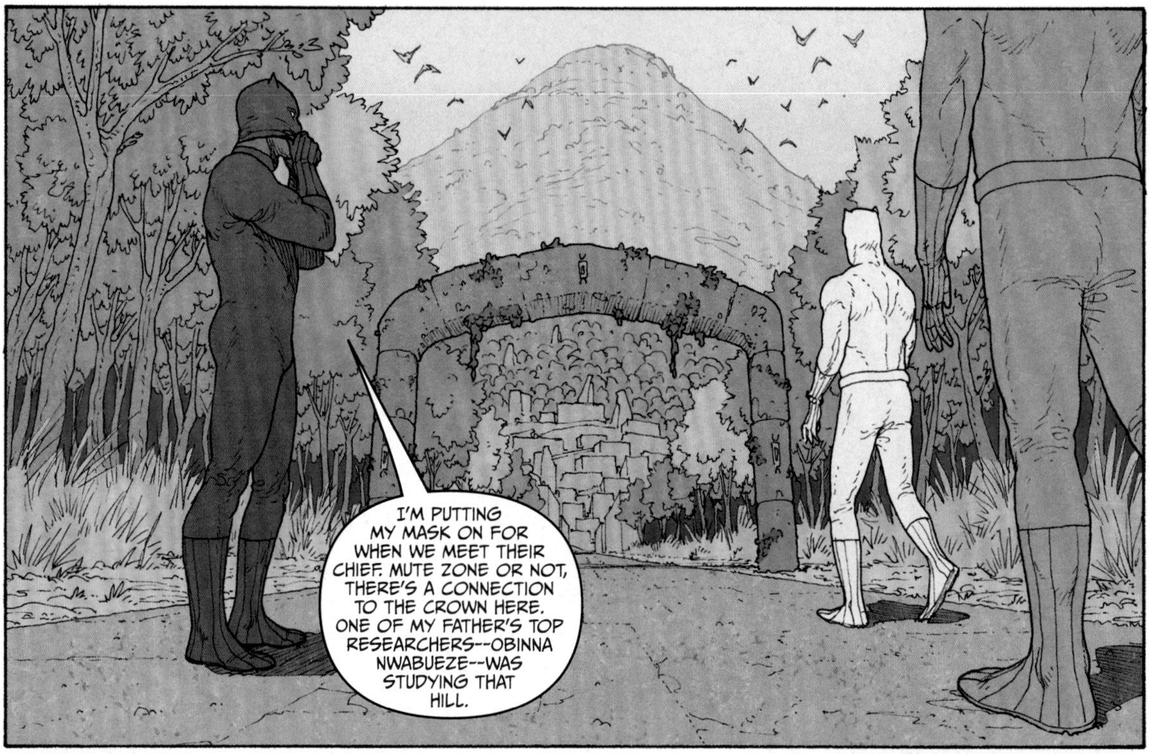
I'M PUTTING MY MASK ON FOR WHEN WE MEET THEIR CHIEF. MUTE ZONE OR NOT, THERE'S A CONNECTION TO THE CROWN HERE. ONE OF MY FATHER'S TOP RESEARCHERS--OBINNA NWABUEZE--WAS STUDYING THAT HILL.

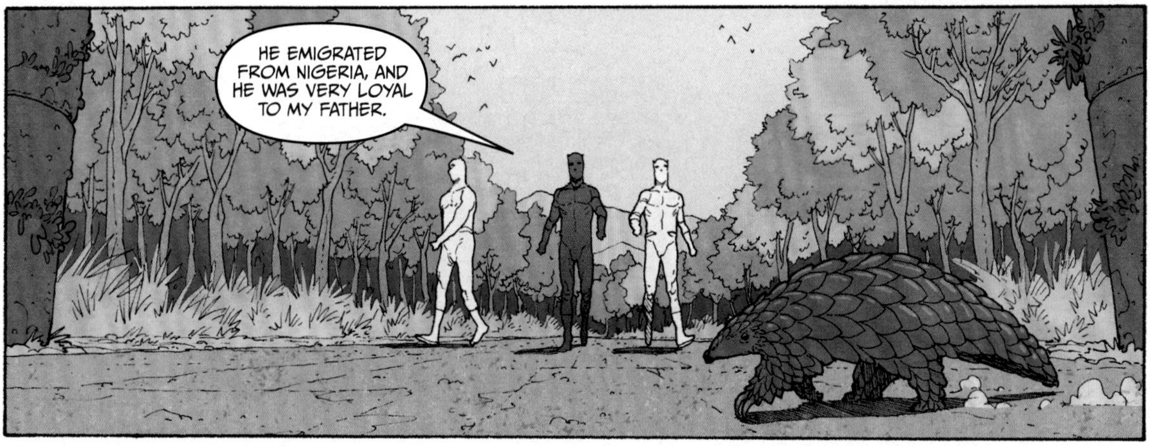
HE EMIGRATED FROM NIGERIA, AND HE WAS VERY LOYAL TO MY FATHER.

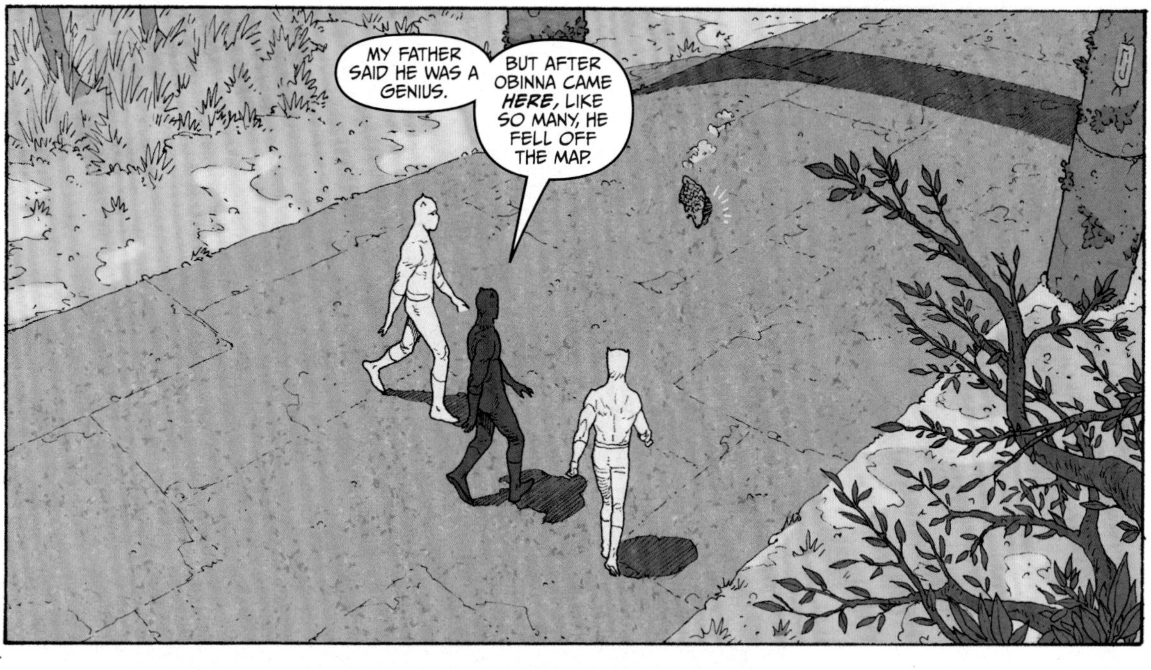
MY FATHER SAID HE WAS A GENIUS.
BUT AFTER OBINNA CAME *HERE,* LIKE SO MANY, HE FELL OFF THE MAP.

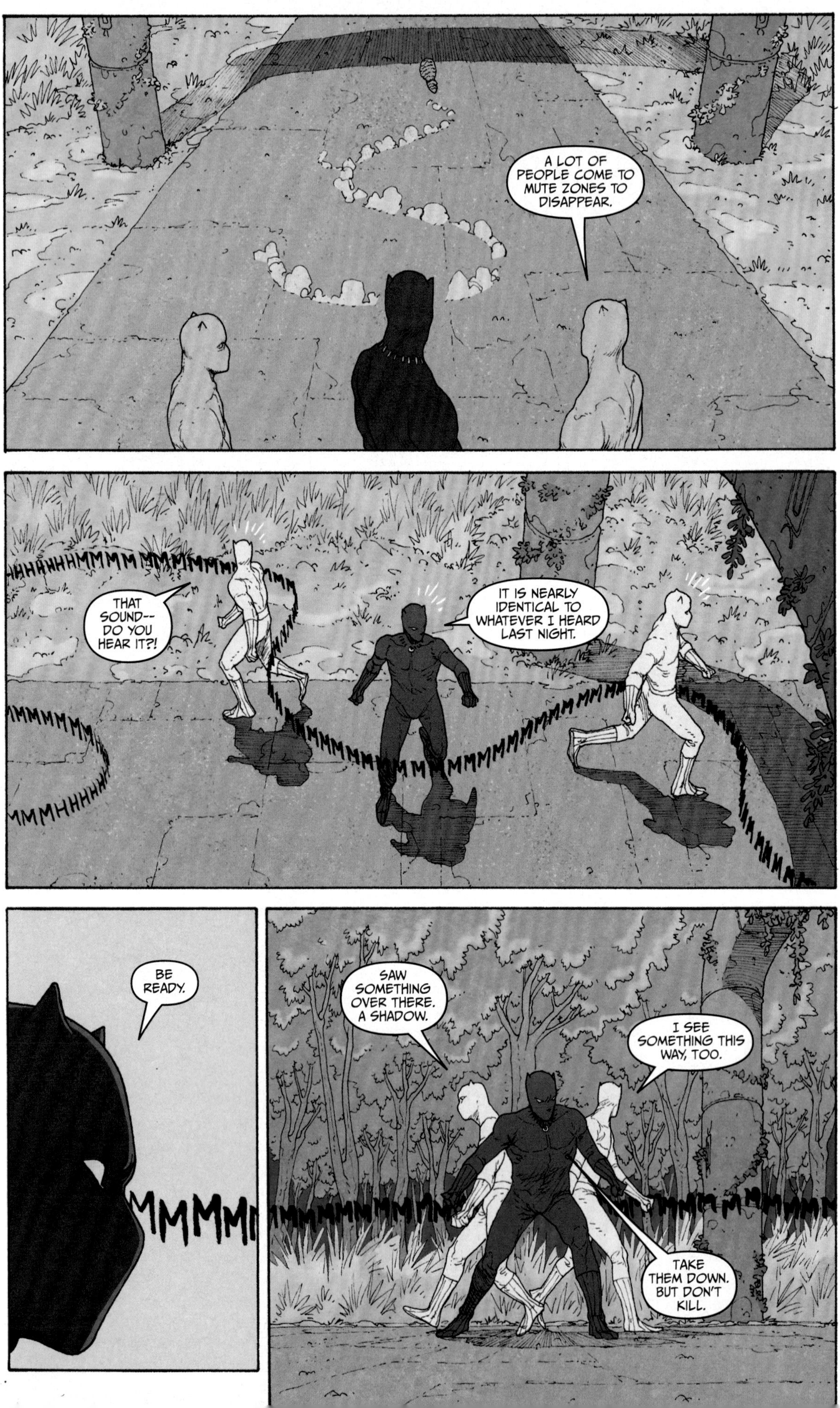
A LOT OF PEOPLE COME TO MUTE ZONES TO DISAPPEAR.
MMMMMMMMMMMMMMMMMMMMMMMMHHHH
THAT SOUND-- DO YOU HEAR IT?!
IT IS NEARLY IDENTICAL TO WHATEVER I HEARD LAST NIGHT.
BE READY.
MMMM
SAW SOMETHING OVER THERE. A SHADOW.
I SEE SOMETHING THIS WAY, TOO.
TAKE THEM DOWN. BUT DON'T KILL.

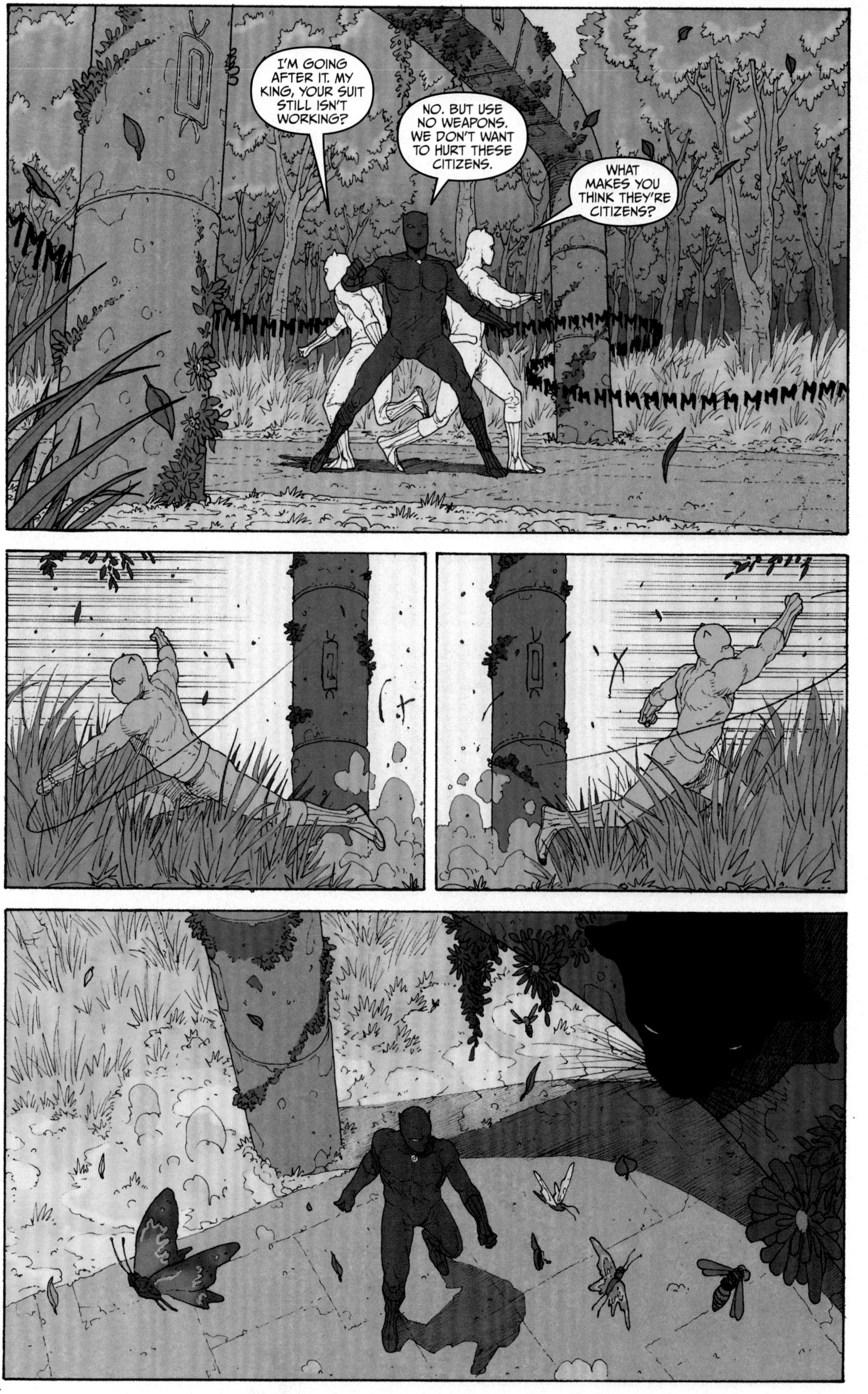
I'M GOING AFTER IT. MY KING, YOUR SUIT STILL ISN'T WORKING?
NO. BUT USE NO WEAPONS. WE DON'T WANT TO HURT THESE CITIZENS.
WHAT MAKES YOU THINK THEY'RE CITIZENS?

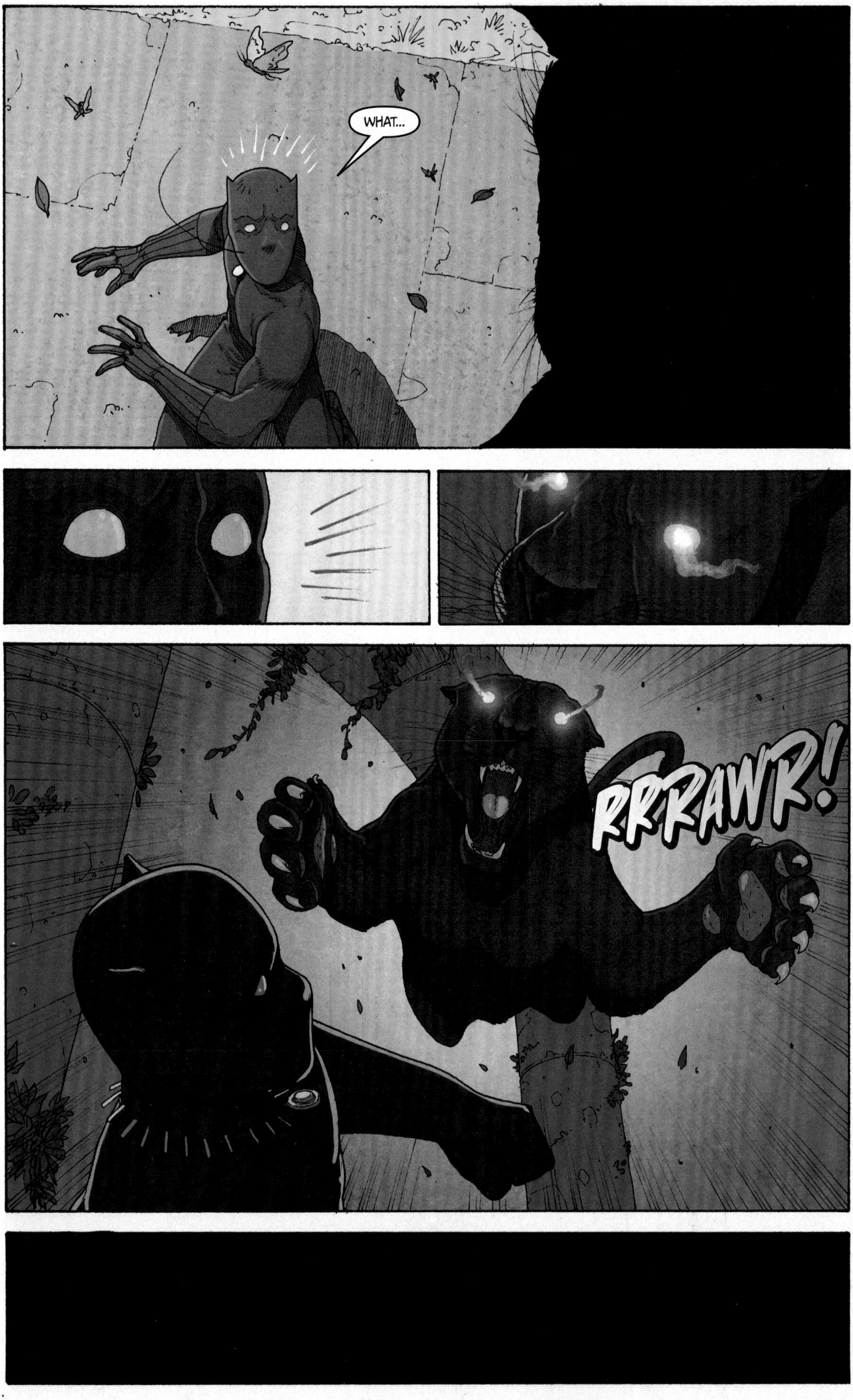
WHAT...
RRRAWR!

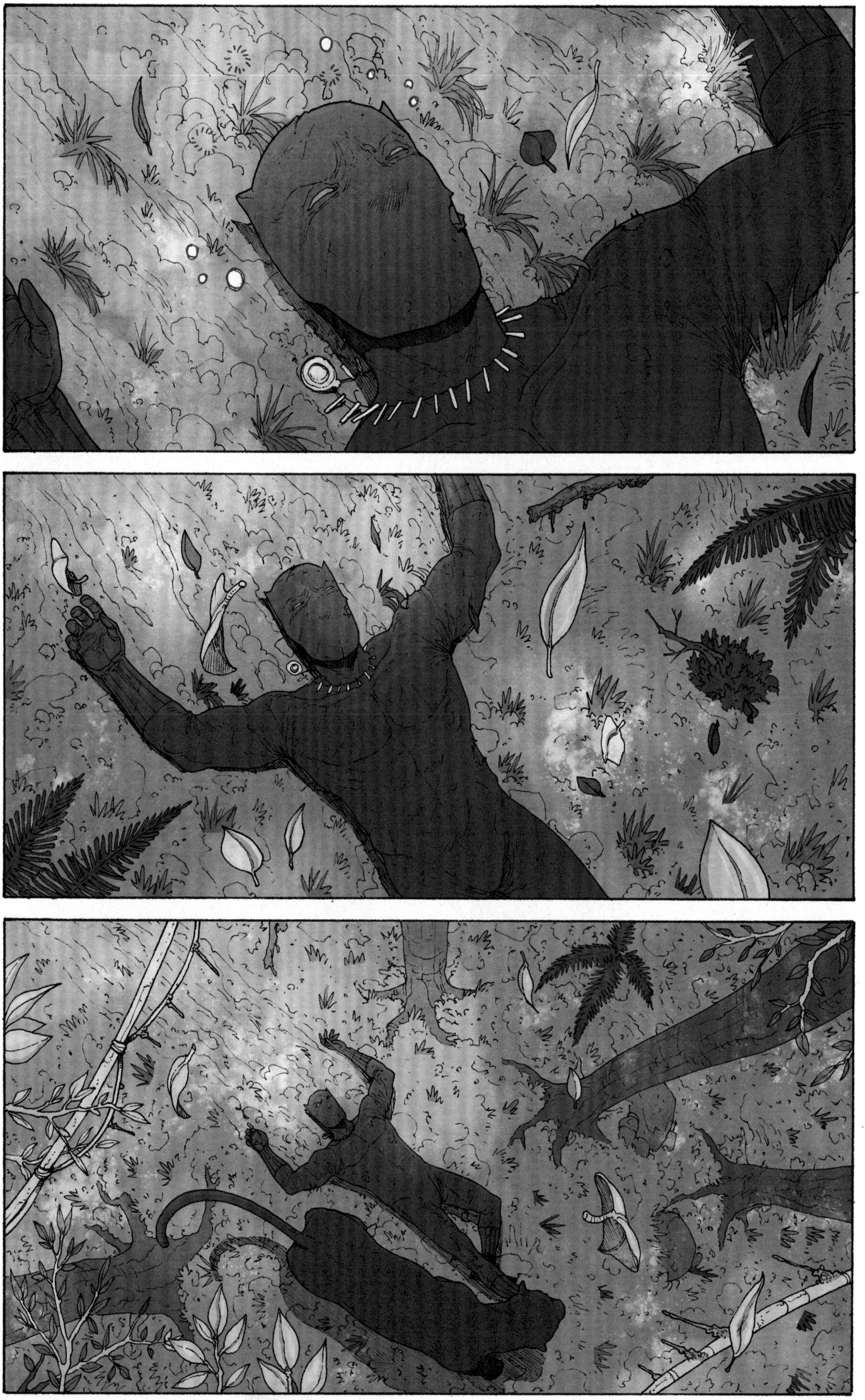

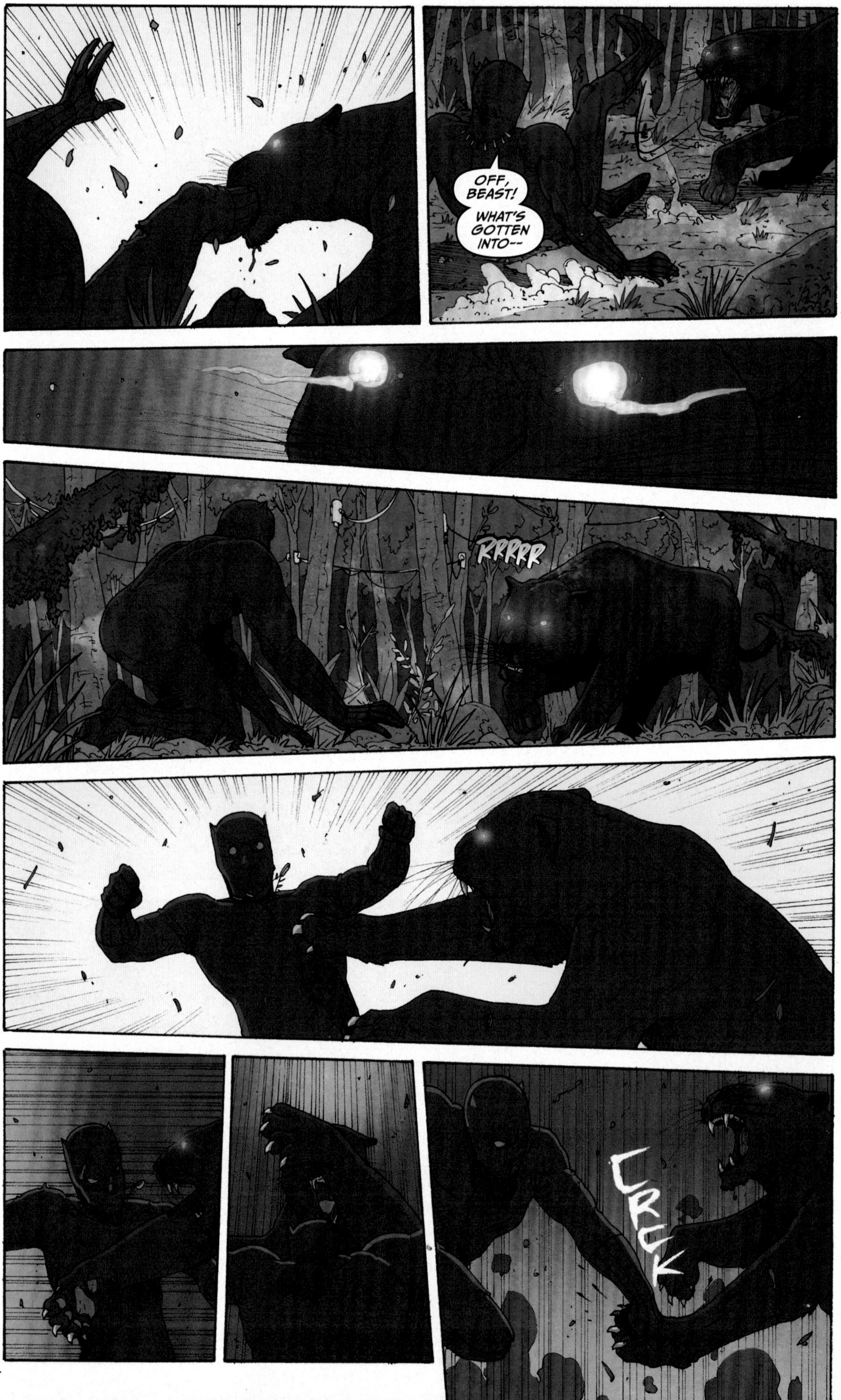
OFF, BEAST!
WHAT'S GOTTEN INTO--
RRRRR
CRCK

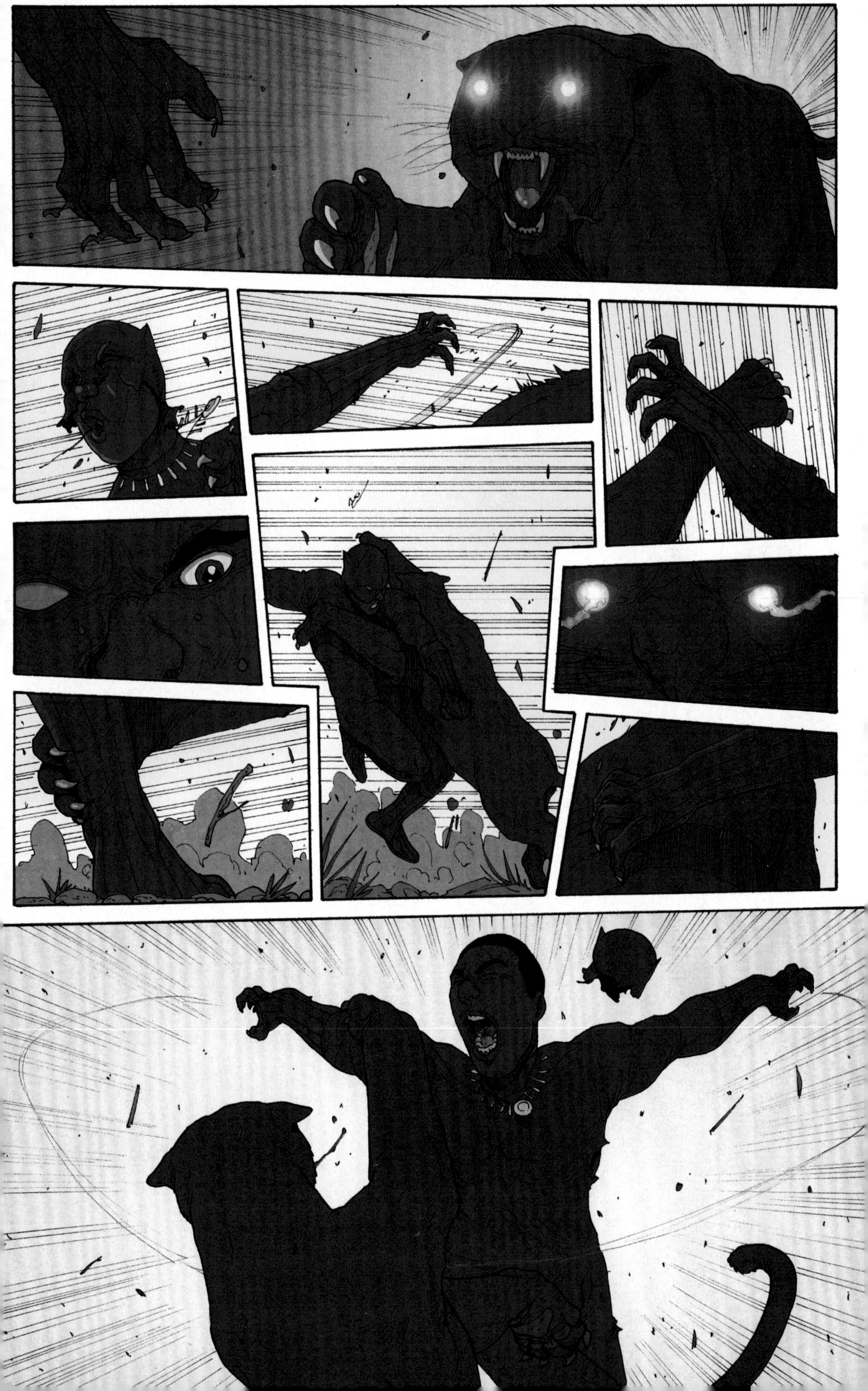

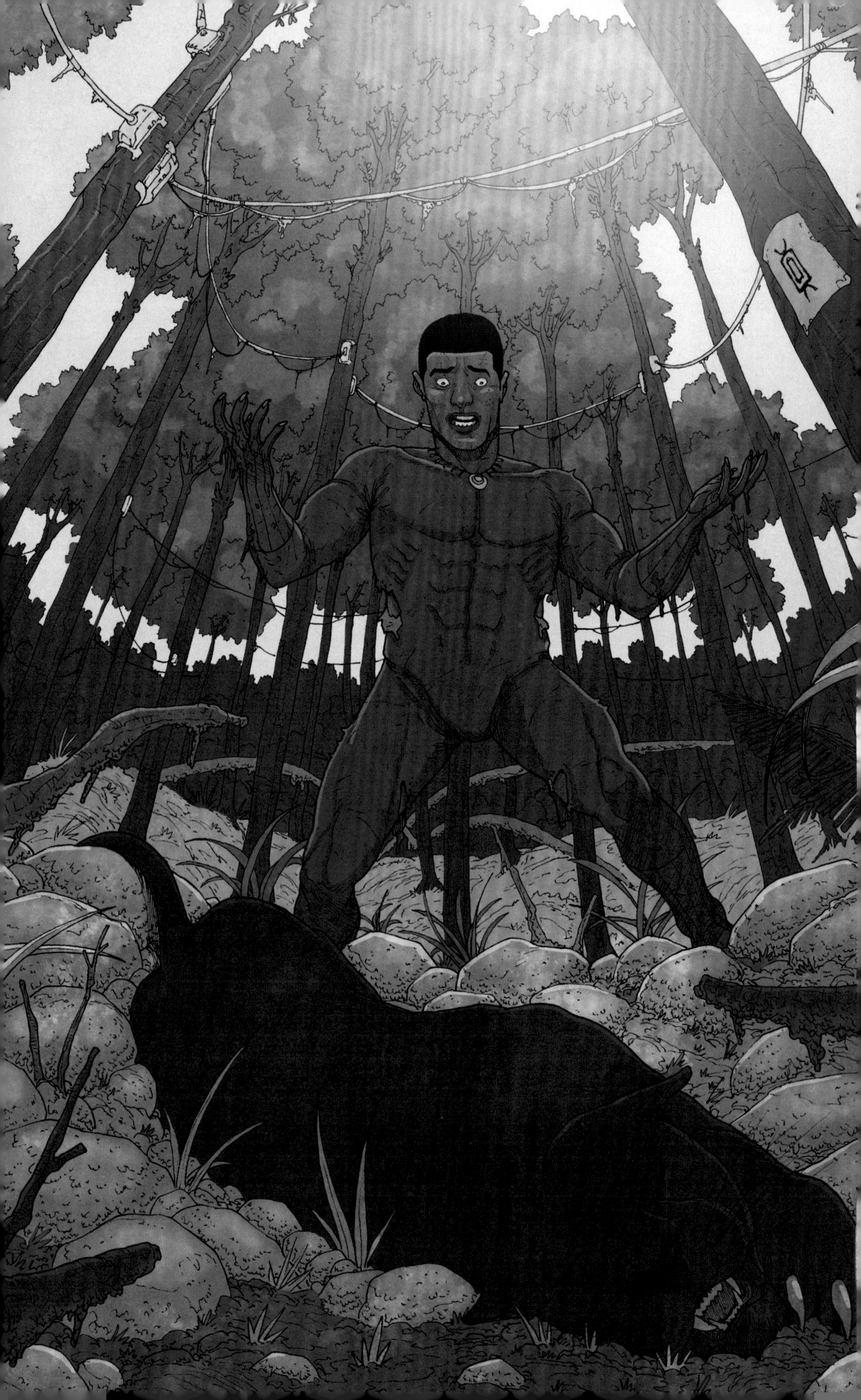

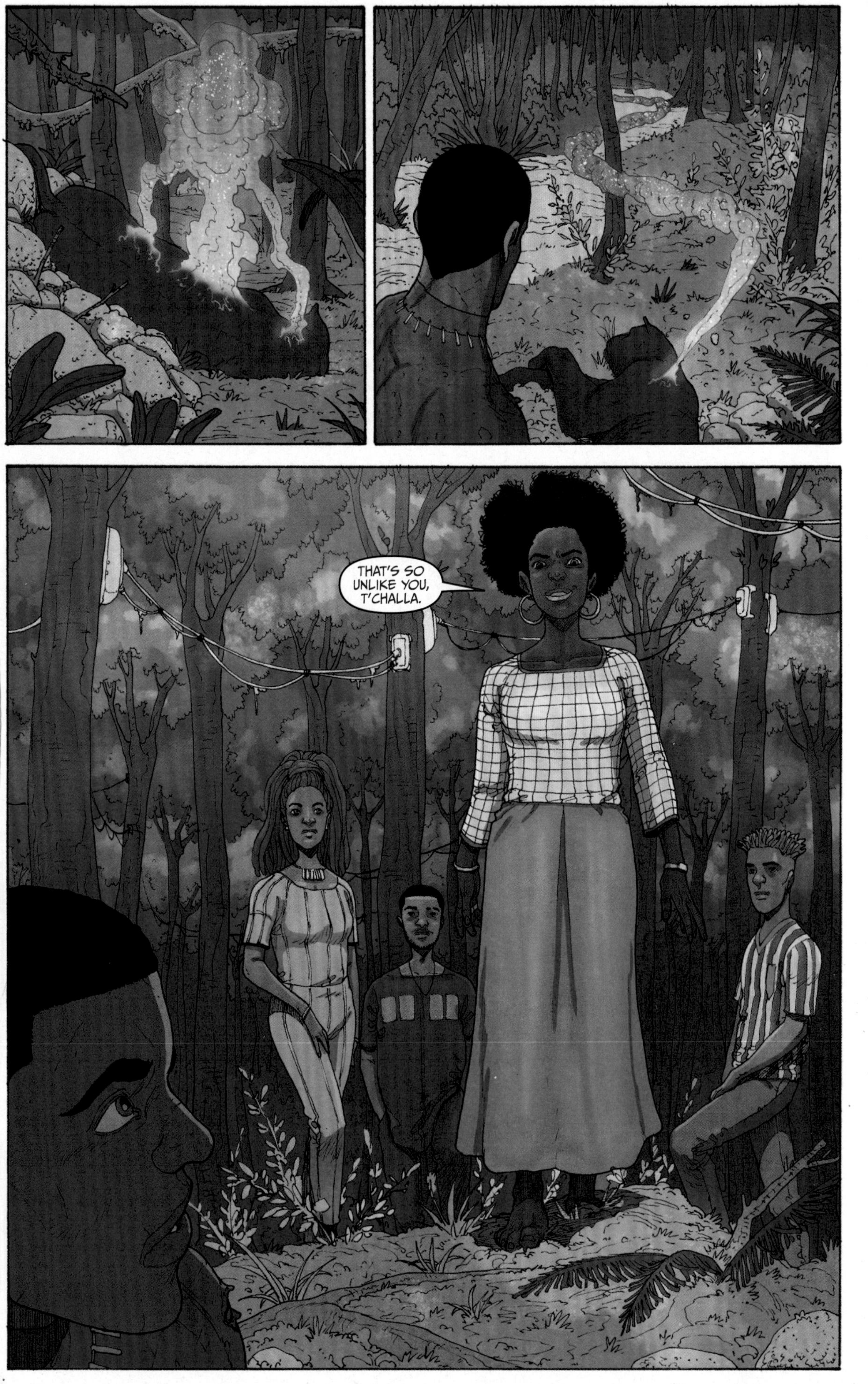
THAT'S SO UNLIKE YOU, T'CHALLA.

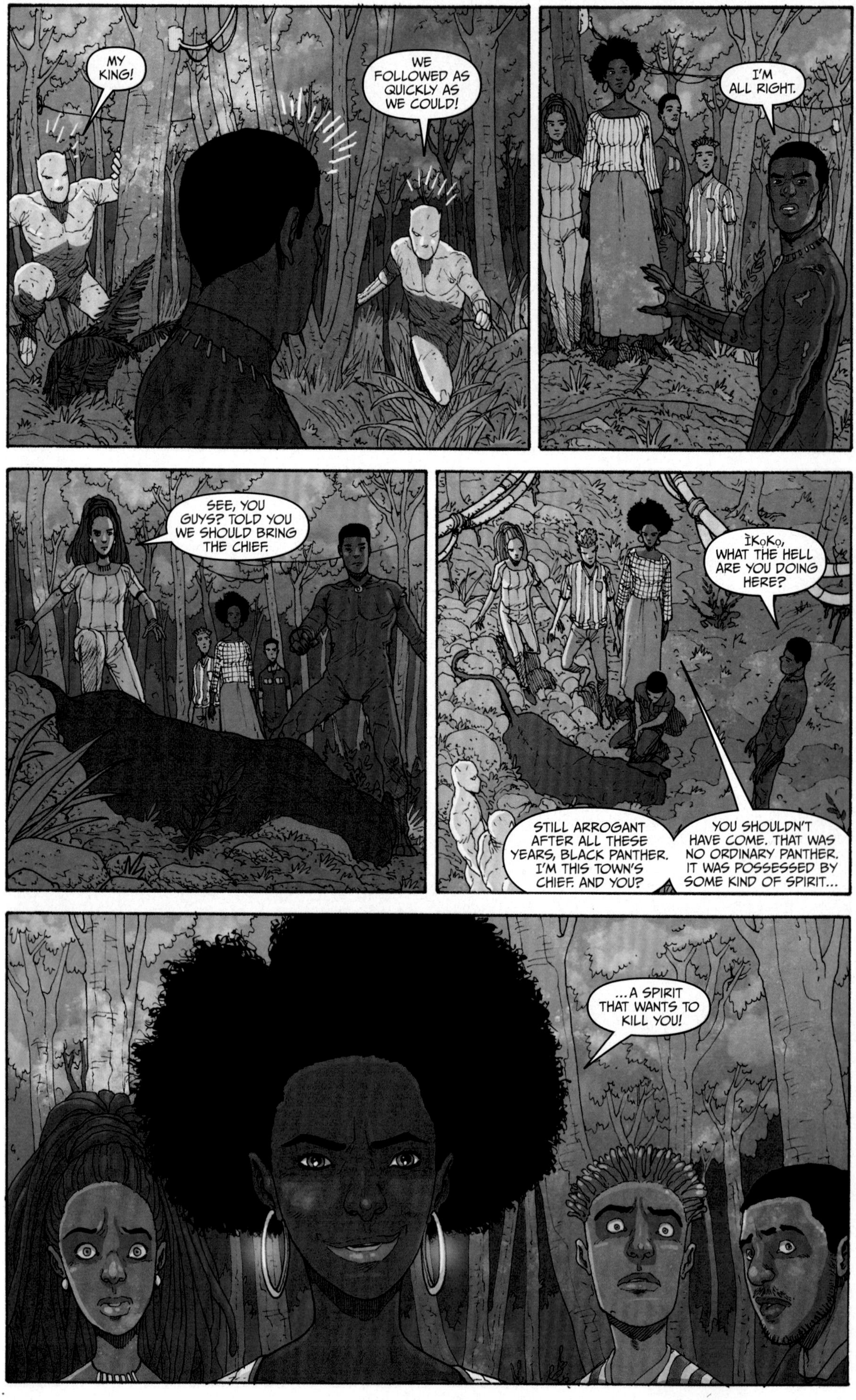
MY KING!
WE FOLLOWED AS QUICKLY AS WE COULD!
I'M ALL RIGHT.
SEE, YOU GUYS? TOLD YOU WE SHOULD BRING THE CHIEF.
ÌKỌKỌ, WHAT THE HELL ARE YOU DOING HERE?
STILL ARROGANT AFTER ALL THESE YEARS, BLACK PANTHER. I'M THIS TOWN'S CHIEF. AND YOU?
YOU SHOULDN'T HAVE COME. THAT WAS NO ORDINARY PANTHER. IT WAS POSSESSED BY SOME KIND OF SPIRIT...
...A SPIRIT THAT WANTS TO KILL YOU!

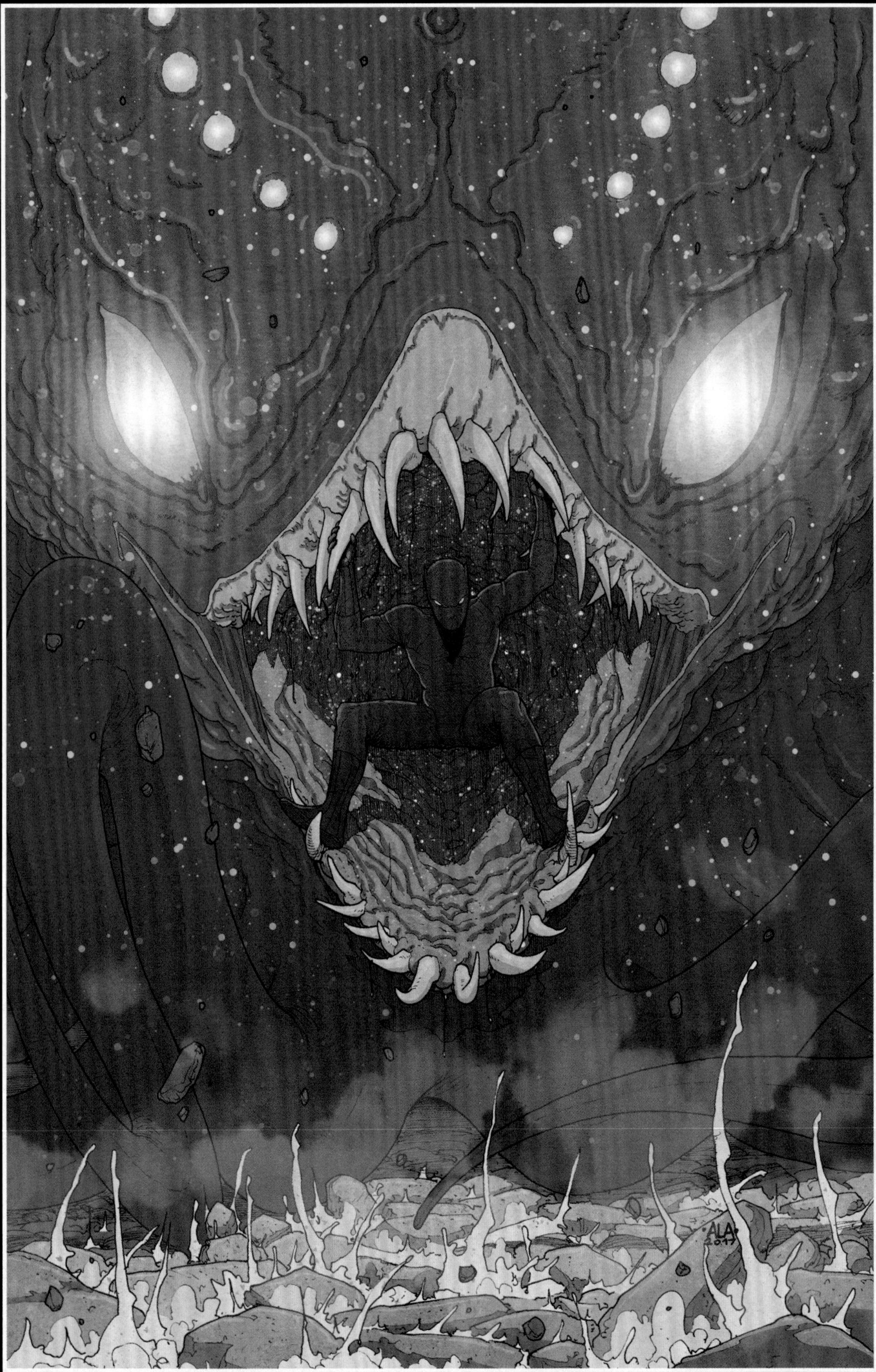
ALA
2017

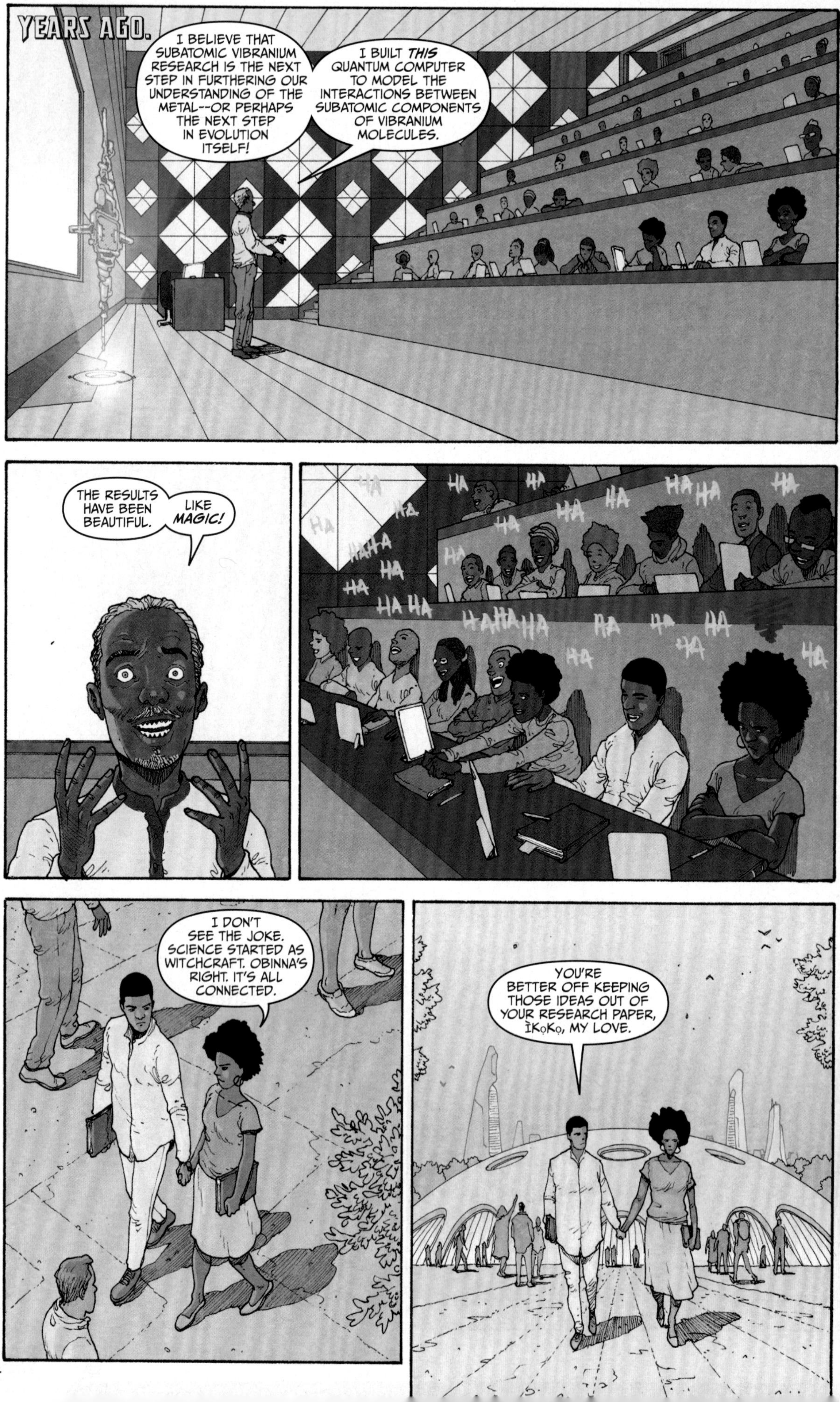
YEARS AGO.
I BELIEVE THAT SUBATOMIC VIBRANIUM RESEARCH IS THE NEXT STEP IN FURTHERING OUR UNDERSTANDING OF THE METAL--OR PERHAPS THE NEXT STEP IN EVOLUTION ITSELF!
I BUILT *THIS* QUANTUM COMPUTER TO MODEL THE INTERACTIONS BETWEEN SUBATOMIC COMPONENTS OF VIBRANIUM MOLECULES.
THE RESULTS HAVE BEEN BEAUTIFUL.
LIKE *MAGIC!*
I DON'T SEE THE JOKE. SCIENCE STARTED AS WITCHCRAFT. OBINNA'S RIGHT. IT'S ALL CONNECTED.
YOU'RE BETTER OFF KEEPING THOSE IDEAS OUT OF YOUR RESEARCH PAPER, ÌKọKọ, MY LOVE.

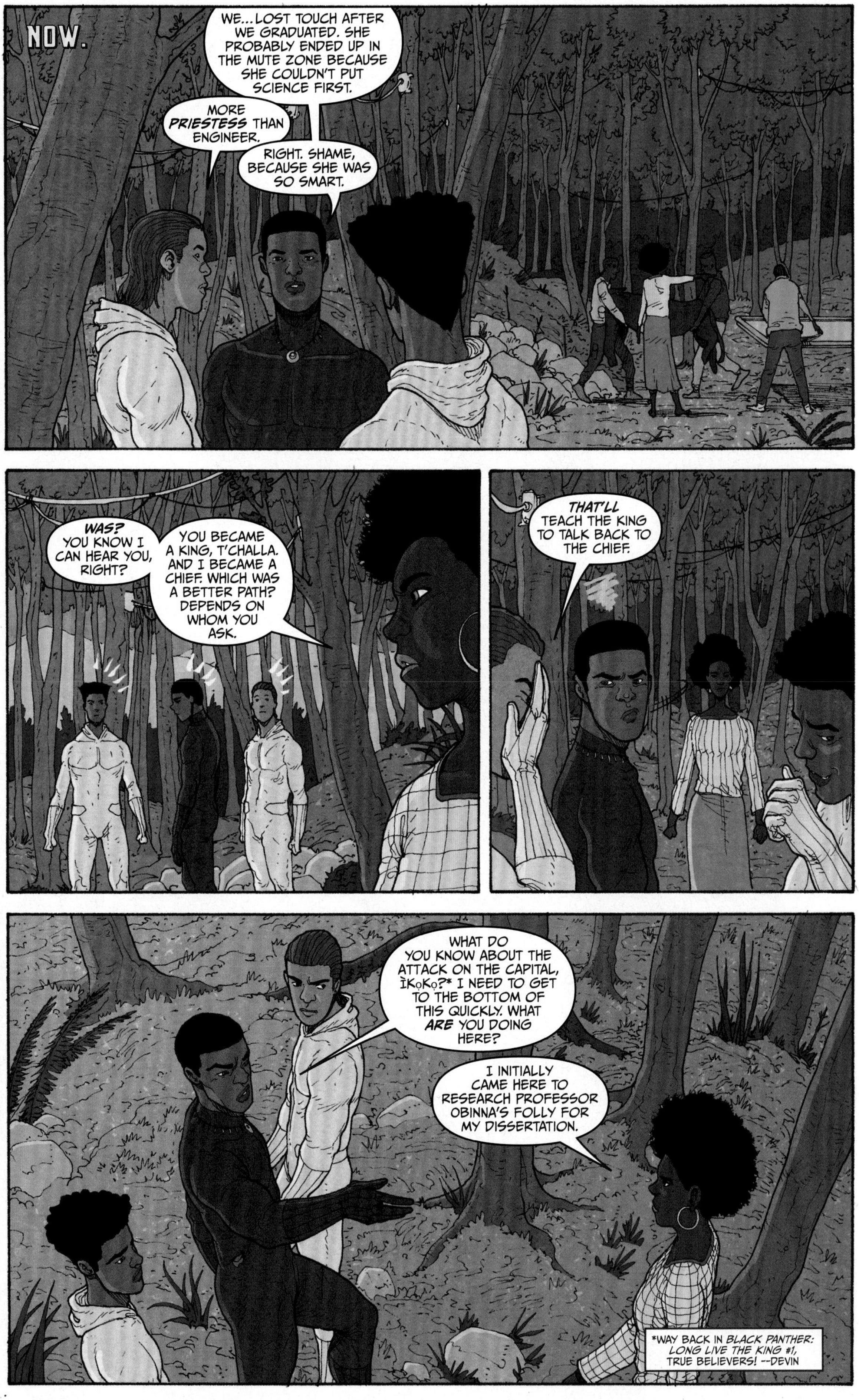
NOW.
WE... LOST TOUCH AFTER WE GRADUATED. SHE PROBABLY ENDED UP IN THE MUTE ZONE BECAUSE SHE COULDN'T PUT SCIENCE FIRST.
MORE PRIESTESS THAN ENGINEER.
RIGHT. SHAME, BECAUSE SHE WAS SO SMART.
WAS? YOU KNOW I CAN HEAR YOU, RIGHT?
YOU BECAME A KING, T'CHALLA. AND I BECAME A CHIEF. WHICH WAS A BETTER PATH? DEPENDS ON WHOM YOU ASK.
THAT'LL TEACH THE KING TO TALK BACK TO THE CHIEF.
WHAT DO YOU KNOW ABOUT THE ATTACK ON THE CAPITAL, ÌKOKO?* I NEED TO GET TO THE BOTTOM OF THIS QUICKLY. WHAT ARE YOU DOING HERE?
I INITIALLY CAME HERE TO RESEARCH PROFESSOR OBINNA'S FOLLY FOR MY DISSERTATION.
*WAY BACK IN BLACK PANTHER: LONG LIVE THE KING #1, TRUE BELIEVERS! --DEVIN

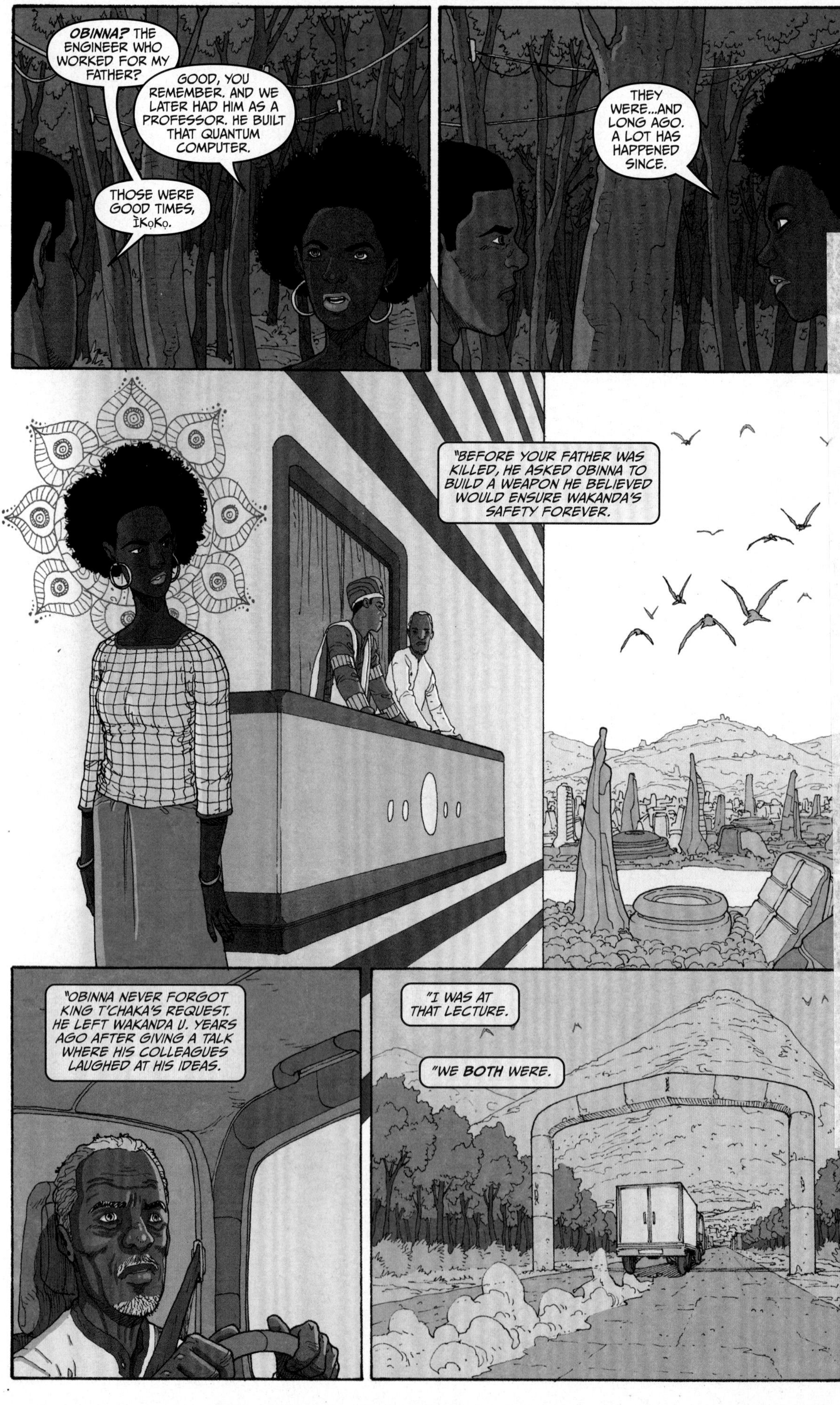
OBINNA? THE ENGINEER WHO WORKED FOR MY FATHER?
GOOD, YOU REMEMBER. AND WE LATER HAD HIM AS A PROFESSOR. HE BUILT THAT QUANTUM COMPUTER.
THOSE WERE GOOD TIMES, ÌKỌKỌ.
THEY WERE...AND LONG AGO. A LOT HAS HAPPENED SINCE.
"BEFORE YOUR FATHER WAS KILLED, HE ASKED OBINNA TO BUILD A WEAPON HE BELIEVED WOULD ENSURE WAKANDA'S SAFETY FOREVER.
"OBINNA NEVER FORGOT KING T'CHAKA'S REQUEST. HE LEFT WAKANDA U. YEARS AGO AFTER GIVING A TALK WHERE HIS COLLEAGUES LAUGHED AT HIS IDEAS.
"I WAS AT THAT LECTURE.
"WE BOTH WERE.

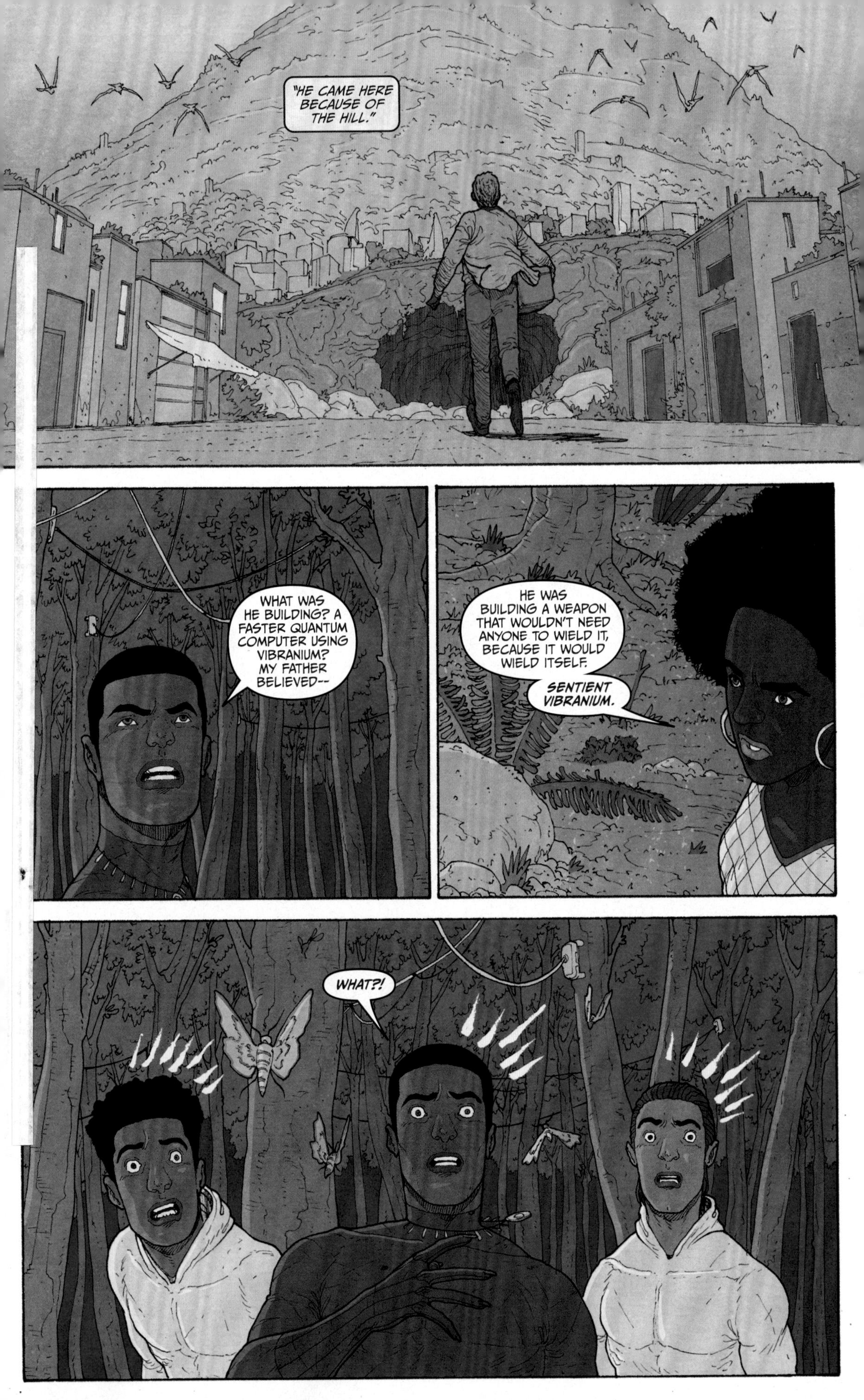
"HE CAME HERE BECAUSE OF THE HILL."
WHAT WAS HE BUILDING? A FASTER QUANTUM COMPUTER USING VIBRANIUM? MY FATHER BELIEVED--
HE WAS BUILDING A WEAPON THAT WOULDN'T NEED ANYONE TO WIELD IT, BECAUSE IT WOULD WIELD ITSELF.
SENTIENT VIBRANIUM.
WHAT?!

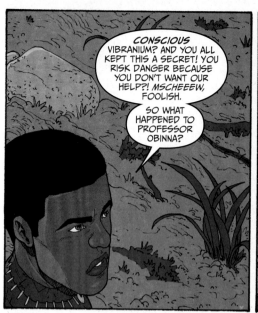

CONSCIOUS VIBRANIUM? AND YOU ALL KEPT THIS A SECRET! YOU RISK DANGER BECAUSE YOU DON'T WANT OUR HELP?! *MSCHEEEW*, FOOLISH.

SO WHAT HAPPENED TO PROFESSOR OBINNA?

THERE'S THE T'CHALLA I KNOW. JUDGMENTAL AND SHORTSIGHTED.

AND SOON *YOU'LL* JUST DISAPPEAR NEVER TO BE HEARD FROM AGAIN. FINISH EXPLAINING EVERYTHING TO ME FIRST THIS TIME.

WE'LL SKIN IT AND PUT THE PELT IN THE TOWN HALL.

THE PELT OF A BLACK PANTHER, THE PERFECT MUTE ZONE SYMBOL.

FUNNY HOW YOU THINK *I* WAS THE ONE WHO DISAPPEARED.

ANYWAY... SOME ELDERS IN THESE PARTS SAY THE HILL ITSELF GREW SO DISGUSTED WITH WHATEVER OBINNA WAS DOING THAT IT SWALLOWED HIM AND THE CAVE HIS LAB WAS IN UP.

I'VE BEEN EVERYWHERE ON THAT HILL--I HAVEN'T SEEN ANY CAVE, SO PERHAPS THERE IS SOME TRUTH TO THE RUMORS.

COME. NOW THAT YOU'VE MADE YOUR SACRIFICE AND OFFERING, LET ME INTRODUCE YOU TO EVERYONE.

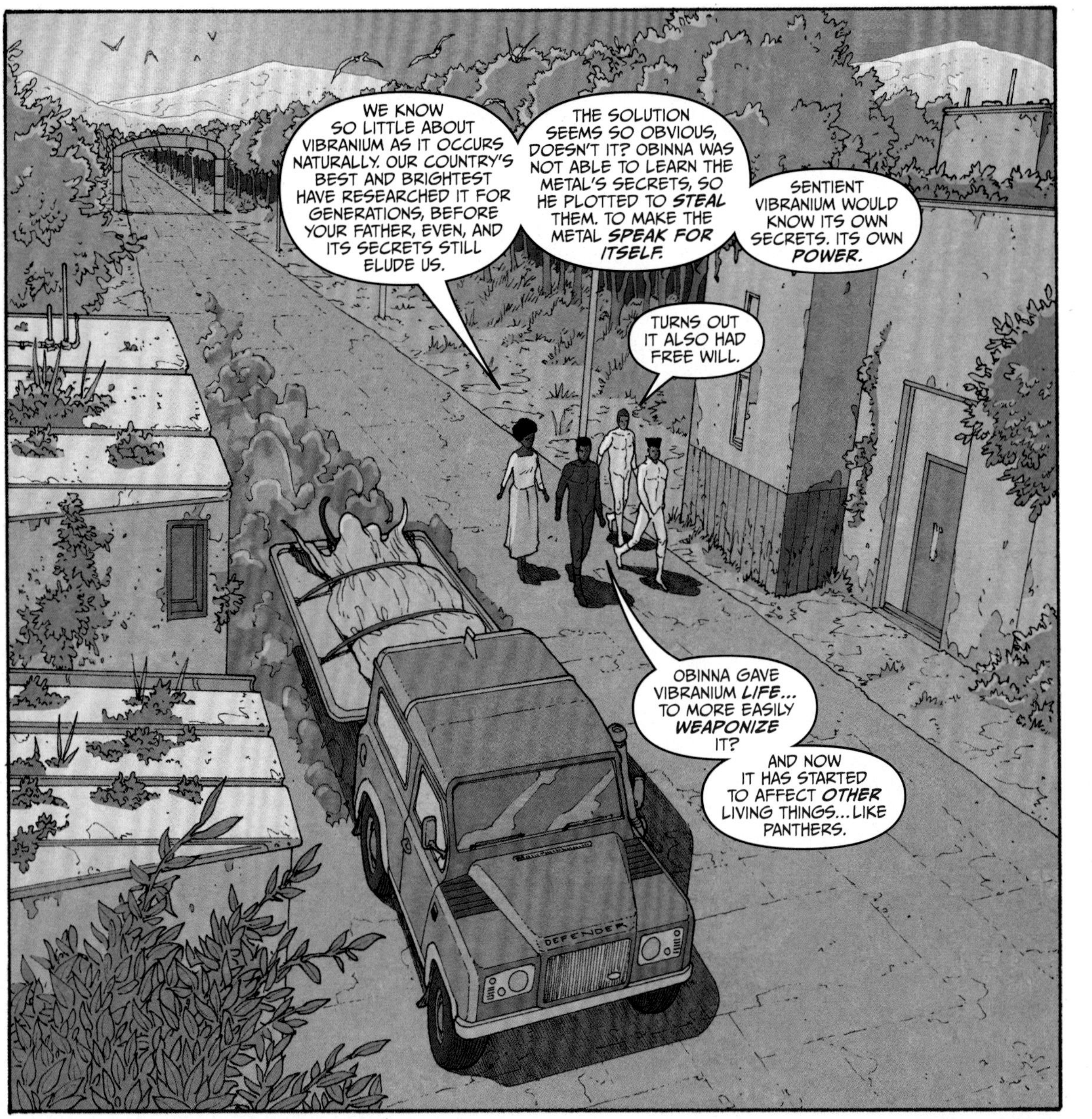
WE KNOW SO LITTLE ABOUT VIBRANIUM AS IT OCCURS NATURALLY. OUR COUNTRY'S BEST AND BRIGHTEST HAVE RESEARCHED IT FOR GENERATIONS, BEFORE YOUR FATHER, EVEN, AND ITS SECRETS STILL ELUDE US.
THE SOLUTION SEEMS SO OBVIOUS, DOESN'T IT? OBINNA WAS NOT ABLE TO LEARN THE METAL'S SECRETS, SO HE PLOTTED TO ***STEAL*** THEM. TO MAKE THE METAL ***SPEAK FOR ITSELF.***
SENTIENT VIBRANIUM WOULD KNOW ITS OWN SECRETS. ITS OWN ***POWER.***
TURNS OUT IT ALSO HAD FREE WILL.
OBINNA GAVE VIBRANIUM ***LIFE...*** TO MORE EASILY ***WEAPONIZE*** IT?
AND NOW IT HAS STARTED TO AFFECT ***OTHER*** LIVING THINGS... LIKE PANTHERS.
DEFENDER

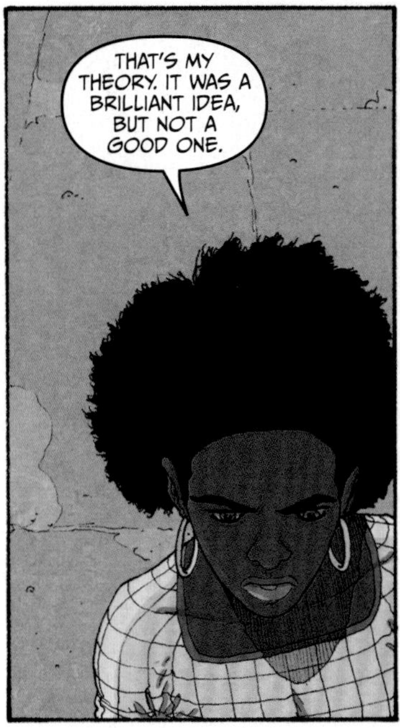
THAT'S MY THEORY. IT WAS A BRILLIANT IDEA, BUT NOT A GOOD ONE.

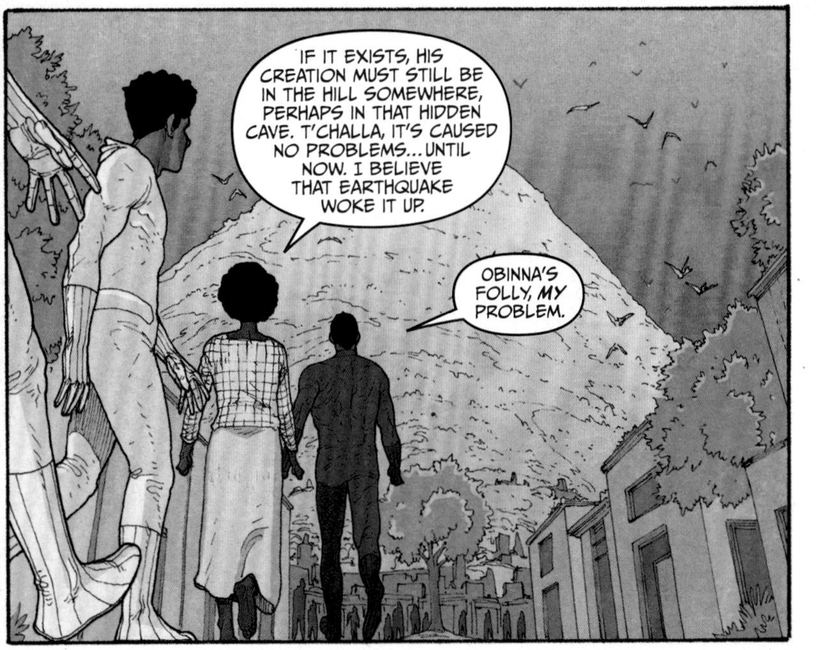
IF IT EXISTS, HIS CREATION MUST STILL BE IN THE HILL SOMEWHERE, PERHAPS IN THAT HIDDEN CAVE. T'CHALLA, IT'S CAUSED NO PROBLEMS... UNTIL NOW. I BELIEVE THAT EARTHQUAKE WOKE IT UP.
OBINNA'S FOLLY, ***MY*** PROBLEM.

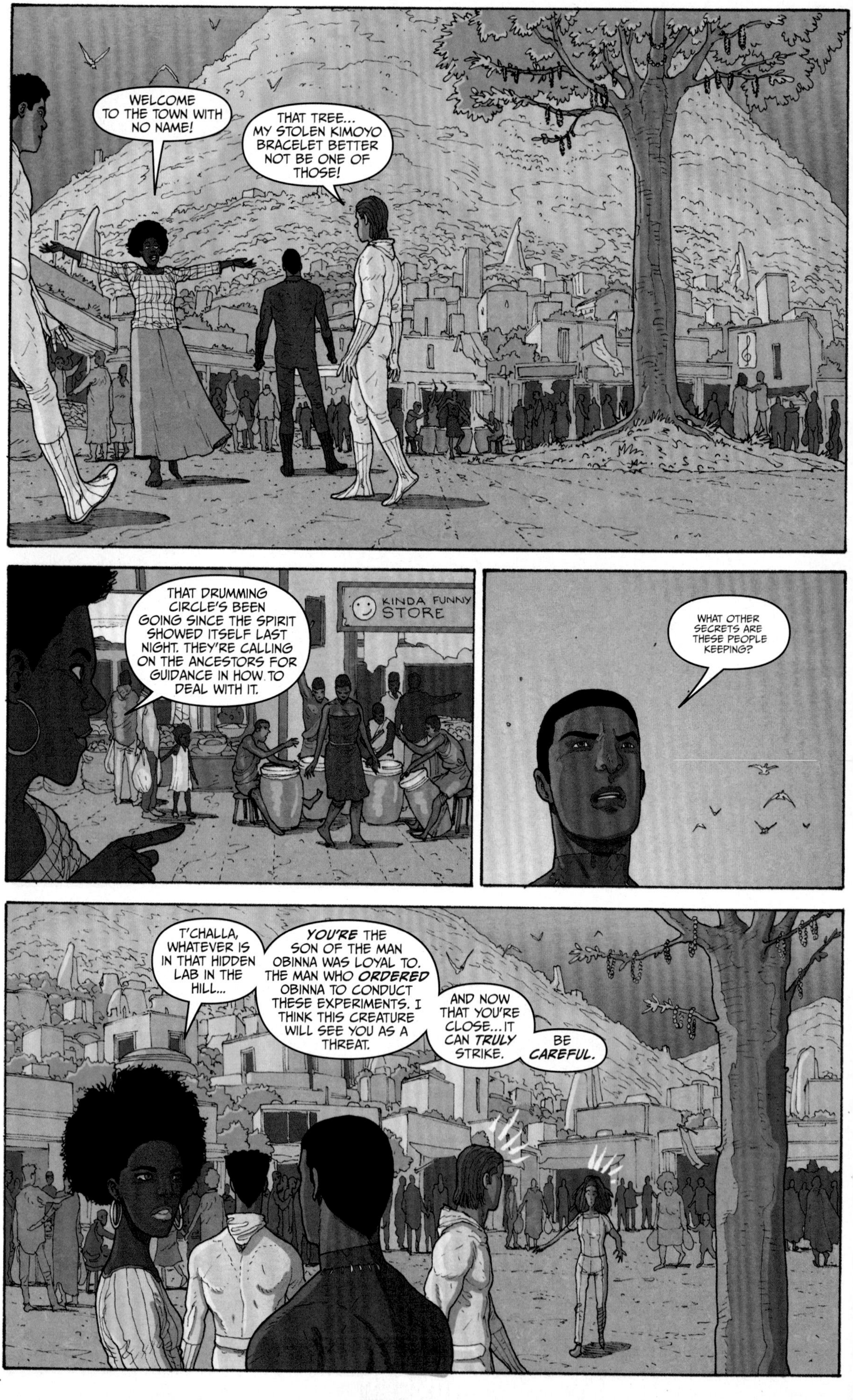
WELCOME TO THE TOWN WITH NO NAME!
THAT TREE... MY STOLEN KIMOYO BRACELET BETTER NOT BE ONE OF THOSE!
THAT DRUMMING CIRCLE'S BEEN GOING SINCE THE SPIRIT SHOWED ITSELF LAST NIGHT. THEY'RE CALLING ON THE ANCESTORS FOR GUIDANCE IN HOW TO DEAL WITH IT.
KINDA FUNNY STORE
WHAT OTHER SECRETS ARE THESE PEOPLE KEEPING?
T'CHALLA, WHATEVER IS IN THAT HIDDEN LAB IN THE HILL...
YOU'RE THE SON OF THE MAN OBINNA WAS LOYAL TO. THE MAN WHO ORDERED OBINNA TO CONDUCT THESE EXPERIMENTS. I THINK THIS CREATURE WILL SEE YOU AS A THREAT.
AND NOW THAT YOU'RE CLOSE...IT CAN TRULY STRIKE.
BE CAREFUL.

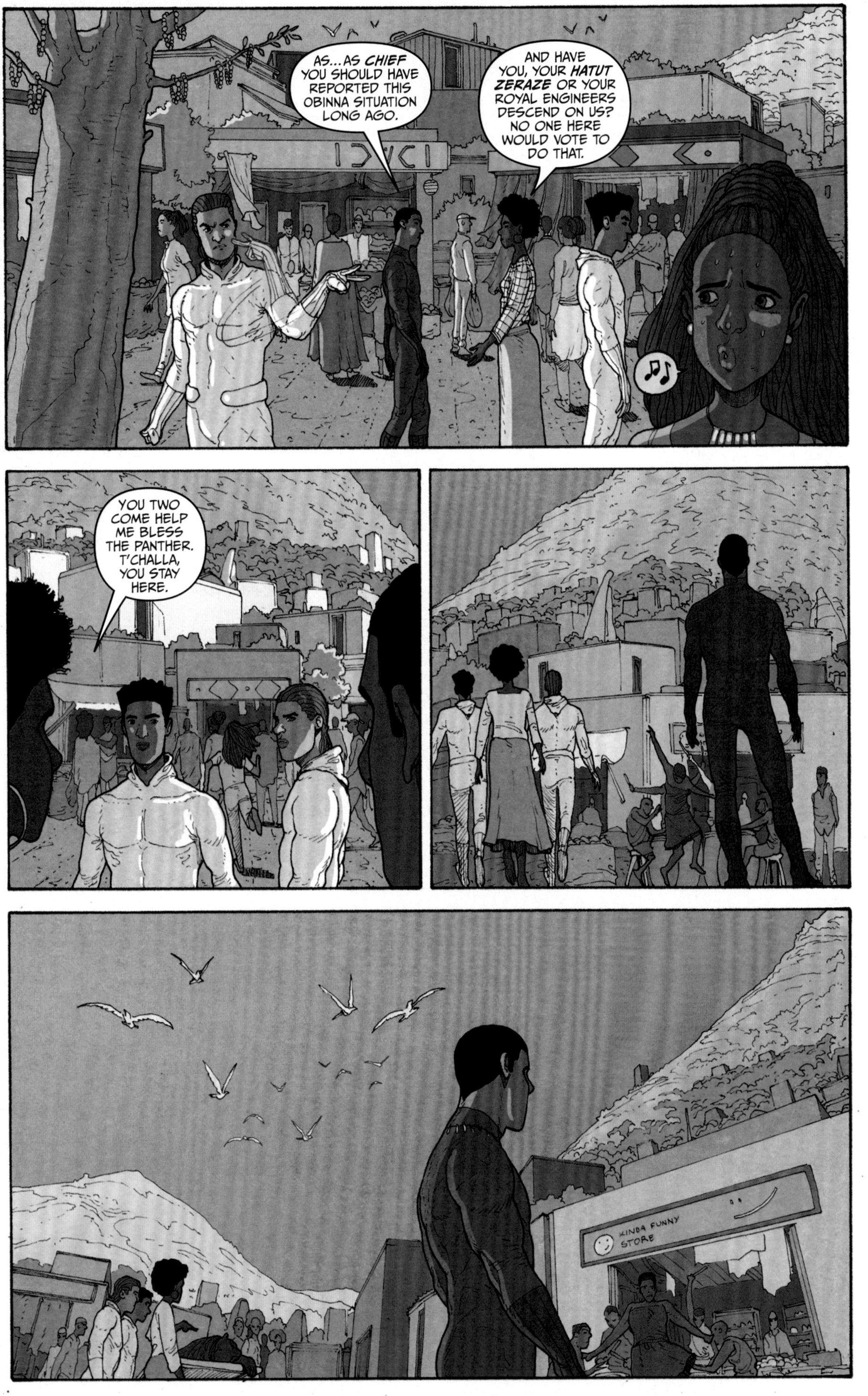
AS...AS *CHIEF* YOU SHOULD HAVE REPORTED THIS OBINNA SITUATION LONG AGO.
AND HAVE YOU, YOUR *HATUT ZERAZE* OR YOUR ROYAL ENGINEERS DESCEND ON US? NO ONE HERE WOULD VOTE TO DO THAT.
YOU TWO COME HELP ME BLESS THE PANTHER. T'CHALLA, YOU STAY HERE.
KINDA FUNNY STORE

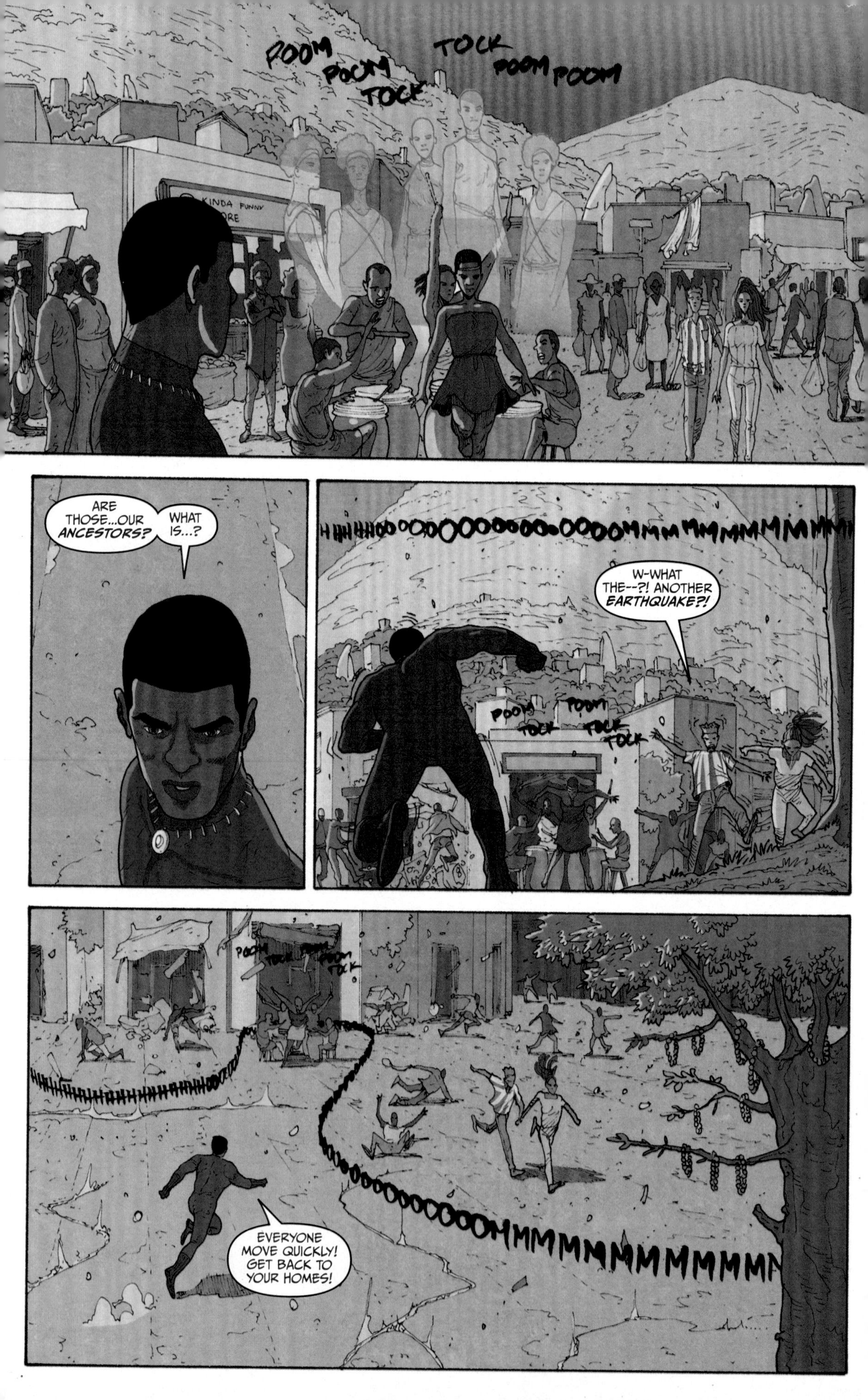
POOM
POOM
TOCK
TOCK
POOM POOM
KINDA FUNNY
ORE
ARE THOSE...OUR ANCESTORS?
WHAT IS...?
HHHHHOOOOOOOOOOOOOOOOOOMMMMMMMMMMMMMM
W-WHAT THE--?! ANOTHER EARTHQUAKE?!
POOM POOM
TOCK TOCK TOCK
POOM TOCK POOM POOM TOCK
HHHHHHHHHHHHHHHHOOOOOOOOOOOOOOOOOOOOOOOMMMMMMMMMMMMM
EVERYONE MOVE QUICKLY! GET BACK TO YOUR HOMES!

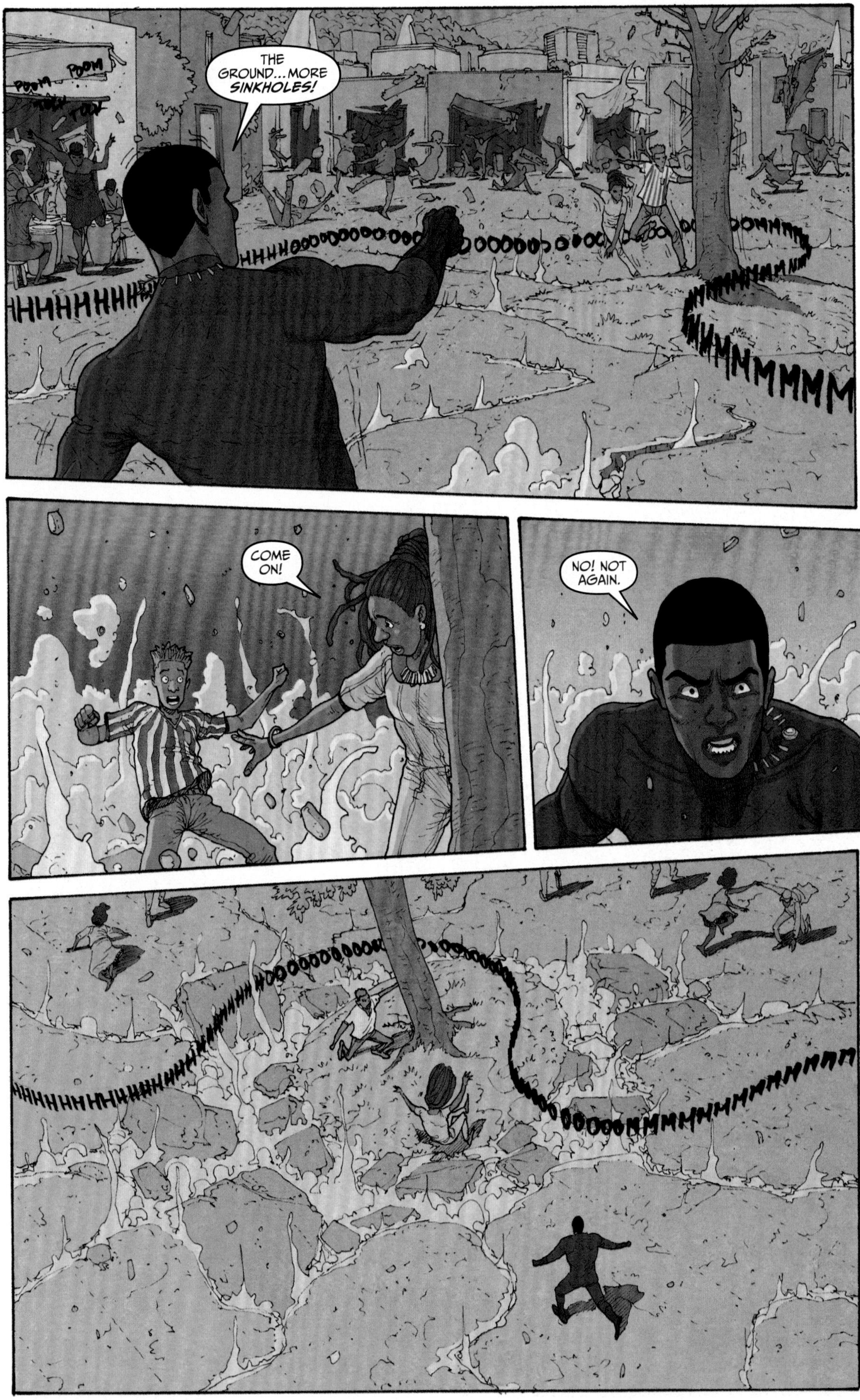

POOM POOM
TOOM TOOM
THE GROUND...MORE *SINKHOLES!*
HHHHHHHHHHHHOOOOOOOOOOOOOOOOOOOOOOOOOOOOOMMMMMMMMMMMMM
COME ON!
NO! NOT AGAIN.
HHHHHHHHHHHHHHHHHHHHHHHHHHOOOOOOOOOOOOOOOOOOOOOOOOOMMMMMMMMMMMMMMMMMMMM

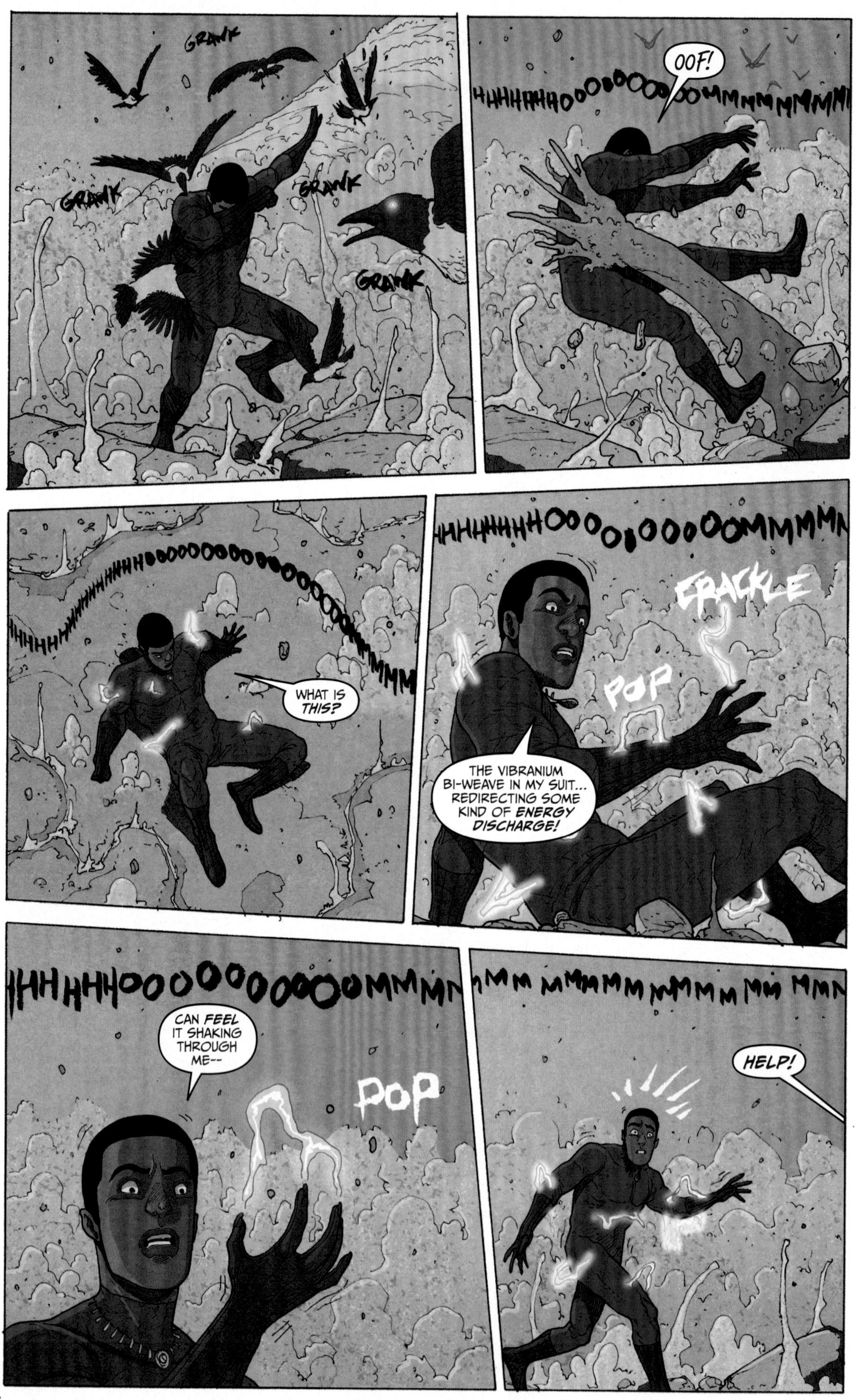
GRANK
GRANK
GRANK
GRANK
HHHHHHOOOOOOOOOOOMMMMMMMMMMM
OOF!
HHHHHHHHHHHHHHHOOOOOOOOOOOOOOOMMMM
WHAT IS *THIS?*
HHHHHHHHOOOOOOOOOOOMMMMM
CRACKLE
POP
THE VIBRANIUM BI-WEAVE IN MY SUIT... REDIRECTING SOME KIND OF *ENERGY DISCHARGE!*
HHHHHHOOOOOOOOOOOMMMMM
CAN *FEEL* IT SHAKING THROUGH ME--
POP
MMMMMMMMMMMMMMMMMM
HELP!

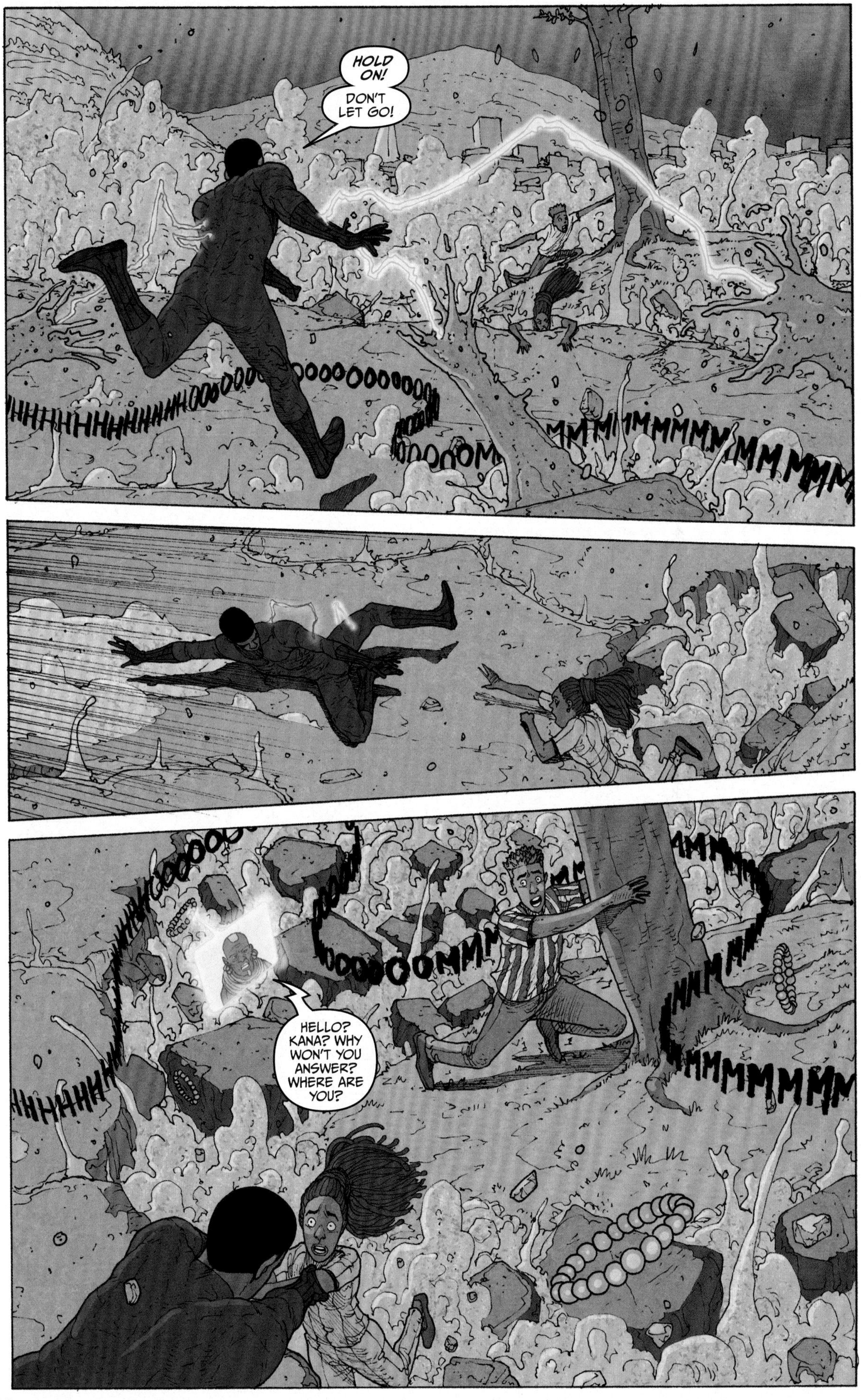
HOLD ON!
DON'T LET GO!
HHHHHHHHHHHHHOOOOOOOOOOOOOOOOOOOOOOM
MMMMMMMMMMMMMM
HHHHHOOOOOOOOOOOOOOOOOOOOOOOOOMMMM
MMMMMMMMMMMMMMMMM
HELLO? KANA? WHY WON'T YOU ANSWER? WHERE ARE YOU?

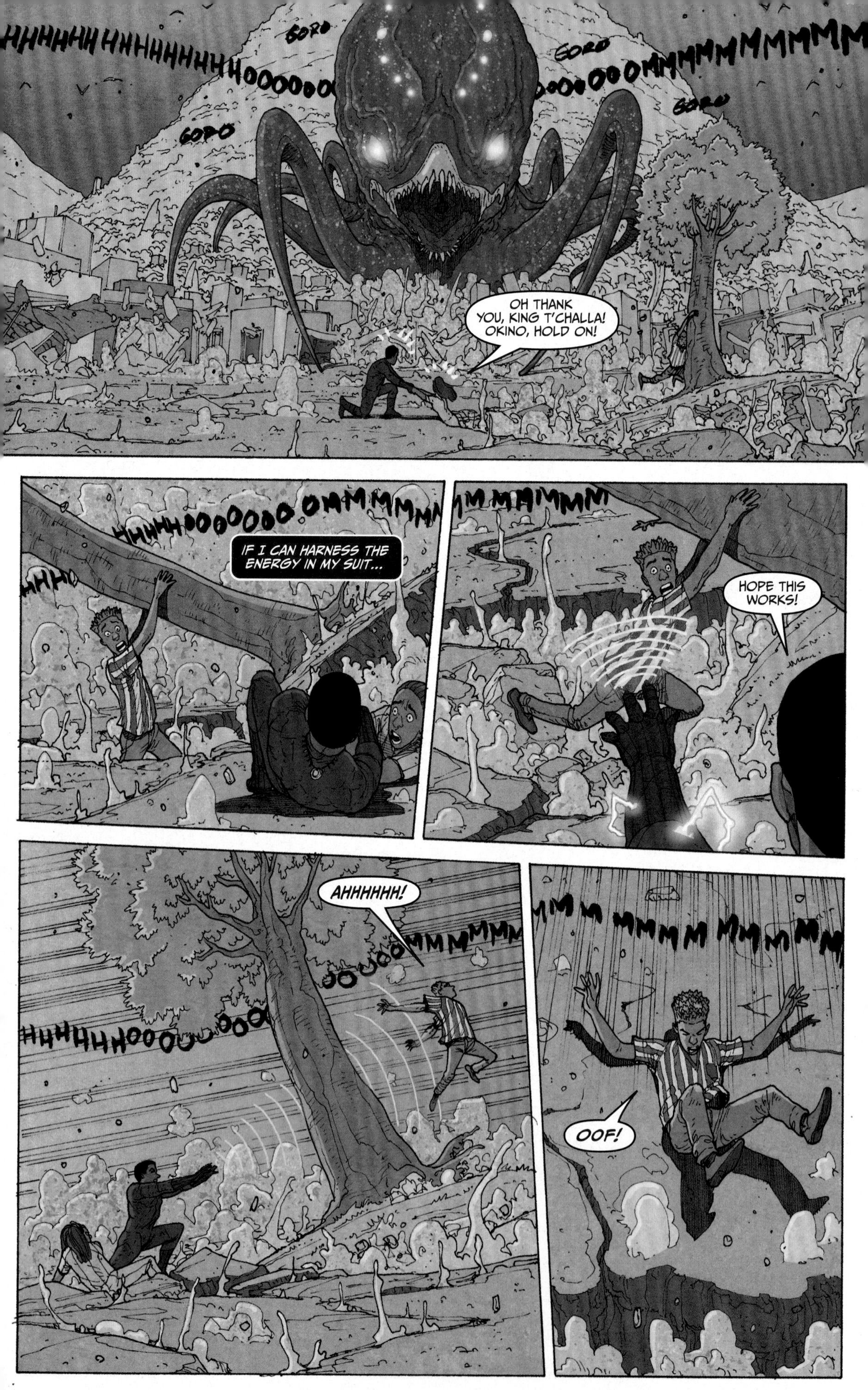

HHHHHHHHHHHHHHHHHHHOOOOOOOOOOOOOOOMMMMMMMMMMM
GORO
GORO
GORO
GORO
OH THANK YOU, KING T'CHALLA! OKINO, HOLD ON!
HHHHHOOOOOOOOOMMMMMMMMMMM
IF I CAN HARNESS THE ENERGY IN MY SUIT...
HOPE THIS WORKS!
AHHHHHH!
HHHHHHHOOOOOOOOOOOOMMMM
OOF!

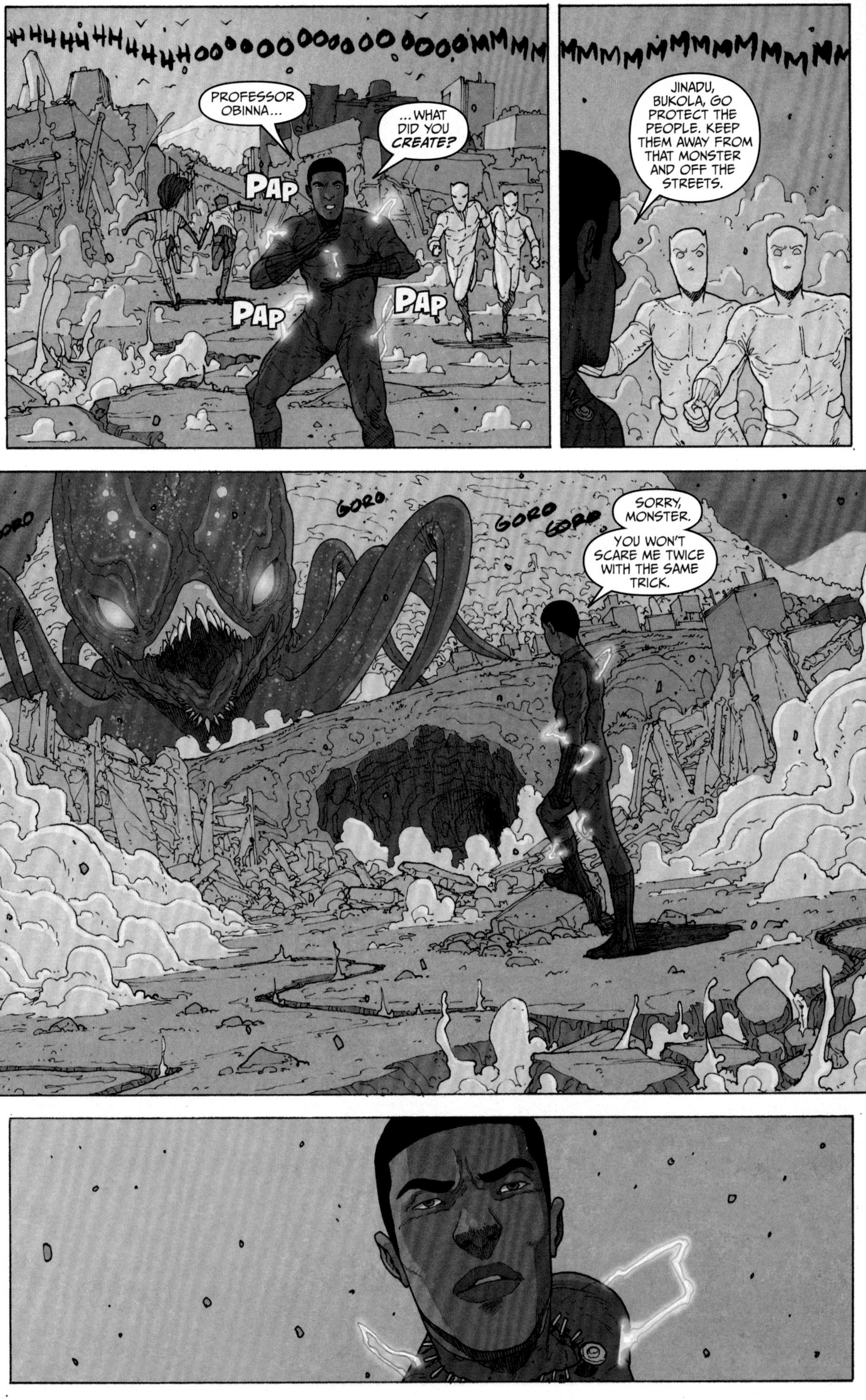
HHHHHHHHHHHOOOOOOOOOOOOOOOMMMMM
PROFESSOR OBINNA...
...WHAT DID YOU CREATE?
PAP
PAP
PAP
MMMMMMMMMMMMMMMM
JINADU, BUKOLA, GO PROTECT THE PEOPLE. KEEP THEM AWAY FROM THAT MONSTER AND OFF THE STREETS.
GORO
GORO
GORO
GORO
SORRY, MONSTER.
YOU WON'T SCARE ME TWICE WITH THE SAME TRICK.

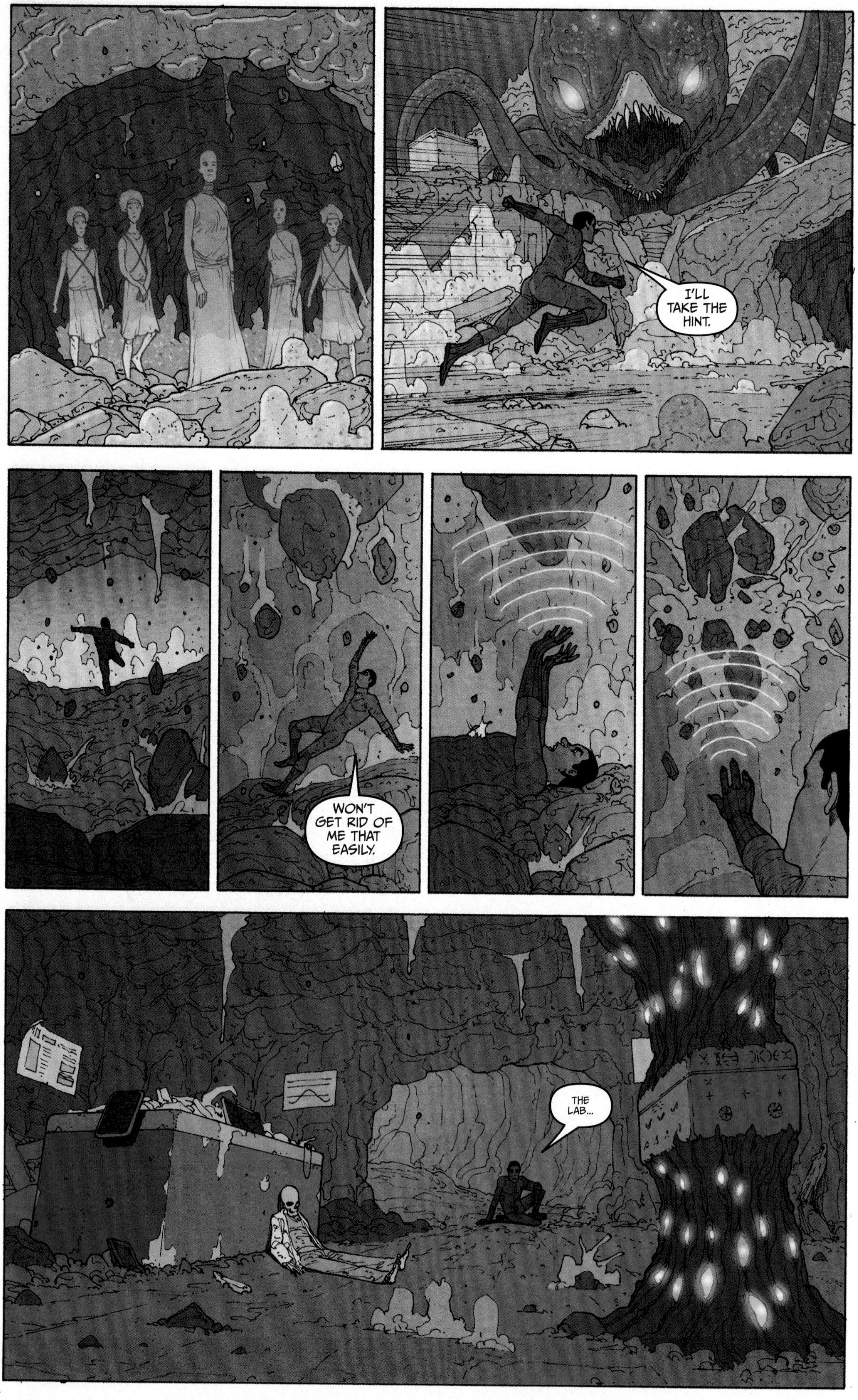
I'LL TAKE THE HINT.
WON'T GET RID OF ME THAT EASILY.
THE LAB...

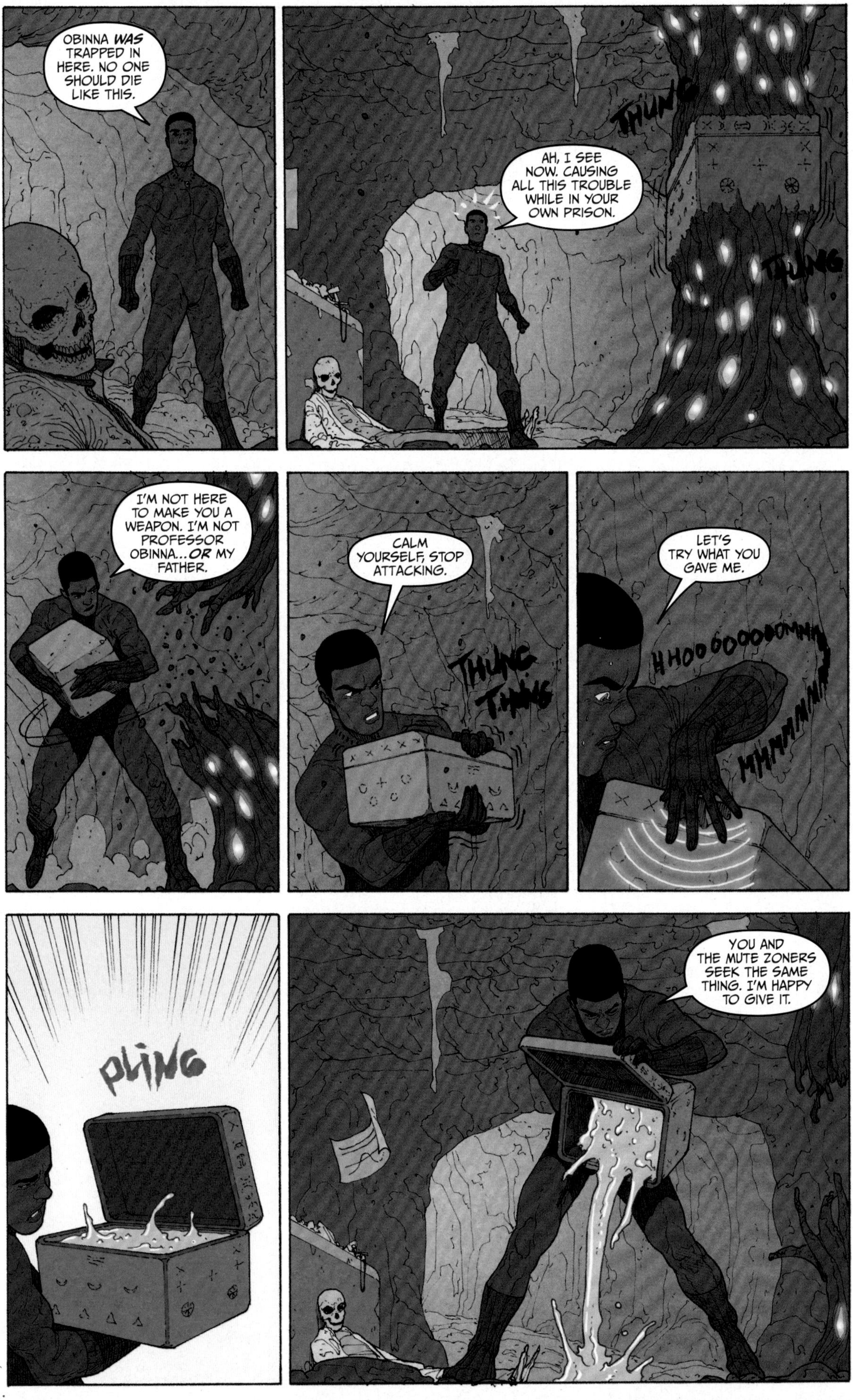
OBINNA WAS TRAPPED IN HERE. NO ONE SHOULD DIE LIKE THIS.
THUNG
AH, I SEE NOW. CAUSING ALL THIS TROUBLE WHILE IN YOUR OWN PRISON.
THUNG
I'M NOT HERE TO MAKE YOU A WEAPON. I'M NOT PROFESSOR OBINNA...OR MY FATHER.
CALM YOURSELF, STOP ATTACKING.
THUNG
THUNG
LET'S TRY WHAT YOU GAVE ME.
HHOOOOOOOMMM
MMMMMMM
PLING
YOU AND THE MUTE ZONERS SEEK THE SAME THING. I'M HAPPY TO GIVE IT.

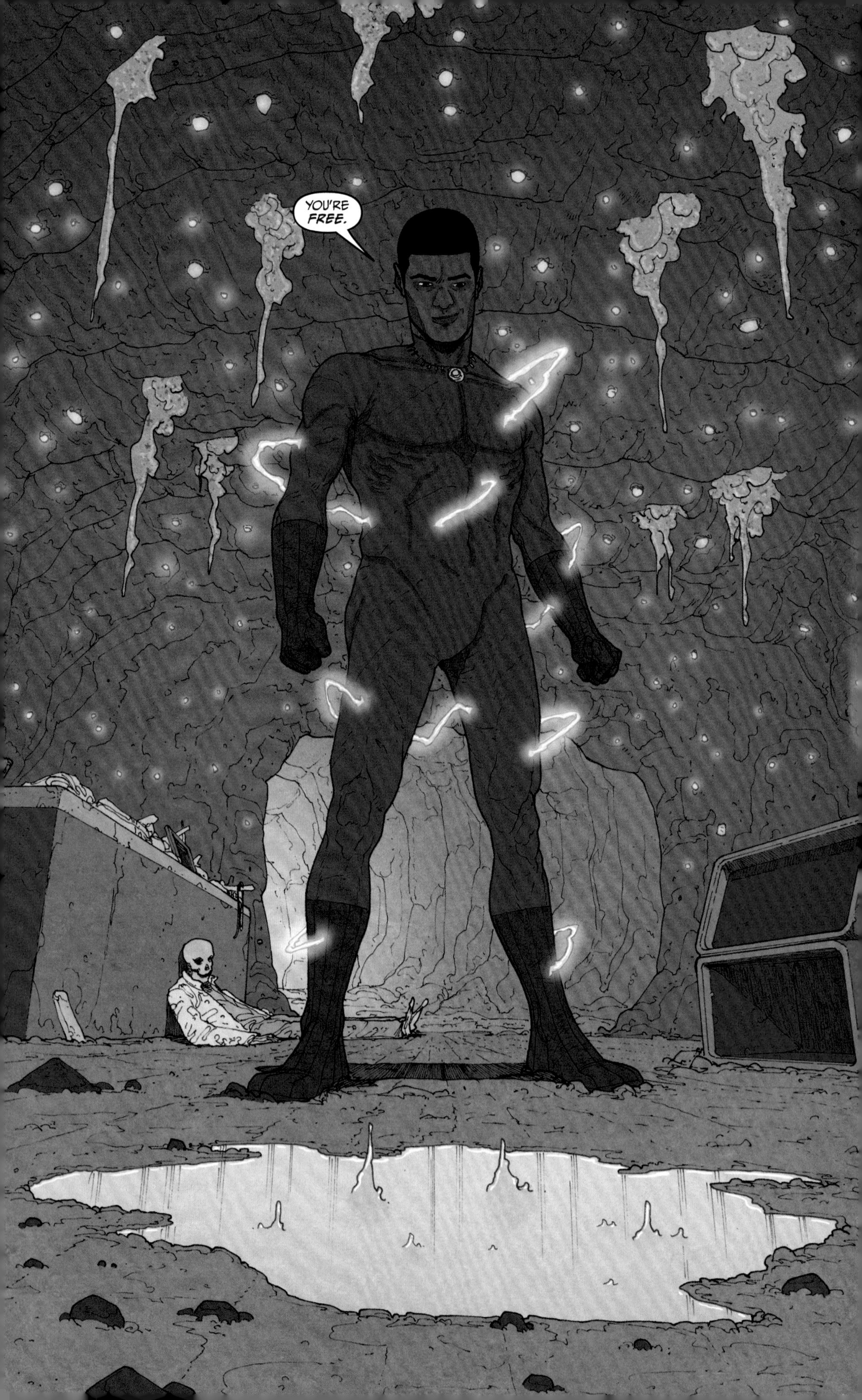
YOU'RE FREE.

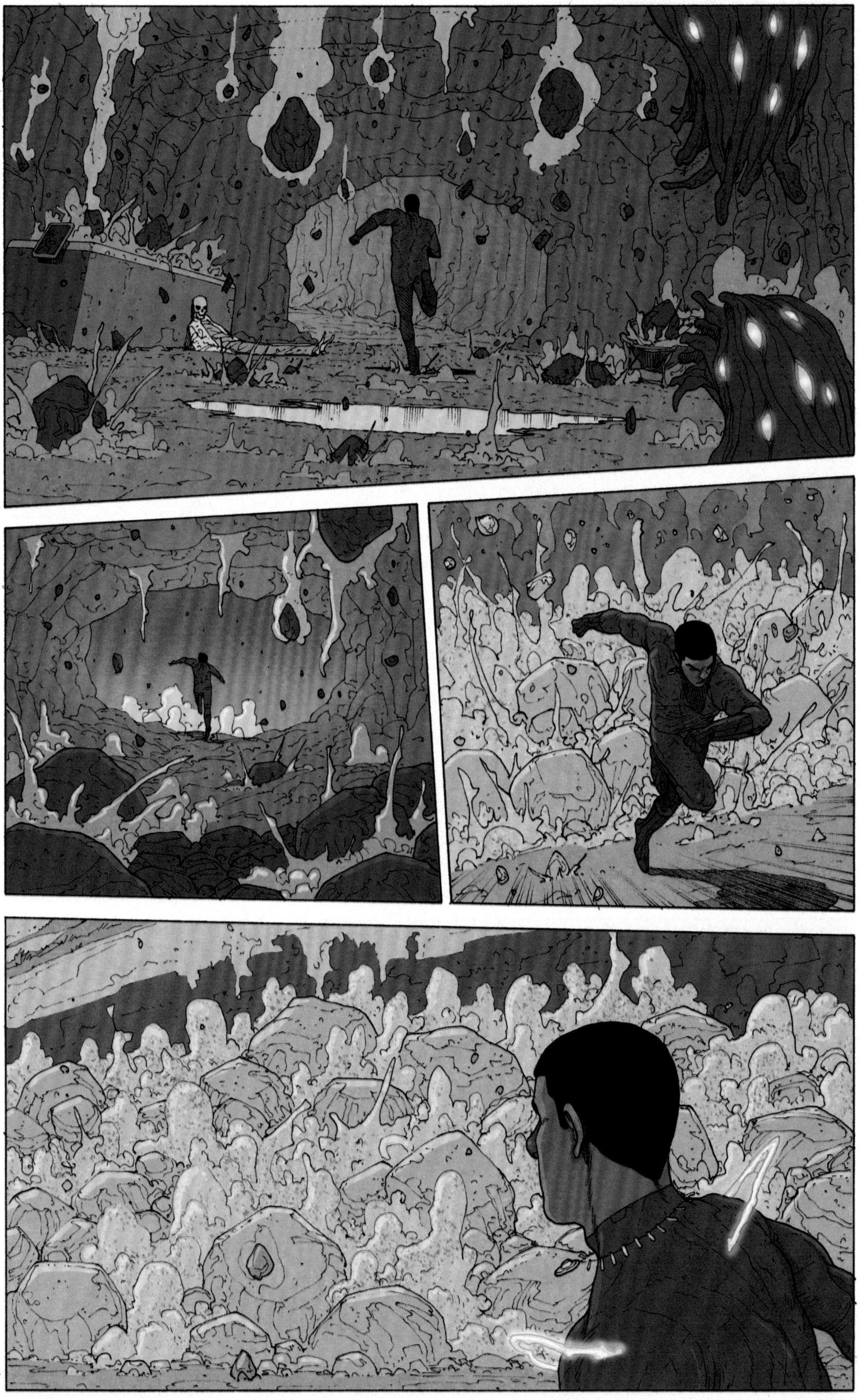

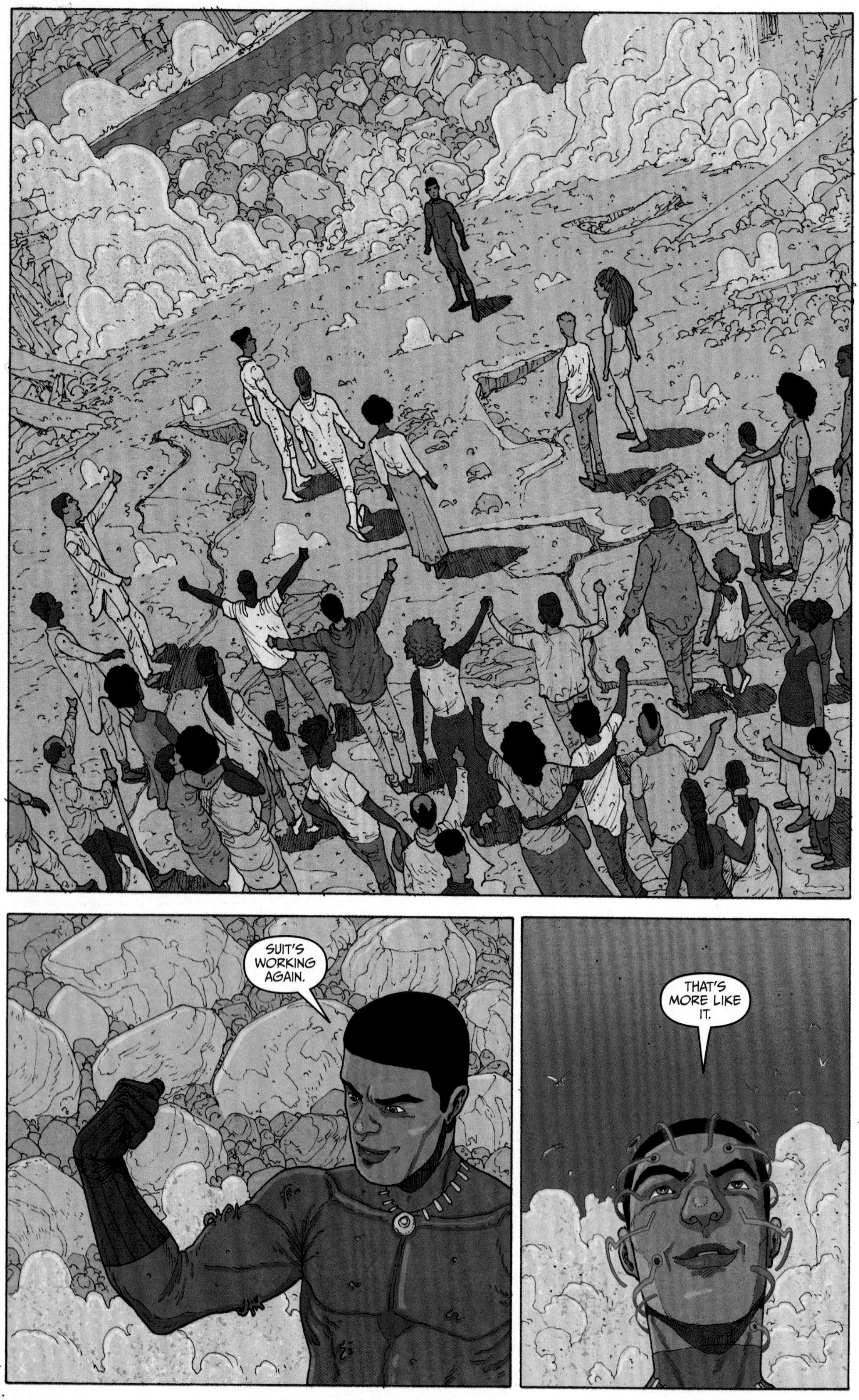
SUIT'S WORKING AGAIN.
THAT'S MORE LIKE IT.

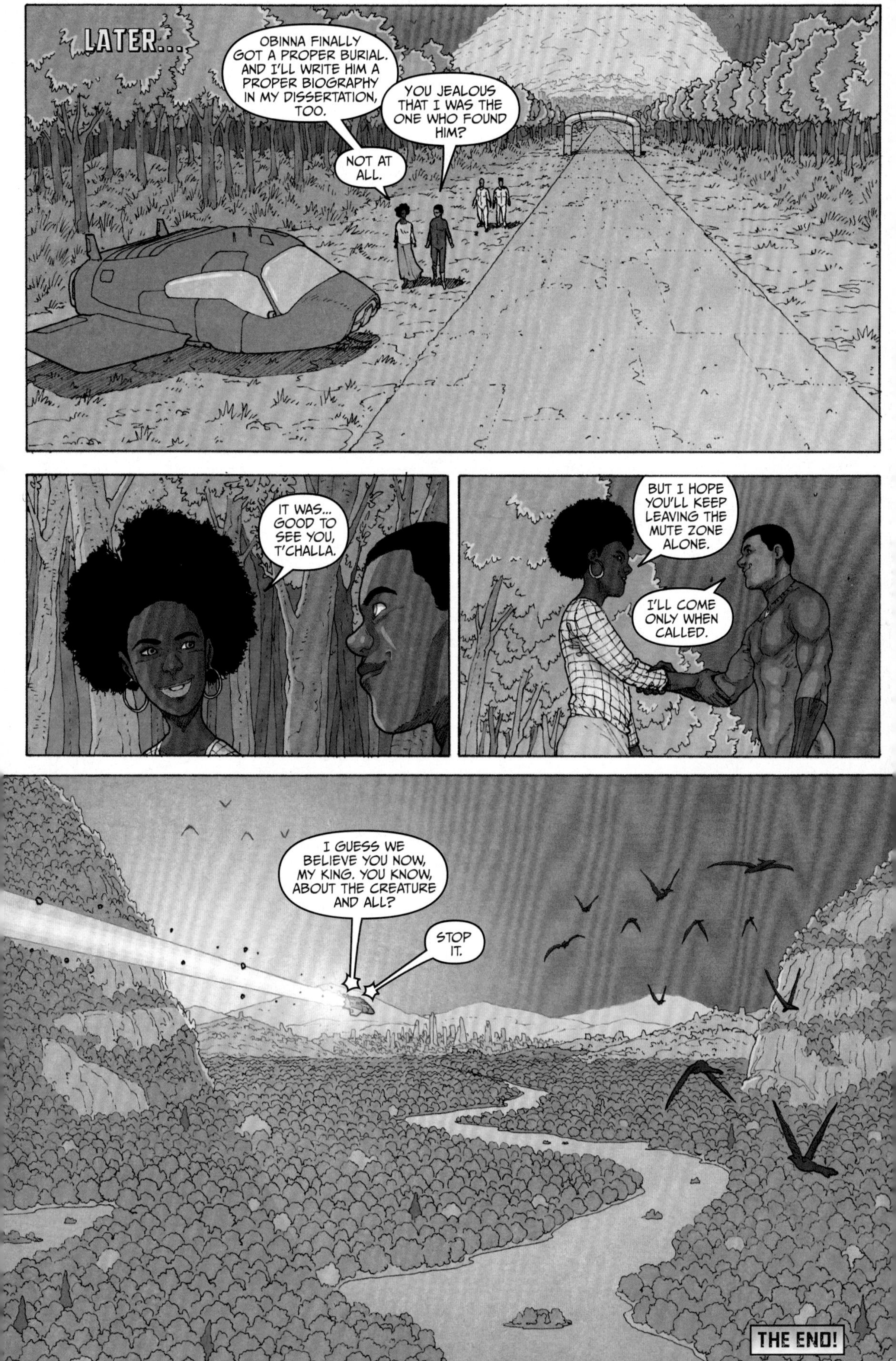
LATER...
OBINNA FINALLY GOT A PROPER BURIAL. AND I'LL WRITE HIM A PROPER BIOGRAPHY IN MY DISSERTATION, TOO.
YOU JEALOUS THAT I WAS THE ONE WHO FOUND HIM?
NOT AT ALL.
IT WAS... GOOD TO SEE YOU, T'CHALLA.
BUT I HOPE YOU'LL KEEP LEAVING THE MUTE ZONE ALONE.
I'LL COME ONLY WHEN CALLED.
I GUESS WE BELIEVE YOU NOW, MY KING. YOU KNOW, ABOUT THE CREATURE AND ALL?
STOP IT.
THE END!
NNEDI + ANDRE

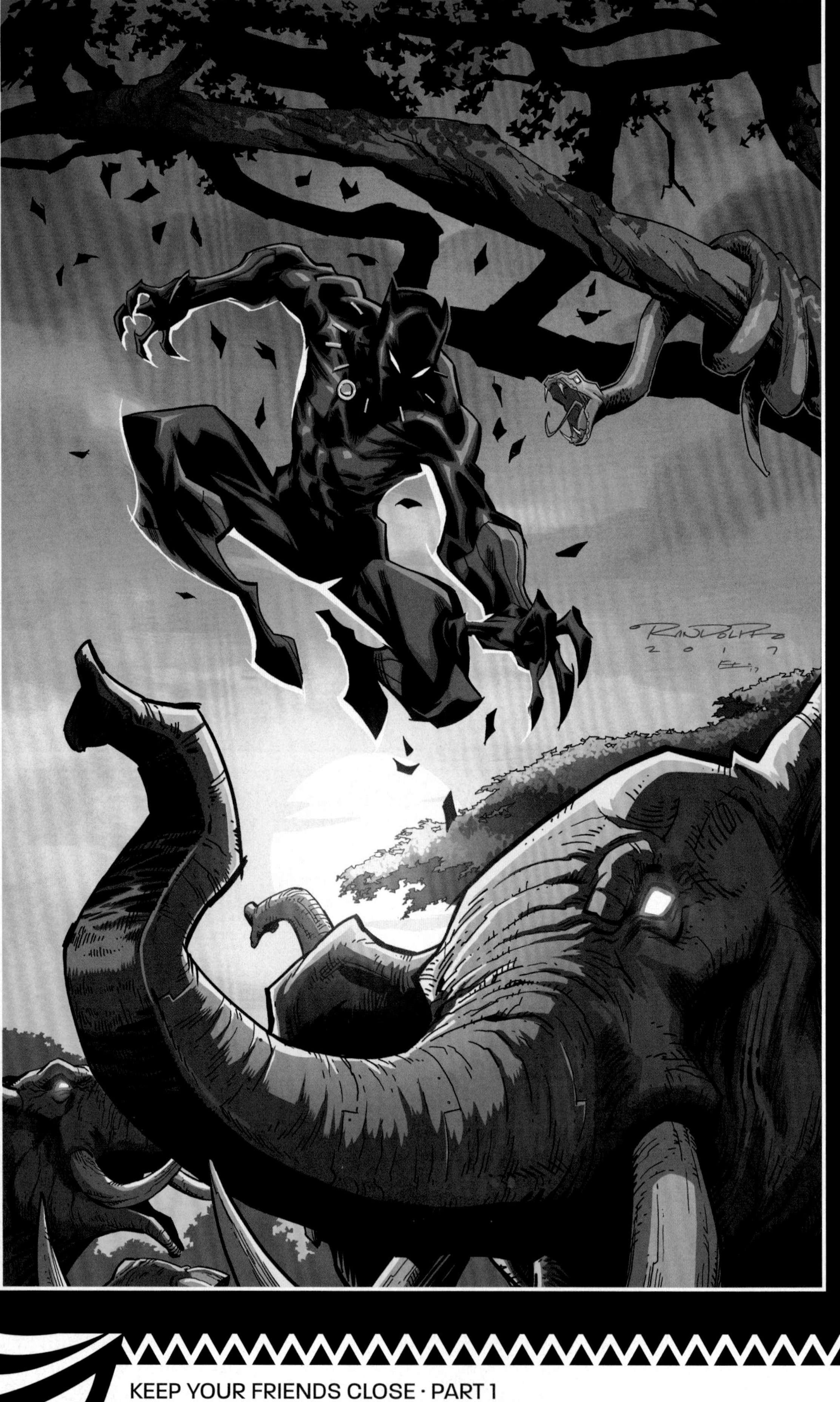
RANDOLPH
2017

KEEP YOUR FRIENDS CLOSE · PART 1

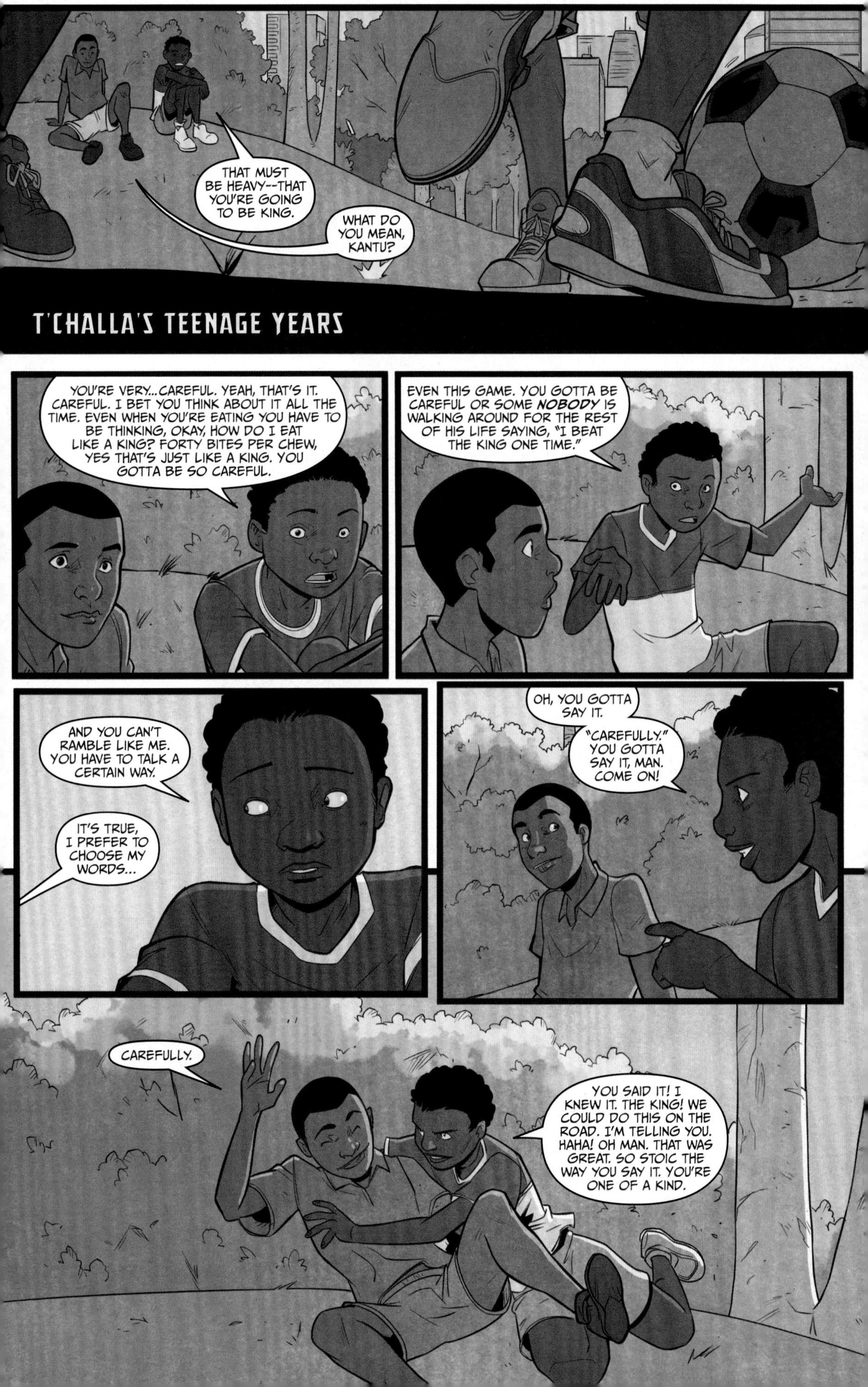
THAT MUST BE HEAVY--THAT YOU'RE GOING TO BE KING.
WHAT DO YOU MEAN, KANTU?
T'CHALLA'S TEENAGE YEARS
YOU'RE VERY...CAREFUL. YEAH, THAT'S IT. CAREFUL. I BET YOU THINK ABOUT IT ALL THE TIME. EVEN WHEN YOU'RE EATING YOU HAVE TO BE THINKING, OKAY, HOW DO I EAT LIKE A KING? FORTY BITES PER CHEW, YES THAT'S JUST LIKE A KING. YOU GOTTA BE SO CAREFUL.
EVEN THIS GAME. YOU GOTTA BE CAREFUL OR SOME NOBODY IS WALKING AROUND FOR THE REST OF HIS LIFE SAYING, "I BEAT THE KING ONE TIME."
AND YOU CAN'T RAMBLE LIKE ME. YOU HAVE TO TALK A CERTAIN WAY.
IT'S TRUE, I PREFER TO CHOOSE MY WORDS...
OH, YOU GOTTA SAY IT.
"CAREFULLY." YOU GOTTA SAY IT, MAN. COME ON!
CAREFULLY.
YOU SAID IT! I KNEW IT. THE KING! WE COULD DO THIS ON THE ROAD. I'M TELLING YOU. HAHA! OH MAN. THAT WAS GREAT. SO STOIC THE WAY YOU SAY IT. YOU'RE ONE OF A KIND.

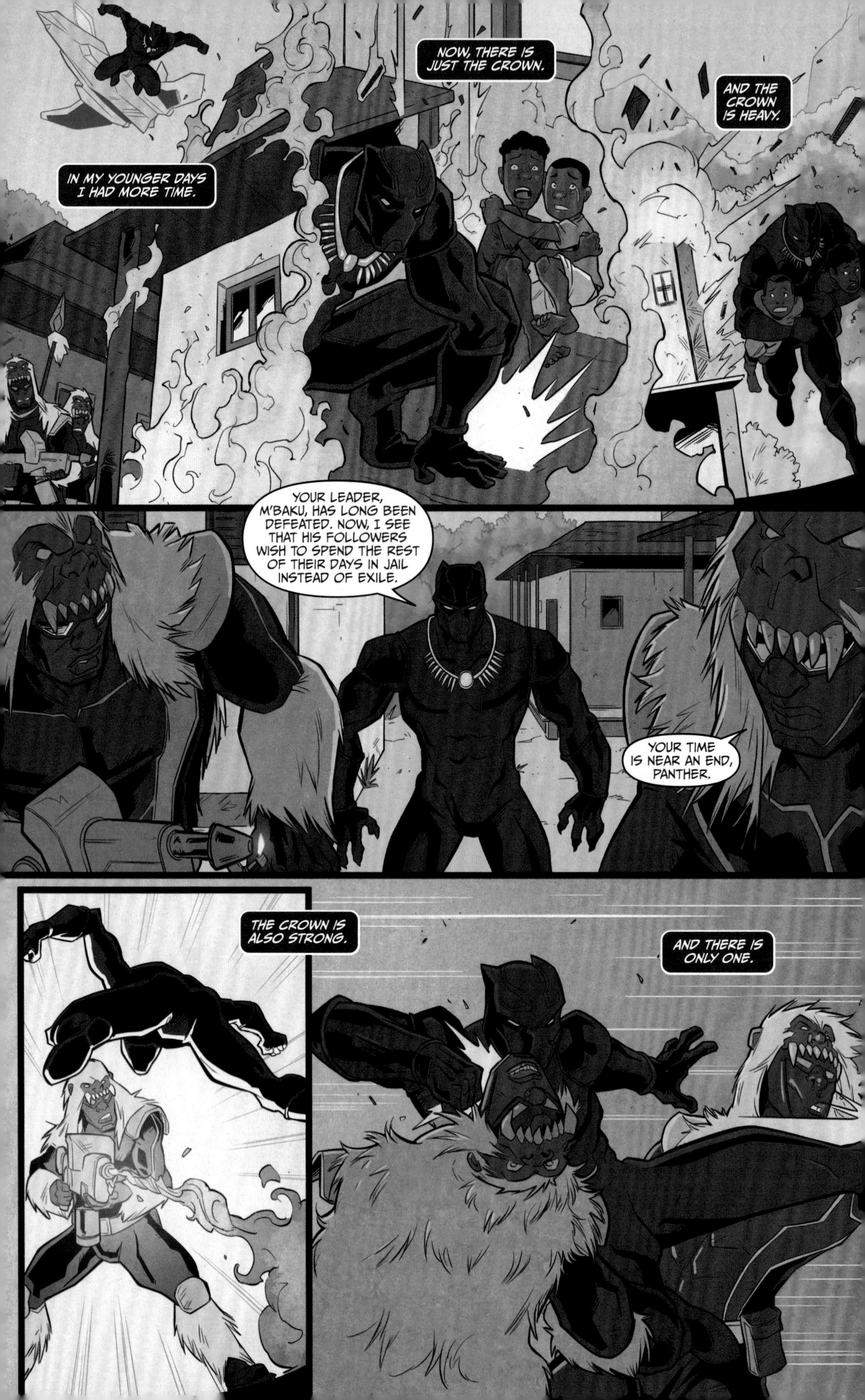
IN MY YOUNGER DAYS I HAD MORE TIME.
NOW, THERE IS JUST THE CROWN.
AND THE CROWN IS HEAVY.
YOUR LEADER, M'BAKU, HAS LONG BEEN DEFEATED. NOW, I SEE THAT HIS FOLLOWERS WISH TO SPEND THE REST OF THEIR DAYS IN JAIL INSTEAD OF EXILE.
YOUR TIME IS NEAR AN END, PANTHER.
THE CROWN IS ALSO STRONG.
AND THERE IS ONLY ONE.

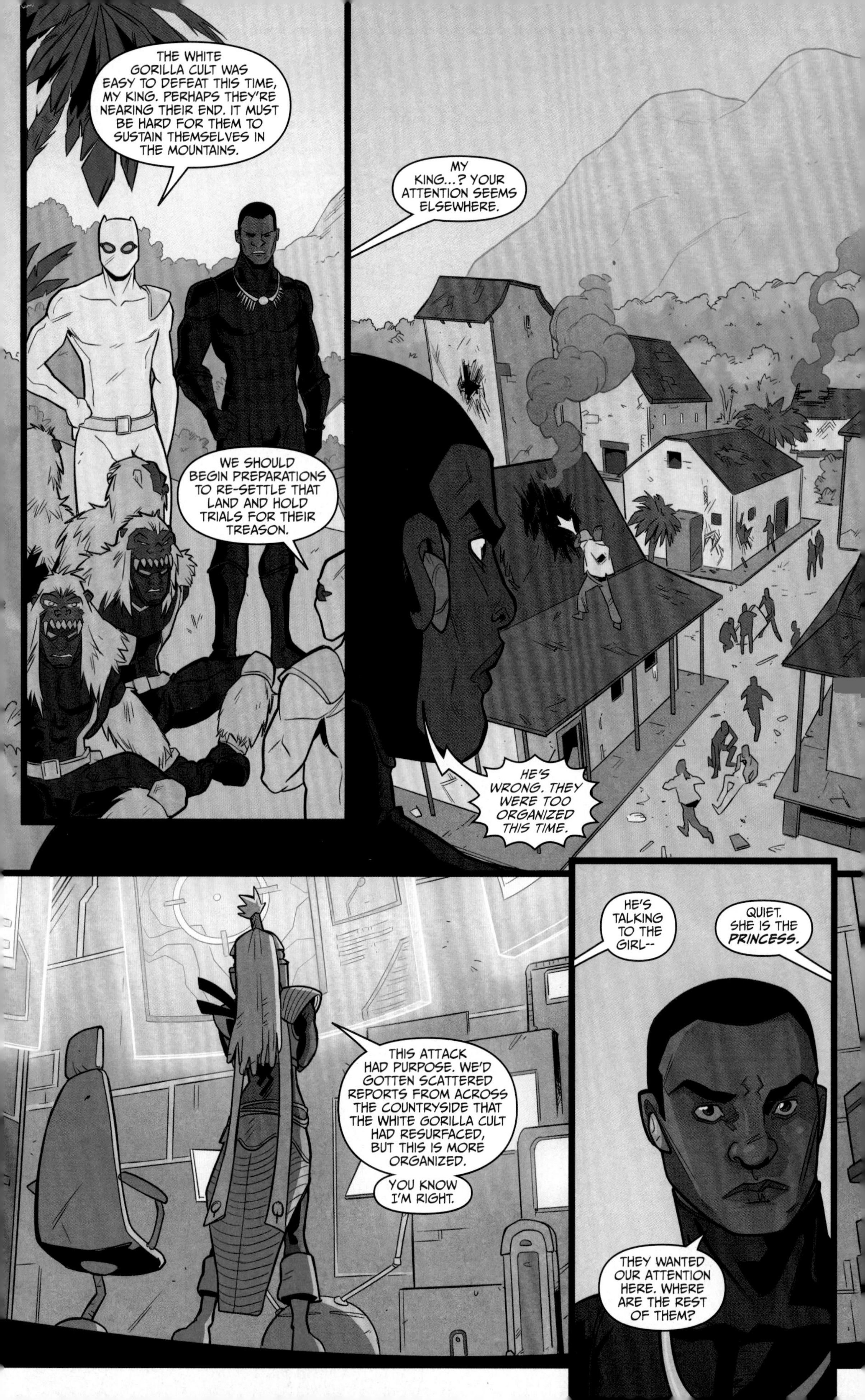
THE WHITE GORILLA CULT WAS EASY TO DEFEAT THIS TIME, MY KING. PERHAPS THEY'RE NEARING THEIR END. IT MUST BE HARD FOR THEM TO SUSTAIN THEMSELVES IN THE MOUNTAINS.
WE SHOULD BEGIN PREPARATIONS TO RE-SETTLE THAT LAND AND HOLD TRIALS FOR THEIR TREASON.
MY KING...? YOUR ATTENTION SEEMS ELSEWHERE.
HE'S WRONG. THEY WERE TOO ORGANIZED THIS TIME.
THIS ATTACK HAD PURPOSE. WE'D GOTTEN SCATTERED REPORTS FROM ACROSS THE COUNTRYSIDE THAT THE WHITE GORILLA CULT HAD RESURFACED, BUT THIS IS MORE ORGANIZED.
YOU KNOW I'M RIGHT.
HE'S TALKING TO THE GIRL--
QUIET. SHE IS THE ***PRINCESS.***
THEY WANTED OUR ATTENTION HERE. WHERE ARE THE REST OF THEM?

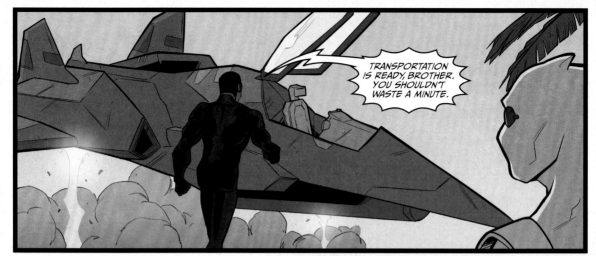

TRANSPORTATION IS READY, BROTHER. YOU SHOULDN'T WASTE A MINUTE.

SECURE THIS AREA. TAKE THESE CRIMINALS TO THE PRISON.

WHERE ARE YOU GOING, MY KING?

I AM GOING TO SCAN THE COUNTRYSIDE. I SUSPECT THIS WAS A MERE DIVERSION.

YOU CONTINUE TO TAKE EVERY THREAT TO WAKANDA AS AN OPPORTUNITY FOR PERSONAL CONQUEST.

YOU SHOULD NOT PURSUE THIS ALONE, T'CHALLA.

I AM NOT ALONE.

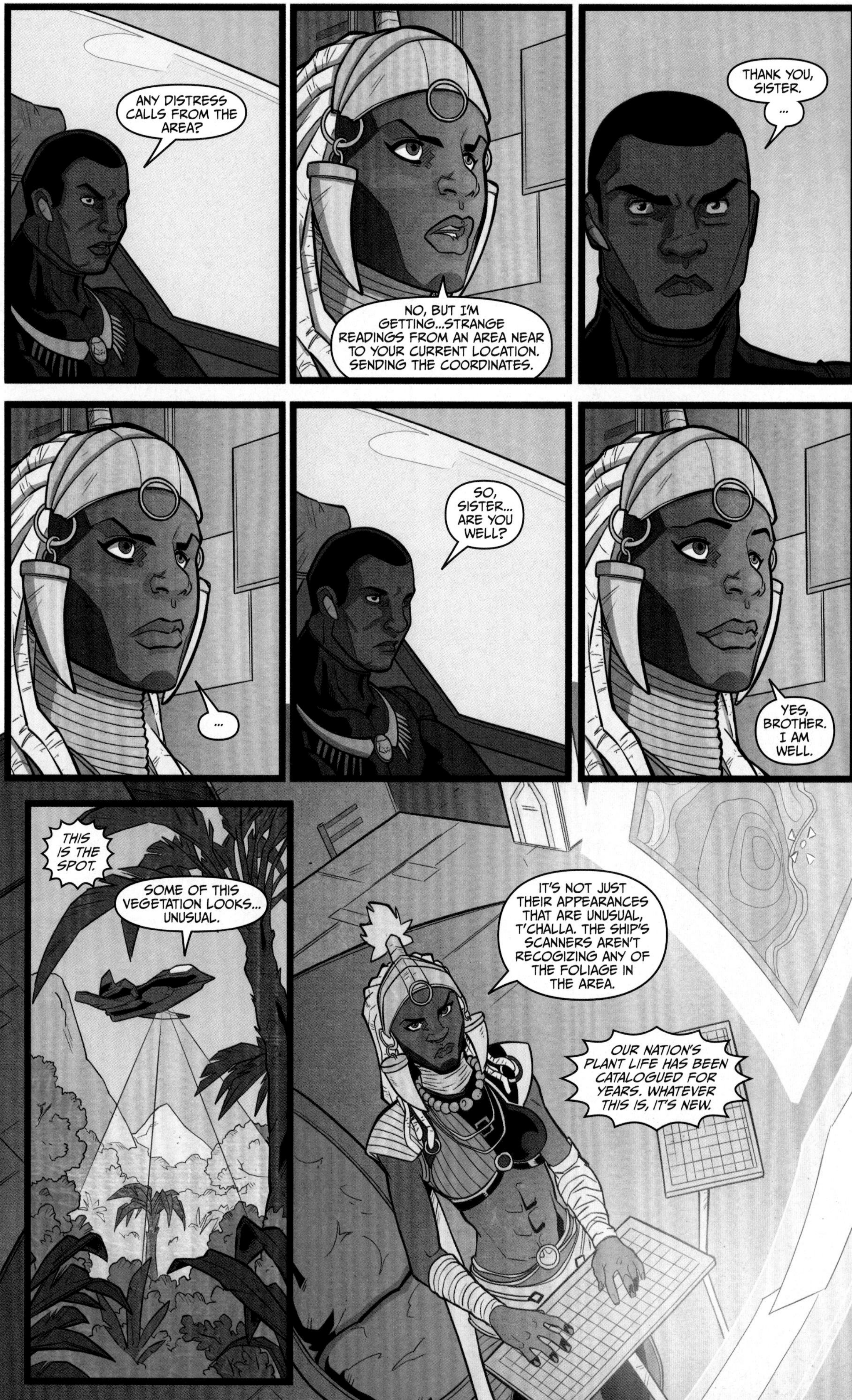
ANY DISTRESS CALLS FROM THE AREA?
NO, BUT I'M GETTING...STRANGE READINGS FROM AN AREA NEAR TO YOUR CURRENT LOCATION. SENDING THE COORDINATES.
THANK YOU, SISTER.
...
...
SO, SISTER... ARE YOU WELL?
YES, BROTHER. I AM WELL.
THIS IS THE SPOT.
SOME OF THIS VEGETATION LOOKS... UNUSUAL.
IT'S NOT JUST THEIR APPEARANCES THAT ARE UNUSUAL, T'CHALLA. THE SHIP'S SCANNERS AREN'T RECOGIZING ANY OF THE FOLIAGE IN THE AREA.
OUR NATION'S PLANT LIFE HAS BEEN CATALOGUED FOR YEARS. WHATEVER THIS IS, IT'S NEW.

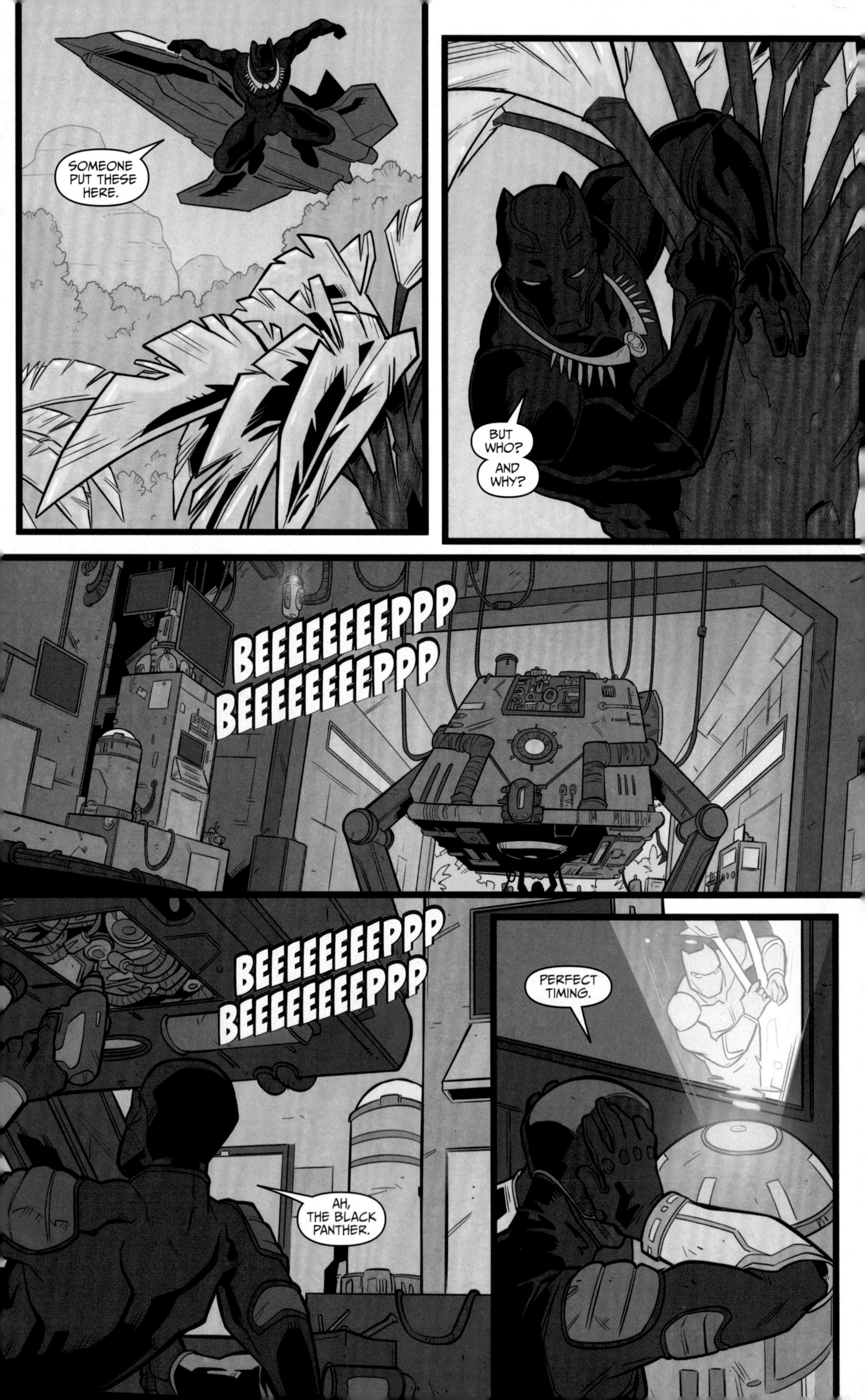
SOMEONE PUT THESE HERE.
BUT WHO?
AND WHY?
BEEEEEEEEPPP
BEEEEEEEEPPP
BEEEEEEEEPPP
BEEEEEEEEPPP
AH, THE BLACK PANTHER.
PERFECT TIMING.

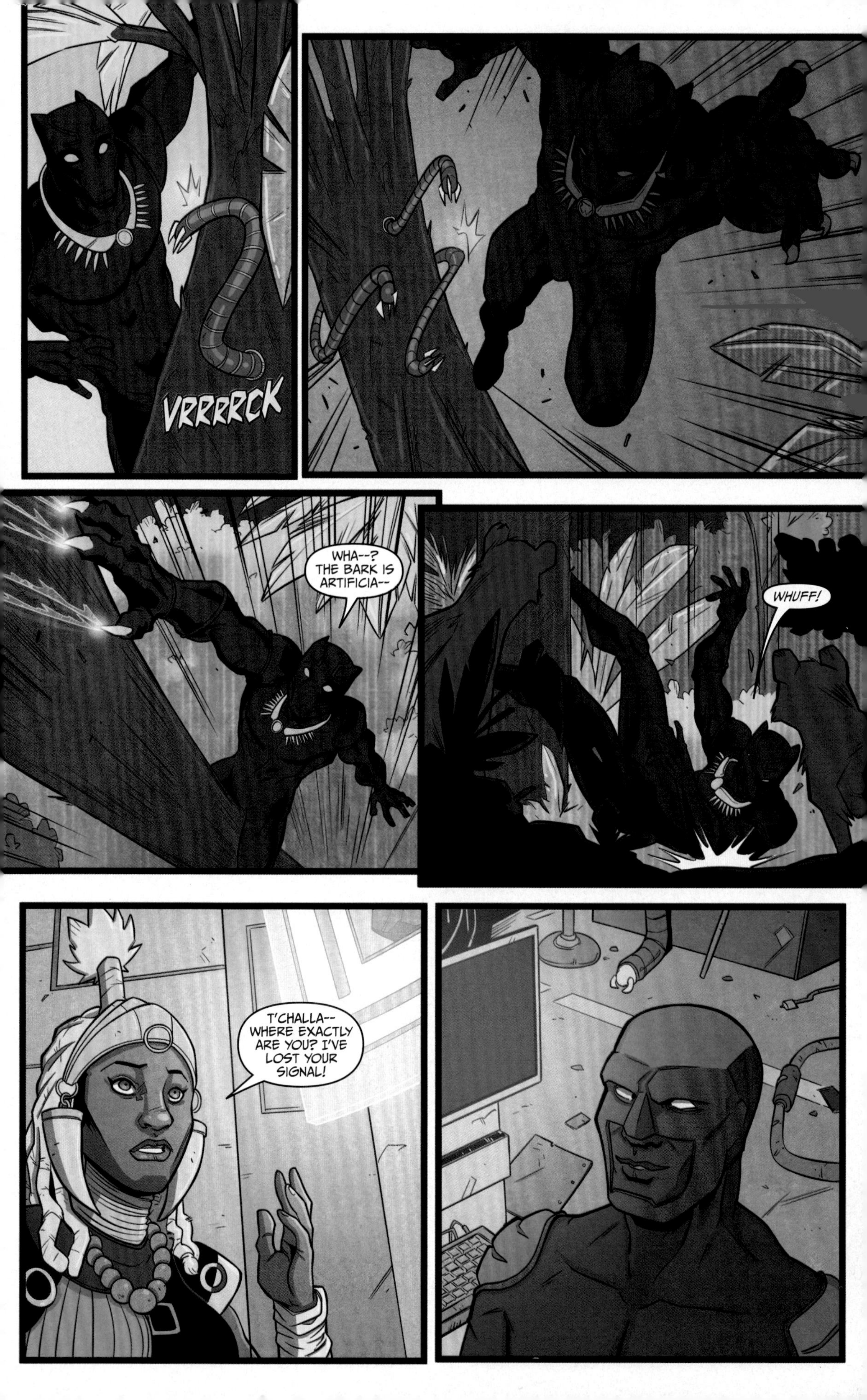
VRRRRCK
WHA--? THE BARK IS ARTIFICIA--
WHUFF!
T'CHALLA-- WHERE EXACTLY ARE YOU? I'VE LOST YOUR SIGNAL!

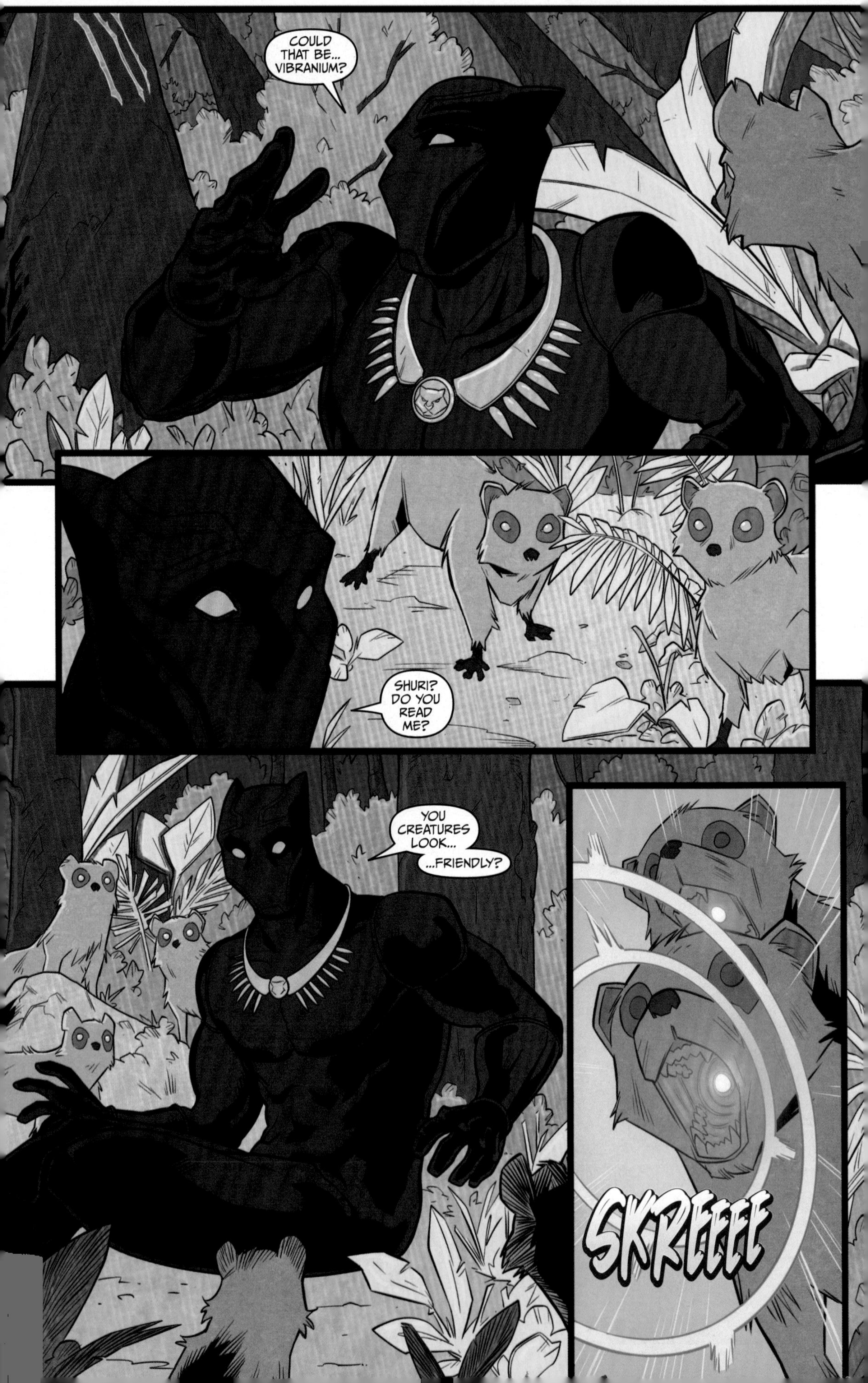
COULD THAT BE... VIBRANIUM?
SHURI? DO YOU READ ME?
YOU CREATURES LOOK...
...FRIENDLY?
SKREEEE

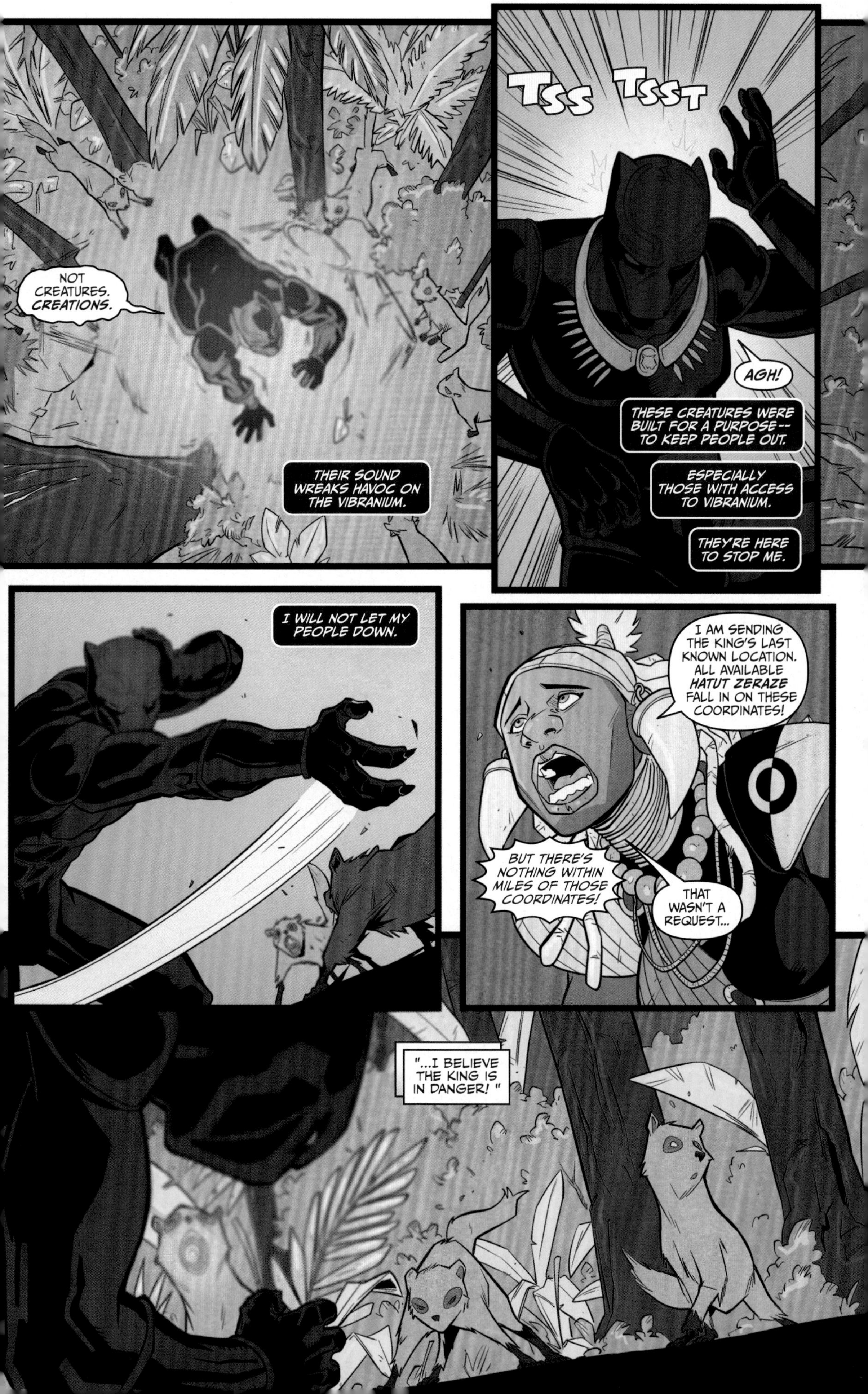
NOT CREATURES. CREATIONS.
THEIR SOUND WREAKS HAVOC ON THE VIBRANIUM.
TSS TSST
AGH!
THESE CREATURES WERE BUILT FOR A PURPOSE-- TO KEEP PEOPLE OUT.
ESPECIALLY THOSE WITH ACCESS TO VIBRANIUM.
THEY'RE HERE TO STOP ME.
I WILL NOT LET MY PEOPLE DOWN.
I AM SENDING THE KING'S LAST KNOWN LOCATION. ALL AVAILABLE HATUT ZERAZE FALL IN ON THESE COORDINATES!
BUT THERE'S NOTHING WITHIN MILES OF THOSE COORDINATES!
THAT WASN'T A REQUEST...
"...I BELIEVE THE KING IS IN DANGER!"

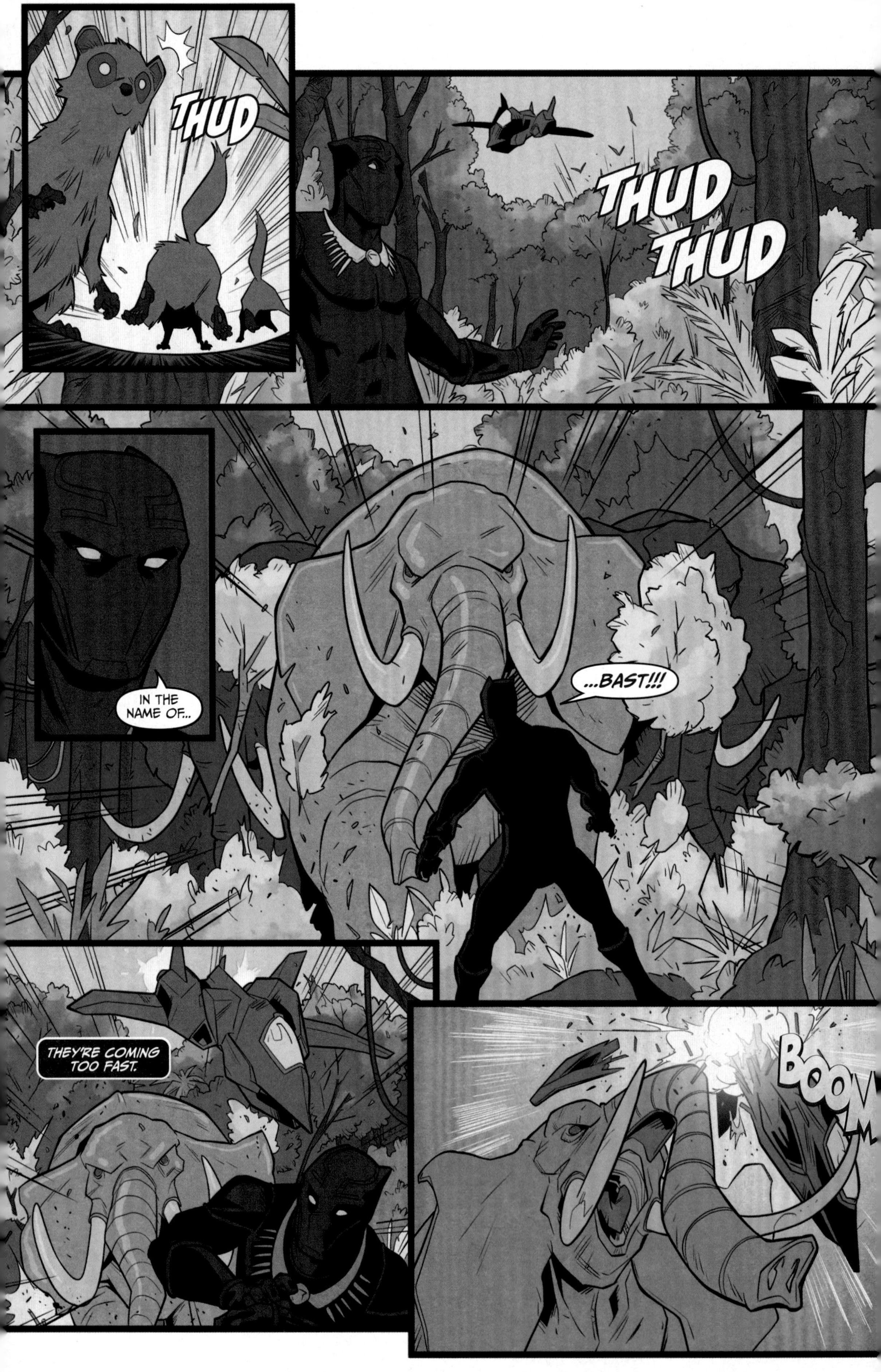
THUD
THUD
THUD
IN THE NAME OF...
...BAST!!!
THEY'RE COMING TOO FAST.
BOOM

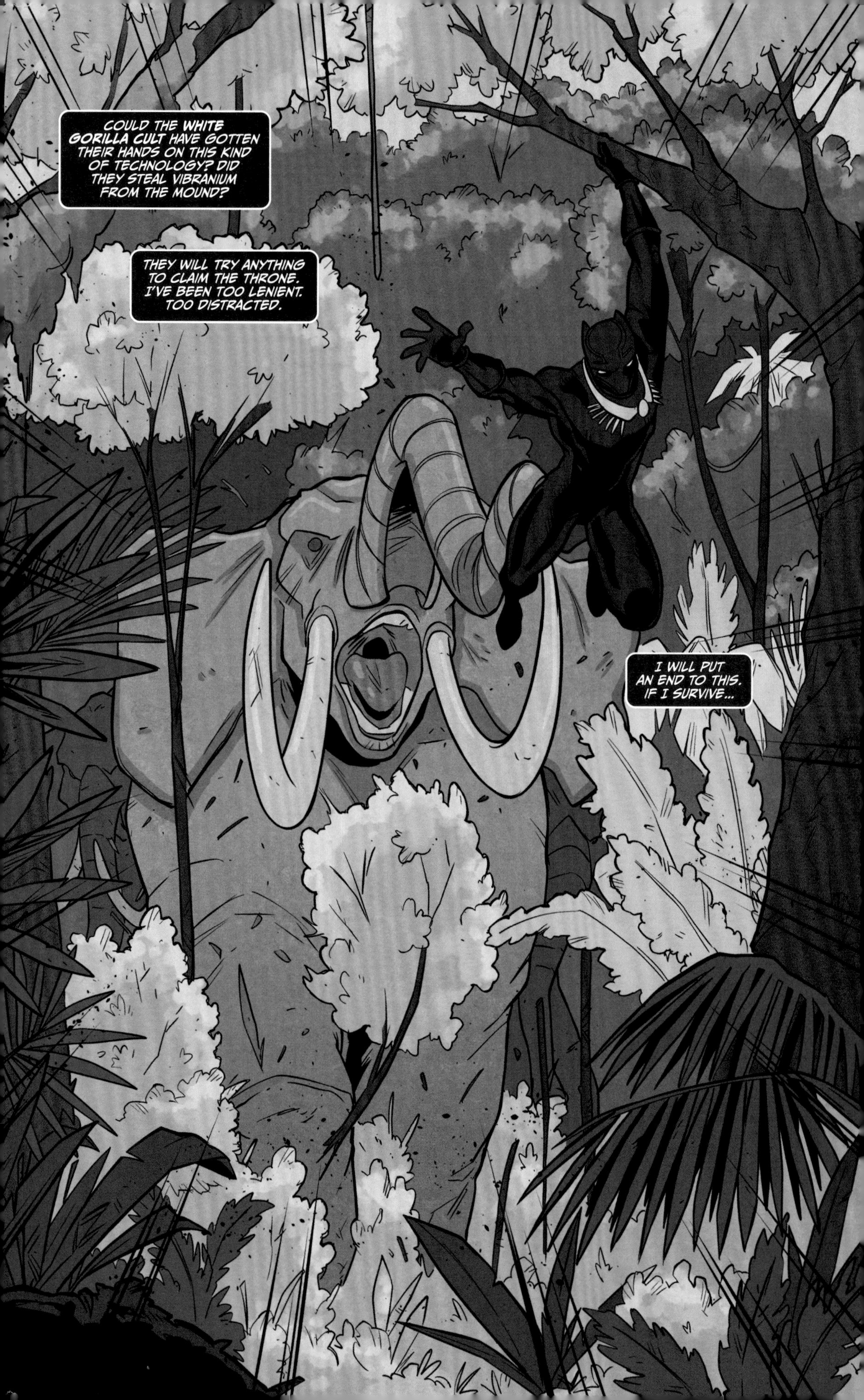
COULD THE WHITE GORILLA CULT HAVE GOTTEN THEIR HANDS ON THIS KIND OF TECHNOLOGY? DID THEY STEAL VIBRANIUM FROM THE MOUND?
THEY WILL TRY ANYTHING TO CLAIM THE THRONE. I'VE BEEN TOO LENIENT. TOO DISTRACTED.
I WILL PUT AN END TO THIS. IF I SURVIVE...

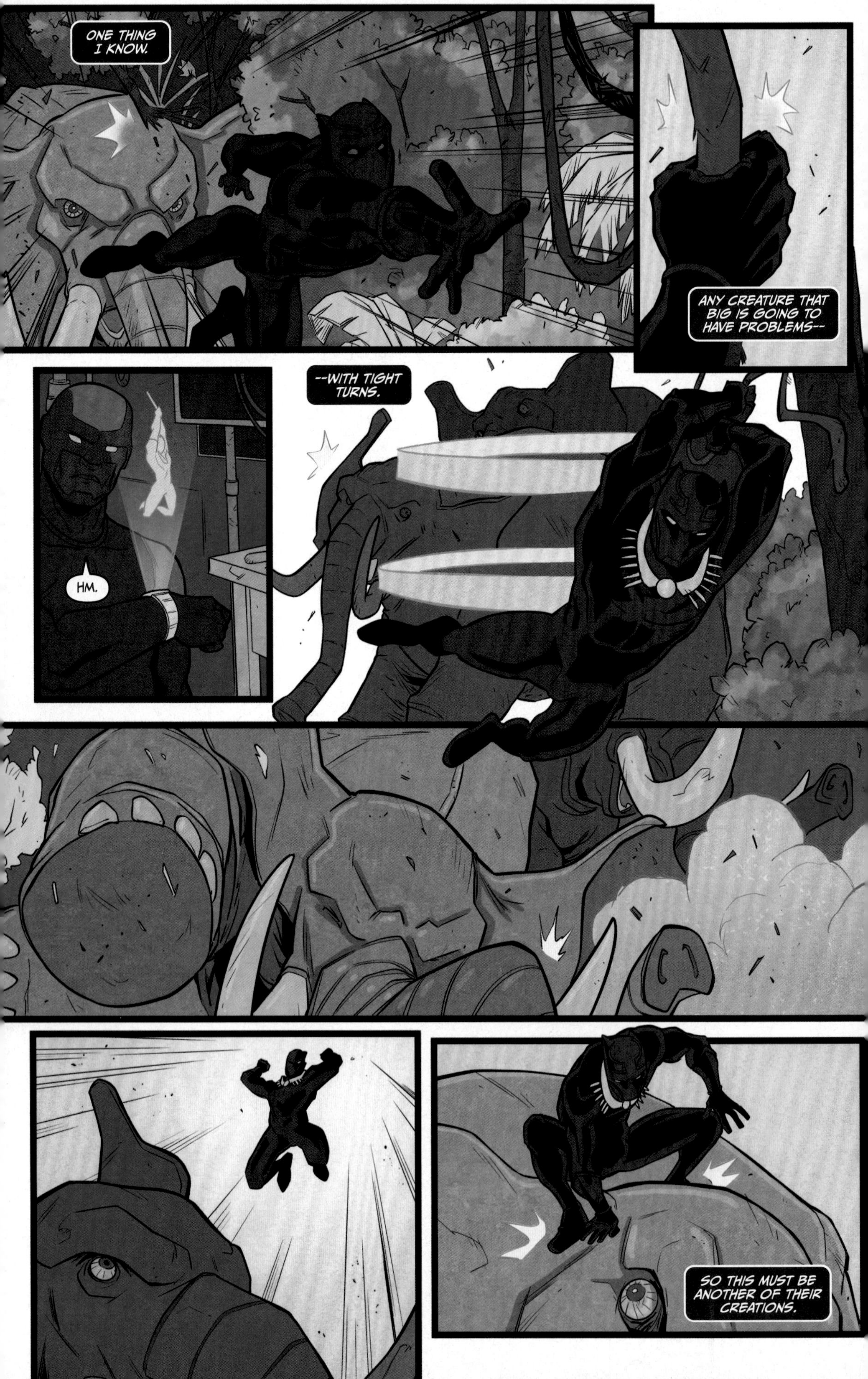
ONE THING I KNOW.
ANY CREATURE THAT BIG IS GOING TO HAVE PROBLEMS--
HM.
--WITH TIGHT TURNS.
SO THIS MUST BE ANOTHER OF THEIR CREATIONS.

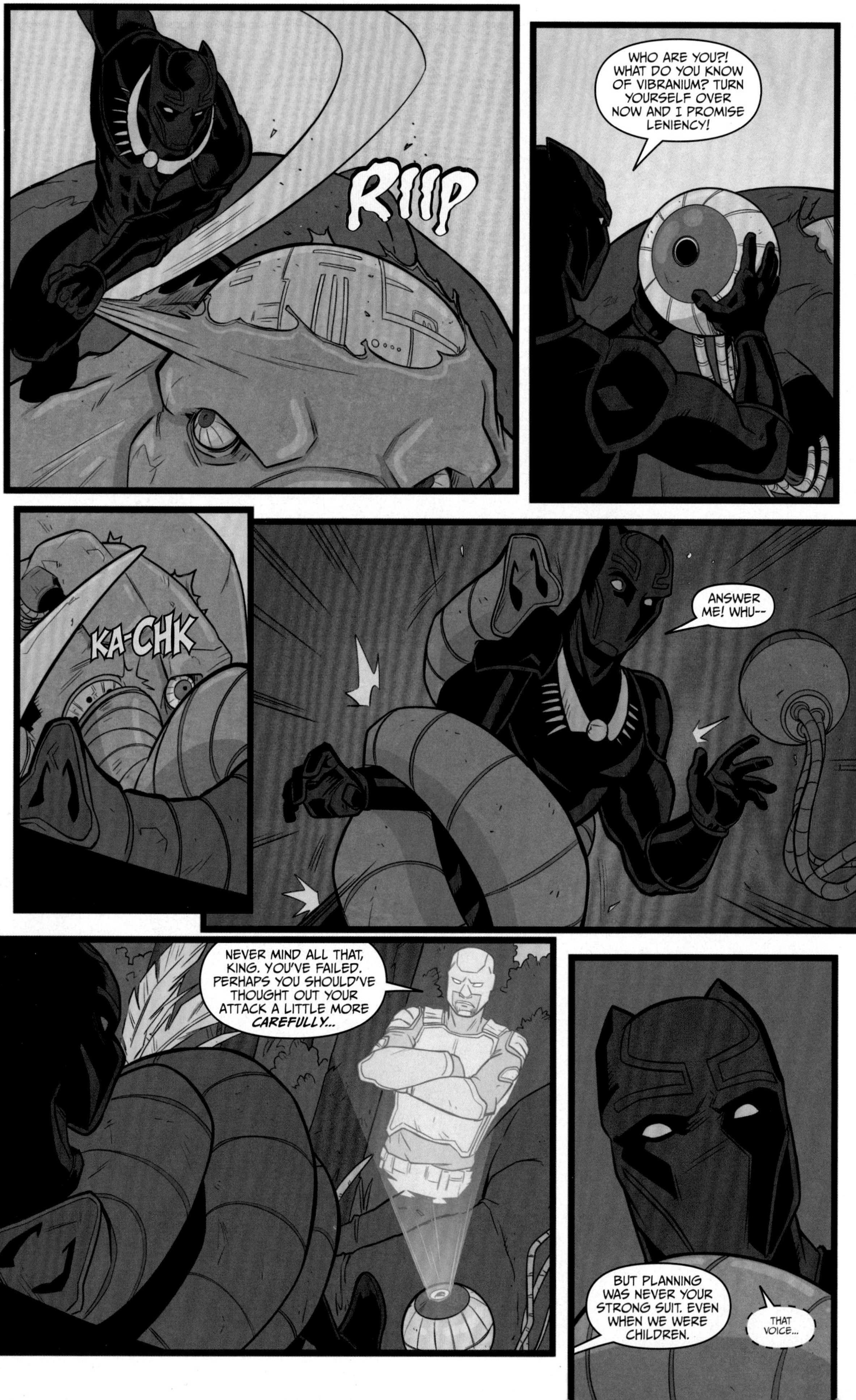
RIIP
WHO ARE YOU?! WHAT DO YOU KNOW OF VIBRANIUM? TURN YOURSELF OVER NOW AND I PROMISE LENIENCY!
KA-CHK
ANSWER ME! WHU--
NEVER MIND ALL THAT, KING. YOU'VE FAILED. PERHAPS YOU SHOULD'VE THOUGHT OUT YOUR ATTACK A LITTLE MORE CAREFULLY...
BUT PLANNING WAS NEVER YOUR STRONG SUIT. EVEN WHEN WE WERE CHILDREN.
THAT VOICE...

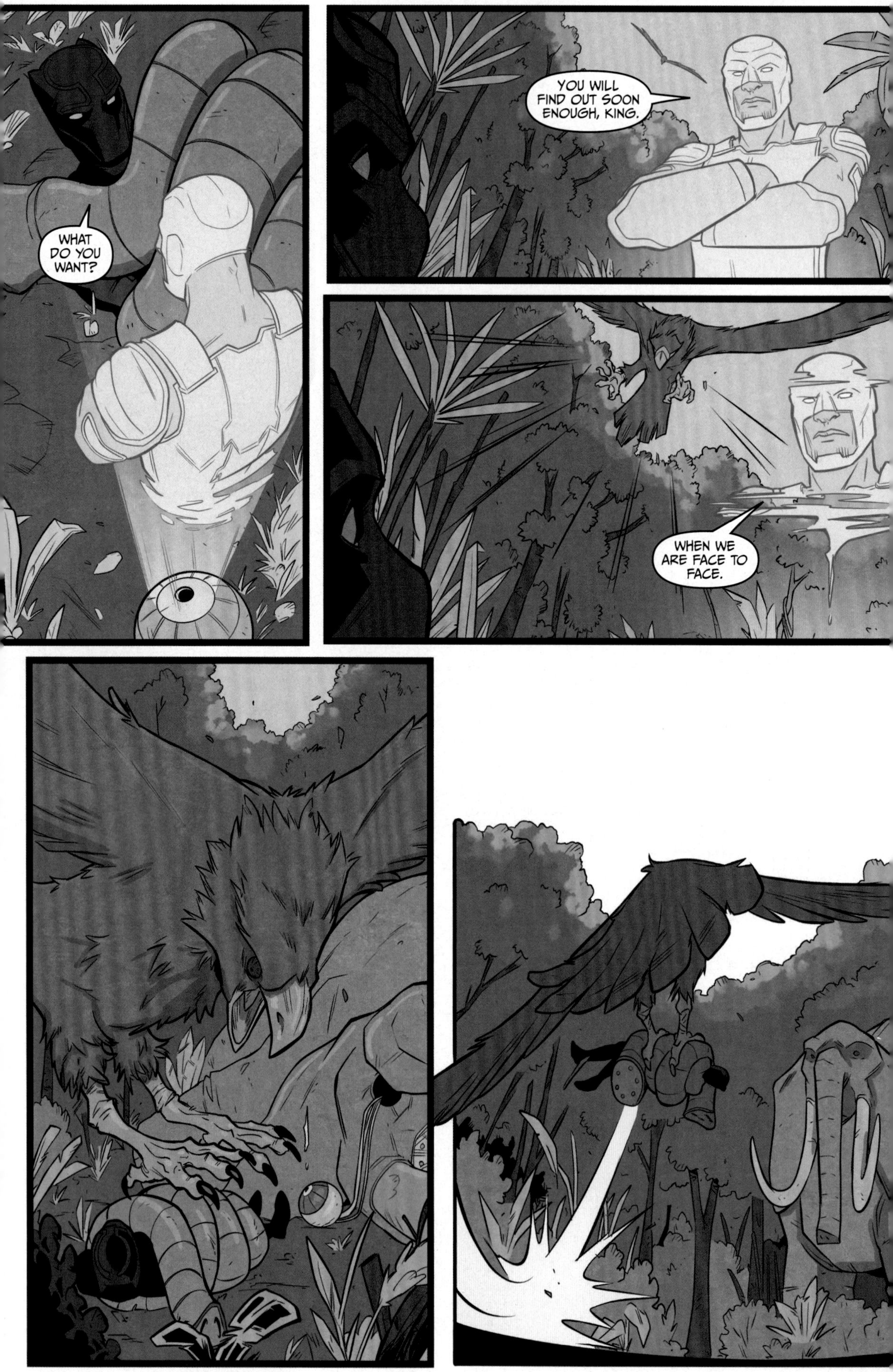
WHAT DO YOU WANT?
YOU WILL FIND OUT SOON ENOUGH, KING.
WHEN WE ARE FACE TO FACE.

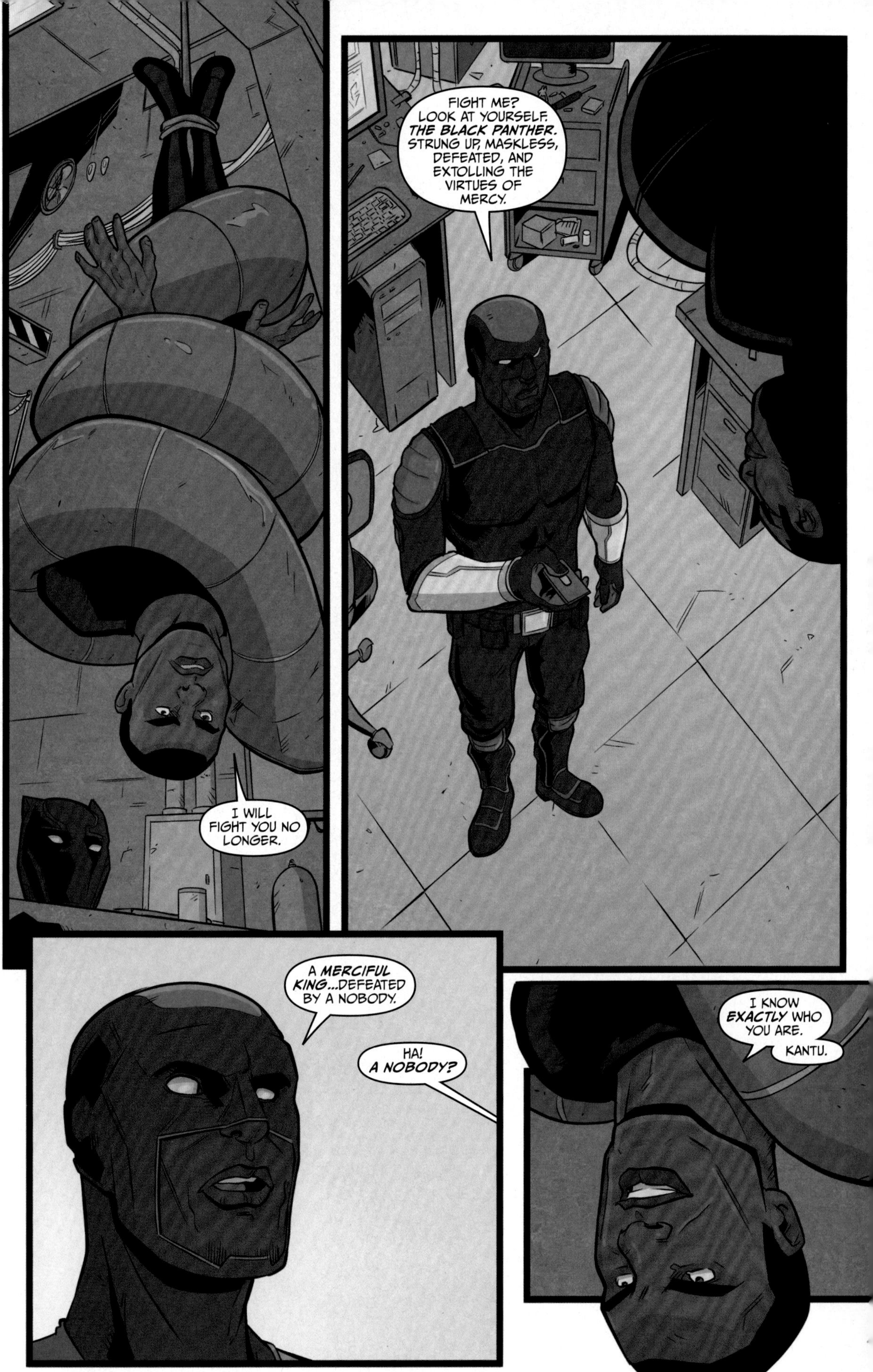
I WILL FIGHT YOU NO LONGER.
FIGHT ME? LOOK AT YOURSELF. THE BLACK PANTHER. STRUNG UP, MASKLESS, DEFEATED, AND EXTOLLING THE VIRTUES OF MERCY.
A MERCIFUL KING...DEFEATED BY A NOBODY.
HA! A NOBODY?
I KNOW EXACTLY WHO YOU ARE.
KANTU.

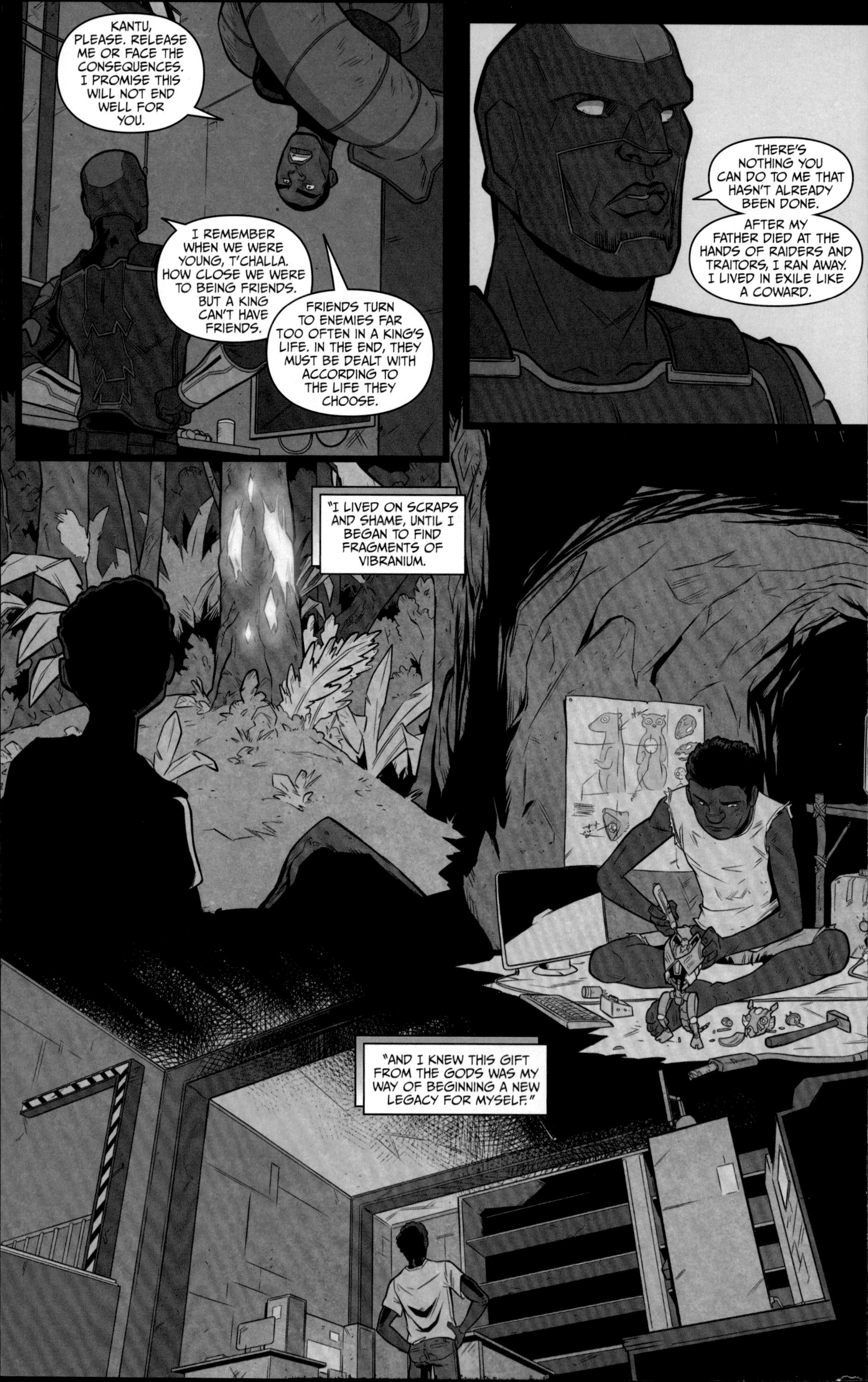
KANTU, PLEASE. RELEASE ME OR FACE THE CONSEQUENCES. I PROMISE THIS WILL NOT END WELL FOR YOU.
I REMEMBER WHEN WE WERE YOUNG, T'CHALLA. HOW CLOSE WE WERE TO BEING FRIENDS. BUT A KING CAN'T HAVE FRIENDS.
FRIENDS TURN TO ENEMIES FAR TOO OFTEN IN A KING'S LIFE. IN THE END, THEY MUST BE DEALT WITH ACCORDING TO THE LIFE THEY CHOOSE.
THERE'S NOTHING YOU CAN DO TO ME THAT HASN'T ALREADY BEEN DONE.
AFTER MY FATHER DIED AT THE HANDS OF RAIDERS AND TRAITORS, I RAN AWAY. I LIVED IN EXILE LIKE A COWARD.
"I LIVED ON SCRAPS AND SHAME, UNTIL I BEGAN TO FIND FRAGMENTS OF VIBRANIUM.
"AND I KNEW THIS GIFT FROM THE GODS WAS MY WAY OF BEGINNING A NEW LEGACY FOR MYSELF."

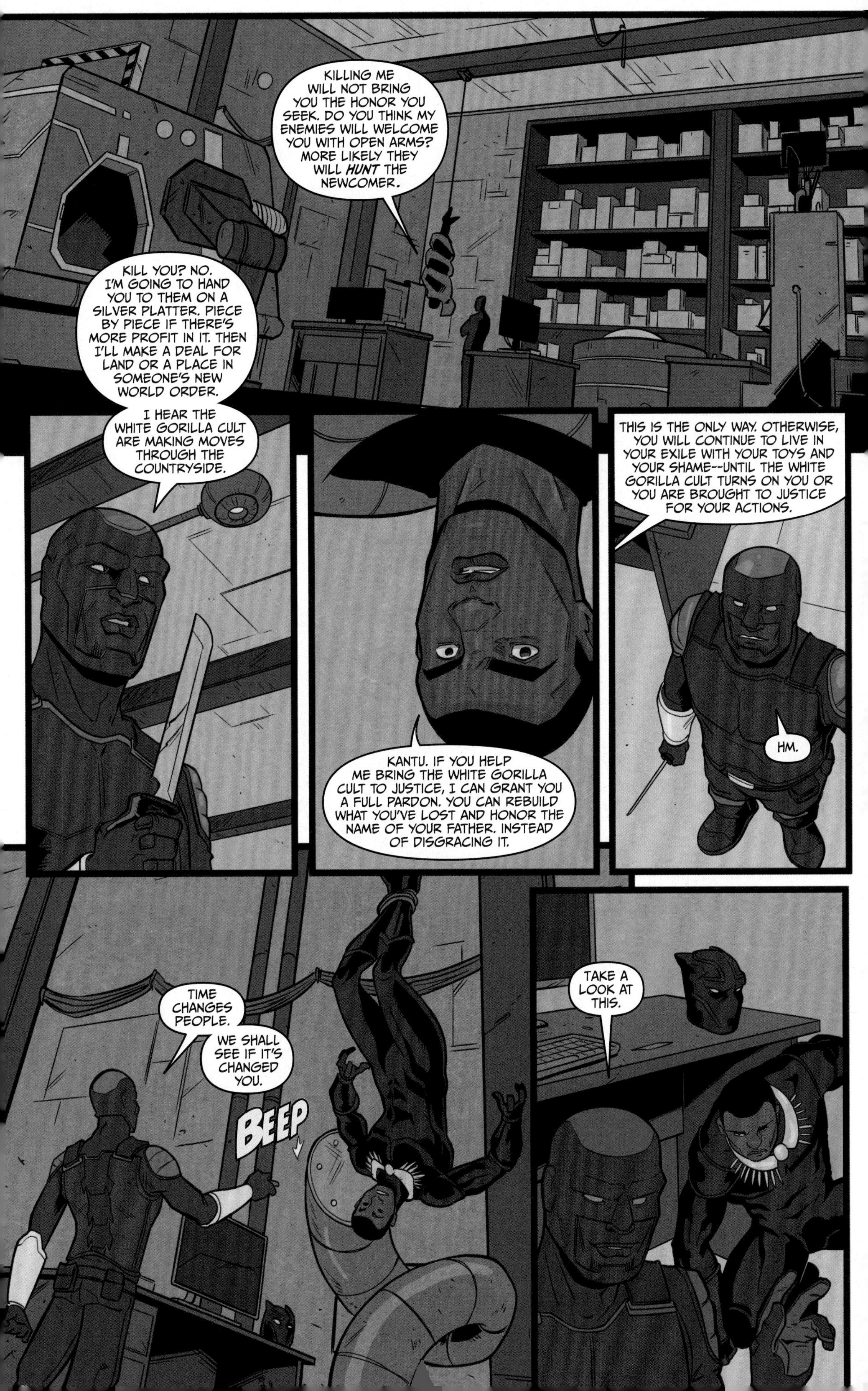

KILLING ME WILL NOT BRING YOU THE HONOR YOU SEEK. DO YOU THINK MY ENEMIES WILL WELCOME YOU WITH OPEN ARMS? MORE LIKELY THEY WILL *HUNT* THE NEWCOMER.
KILL YOU? NO. I'M GOING TO HAND YOU TO THEM ON A SILVER PLATTER. PIECE BY PIECE IF THERE'S MORE PROFIT IN IT. THEN I'LL MAKE A DEAL FOR LAND OR A PLACE IN SOMEONE'S NEW WORLD ORDER.
I HEAR THE WHITE GORILLA CULT ARE MAKING MOVES THROUGH THE COUNTRYSIDE.
KANTU. IF YOU HELP ME BRING THE WHITE GORILLA CULT TO JUSTICE, I CAN GRANT YOU A FULL PARDON. YOU CAN REBUILD WHAT YOU'VE LOST AND HONOR THE NAME OF YOUR FATHER. INSTEAD OF DISGRACING IT.
THIS IS THE ONLY WAY. OTHERWISE, YOU WILL CONTINUE TO LIVE IN YOUR EXILE WITH YOUR TOYS AND YOUR SHAME--UNTIL THE WHITE GORILLA CULT TURNS ON YOU OR YOU ARE BROUGHT TO JUSTICE FOR YOUR ACTIONS.
HM.
TIME CHANGES PEOPLE.
WE SHALL SEE IF IT'S CHANGED YOU.
BEEP
TAKE A LOOK AT THIS.

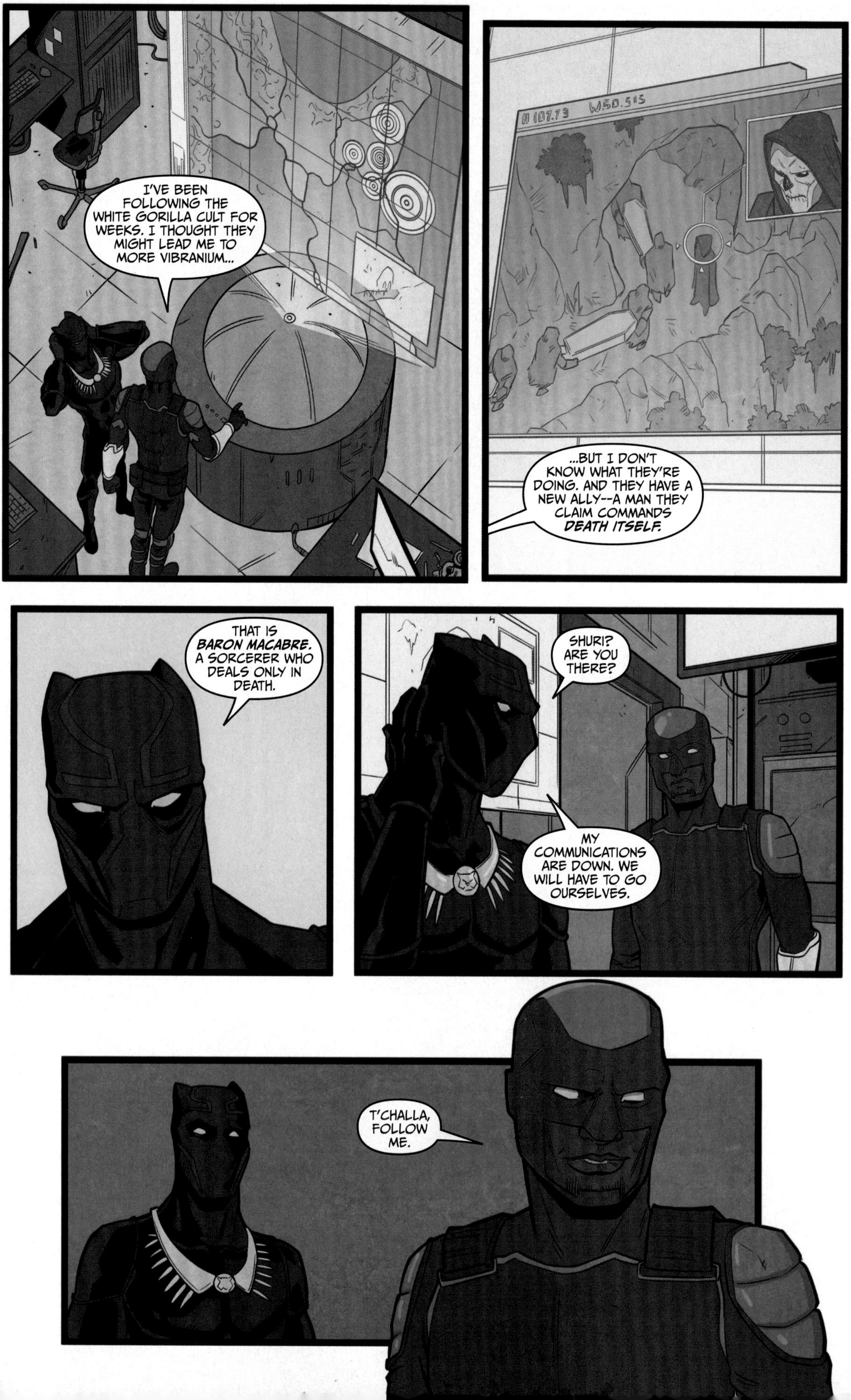
I'VE BEEN FOLLOWING THE WHITE GORILLA CULT FOR WEEKS. I THOUGHT THEY MIGHT LEAD ME TO MORE VIBRANIUM...
N 107.73
W50.515
...BUT I DON'T KNOW WHAT THEY'RE DOING. AND THEY HAVE A NEW ALLY--A MAN THEY CLAIM COMMANDS DEATH ITSELF.
THAT IS BARON MACABRE. A SORCERER WHO DEALS ONLY IN DEATH.
SHURI? ARE YOU THERE?
MY COMMUNICATIONS ARE DOWN. WE WILL HAVE TO GO OURSELVES.
T'CHALLA, FOLLOW ME.

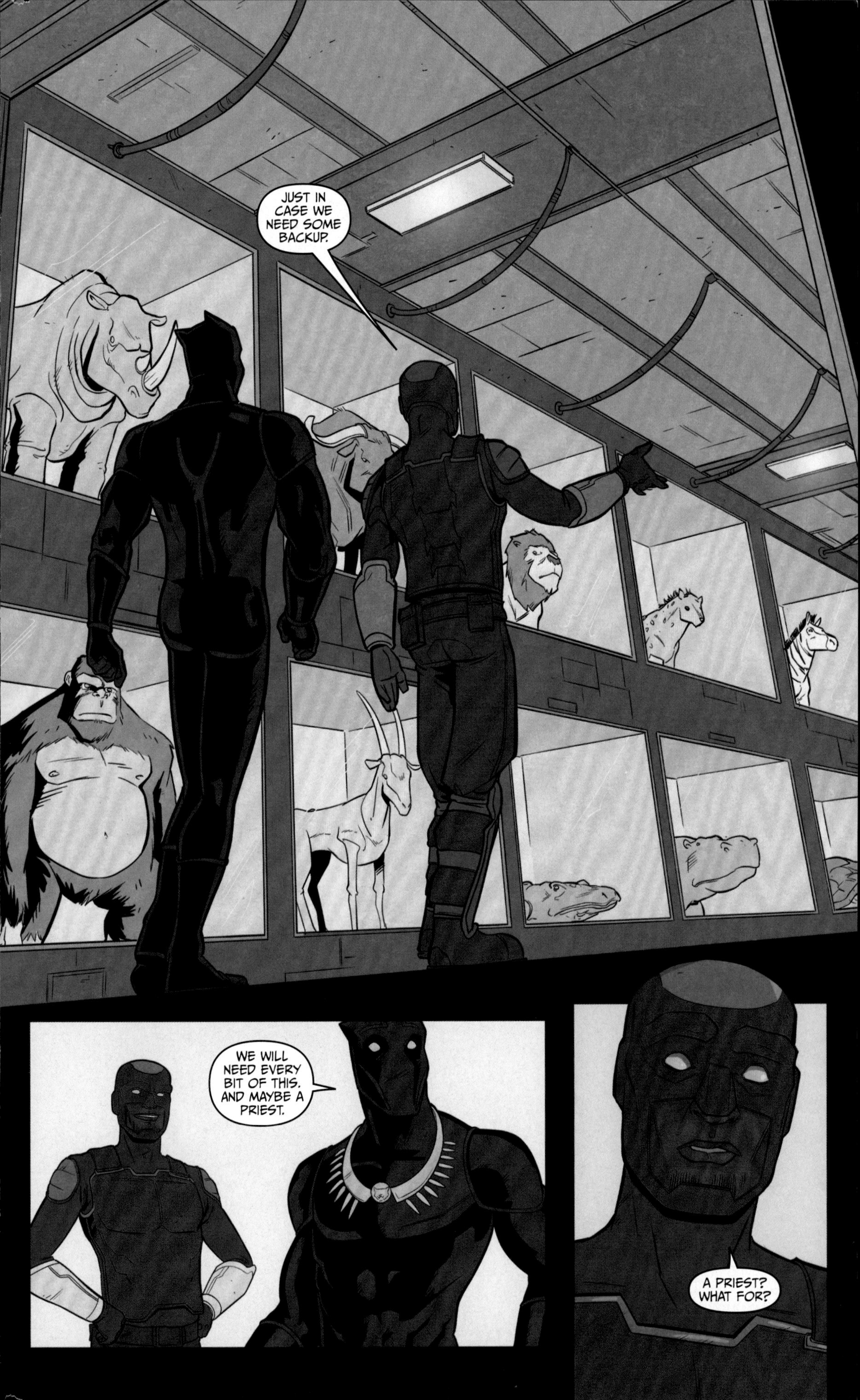
JUST IN CASE WE NEED SOME BACKUP.
WE WILL NEED EVERY BIT OF THIS. AND MAYBE A PRIEST.
A PRIEST? WHAT FOR?

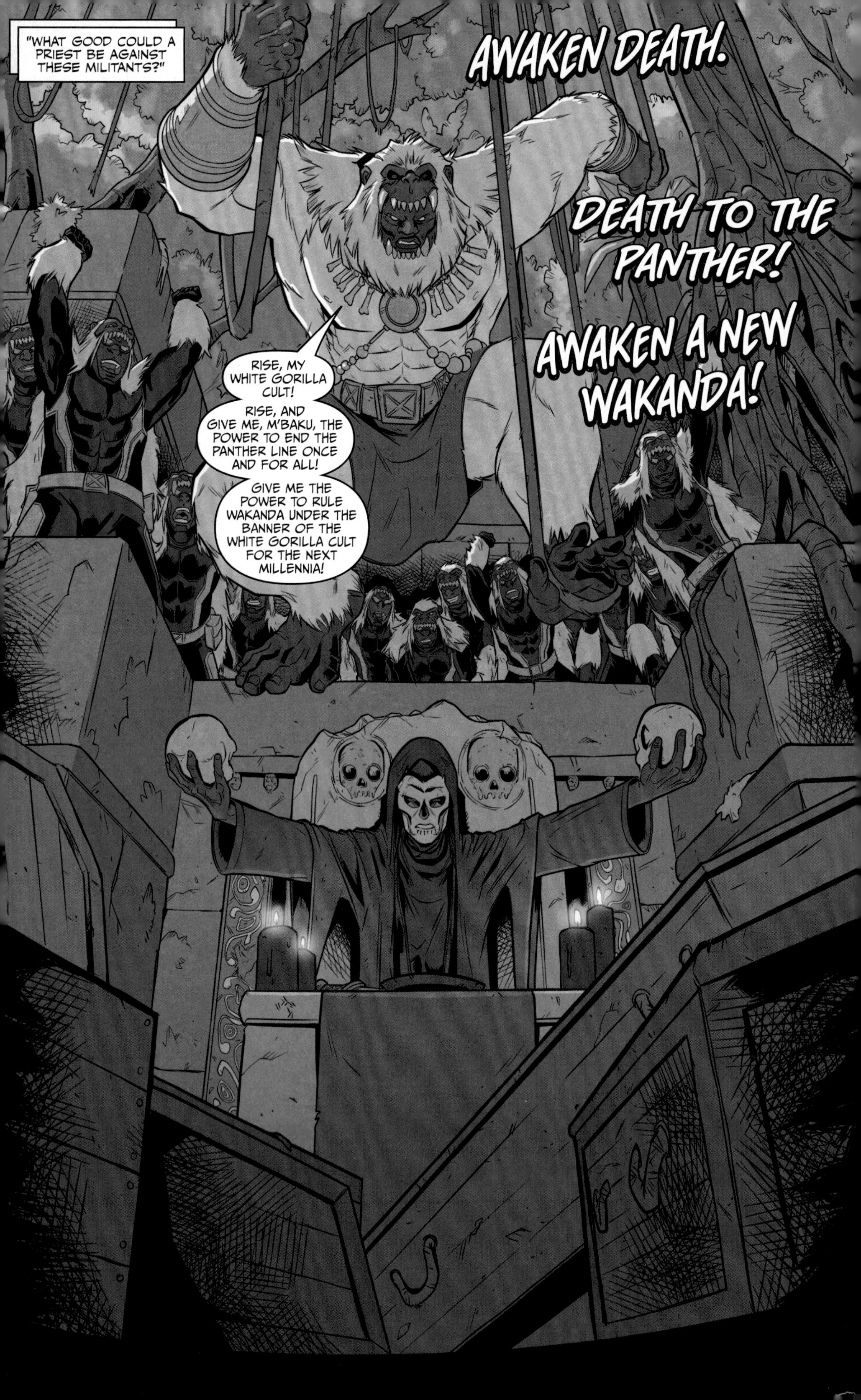
"WHAT GOOD COULD A PRIEST BE AGAINST THESE MILITANTS?"
RISE, MY WHITE GORILLA CULT!
RISE, AND GIVE ME, M'BAKU, THE POWER TO END THE PANTHER LINE ONCE AND FOR ALL!
GIVE ME THE POWER TO RULE WAKANDA UNDER THE BANNER OF THE WHITE GORILLA CULT FOR THE NEXT MILLENNIA!
AWAKEN DEATH.
DEATH TO THE PANTHER!
AWAKEN A NEW WAKANDA!

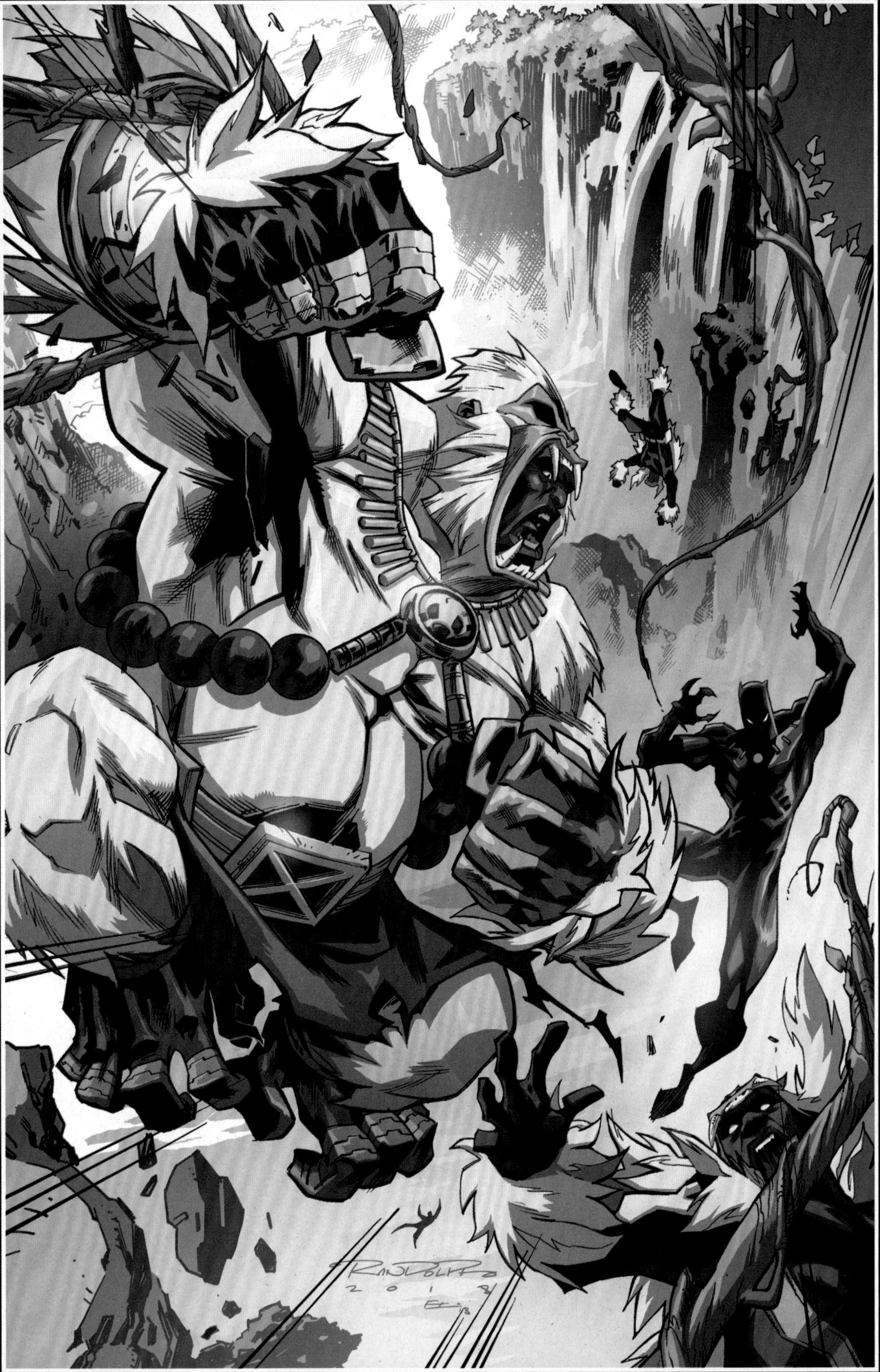

KEEP YOUR FRIENDS CLOSE · PART 2

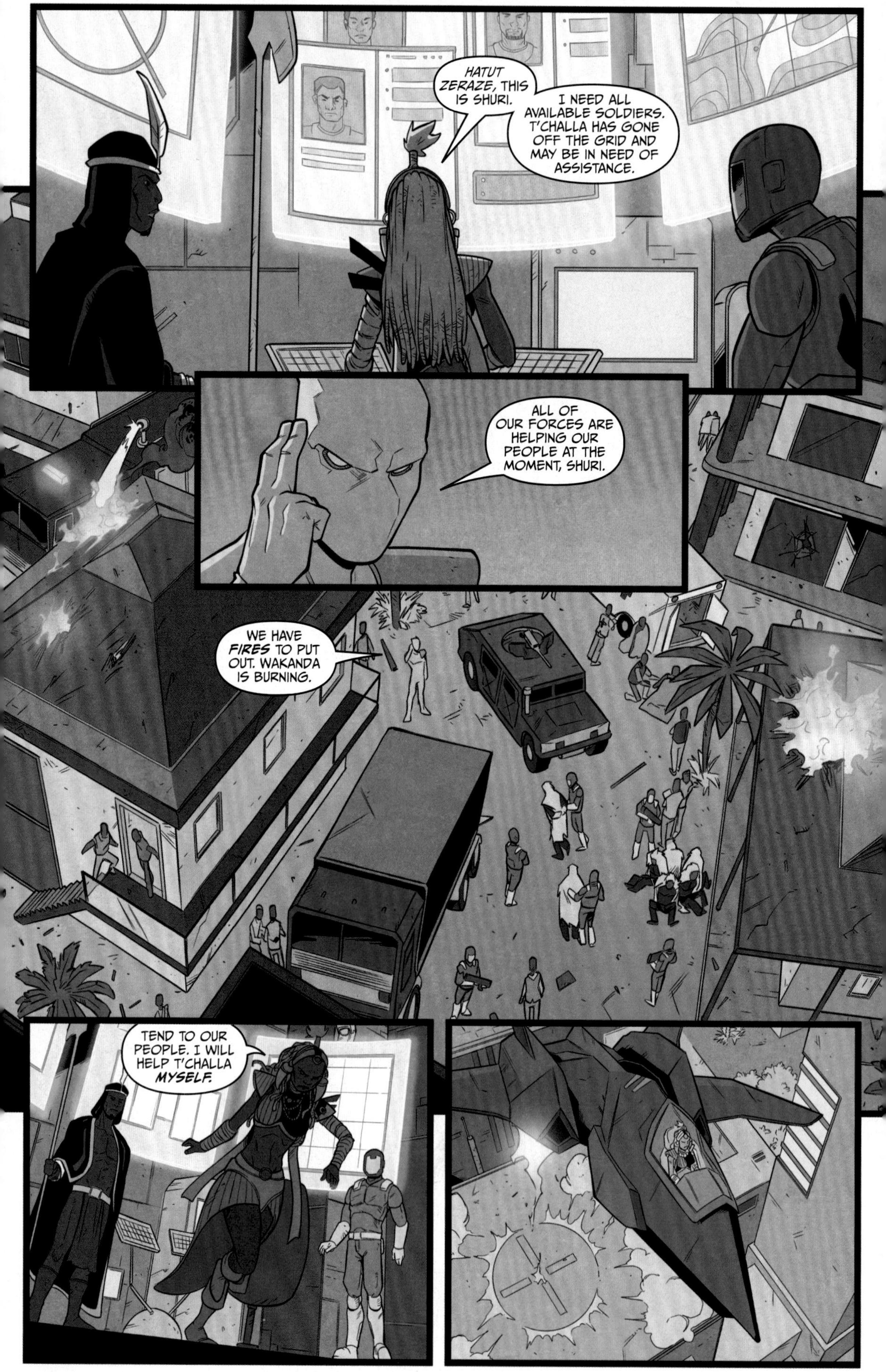
HATUT ZERAZE, THIS IS SHURI.
I NEED ALL AVAILABLE SOLDIERS. T'CHALLA HAS GONE OFF THE GRID AND MAY BE IN NEED OF ASSISTANCE.
ALL OF OUR FORCES ARE HELPING OUR PEOPLE AT THE MOMENT, SHURI.
WE HAVE *FIRES* TO PUT OUT. WAKANDA IS BURNING.
TEND TO OUR PEOPLE. I WILL HELP T'CHALLA *MYSELF.*

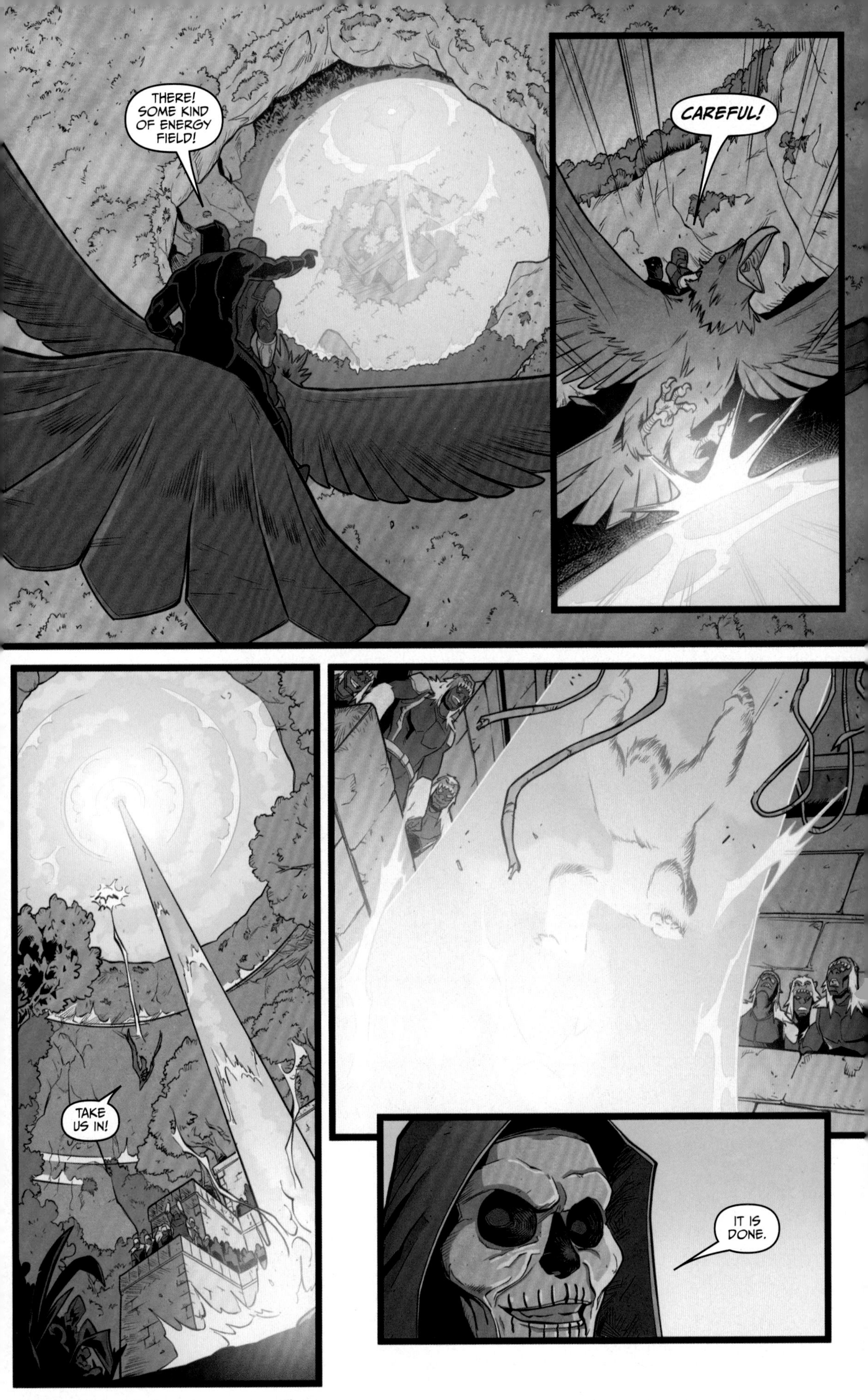
THERE! SOME KIND OF ENERGY FIELD!
CAREFUL!
TAKE US IN!
IT IS DONE.

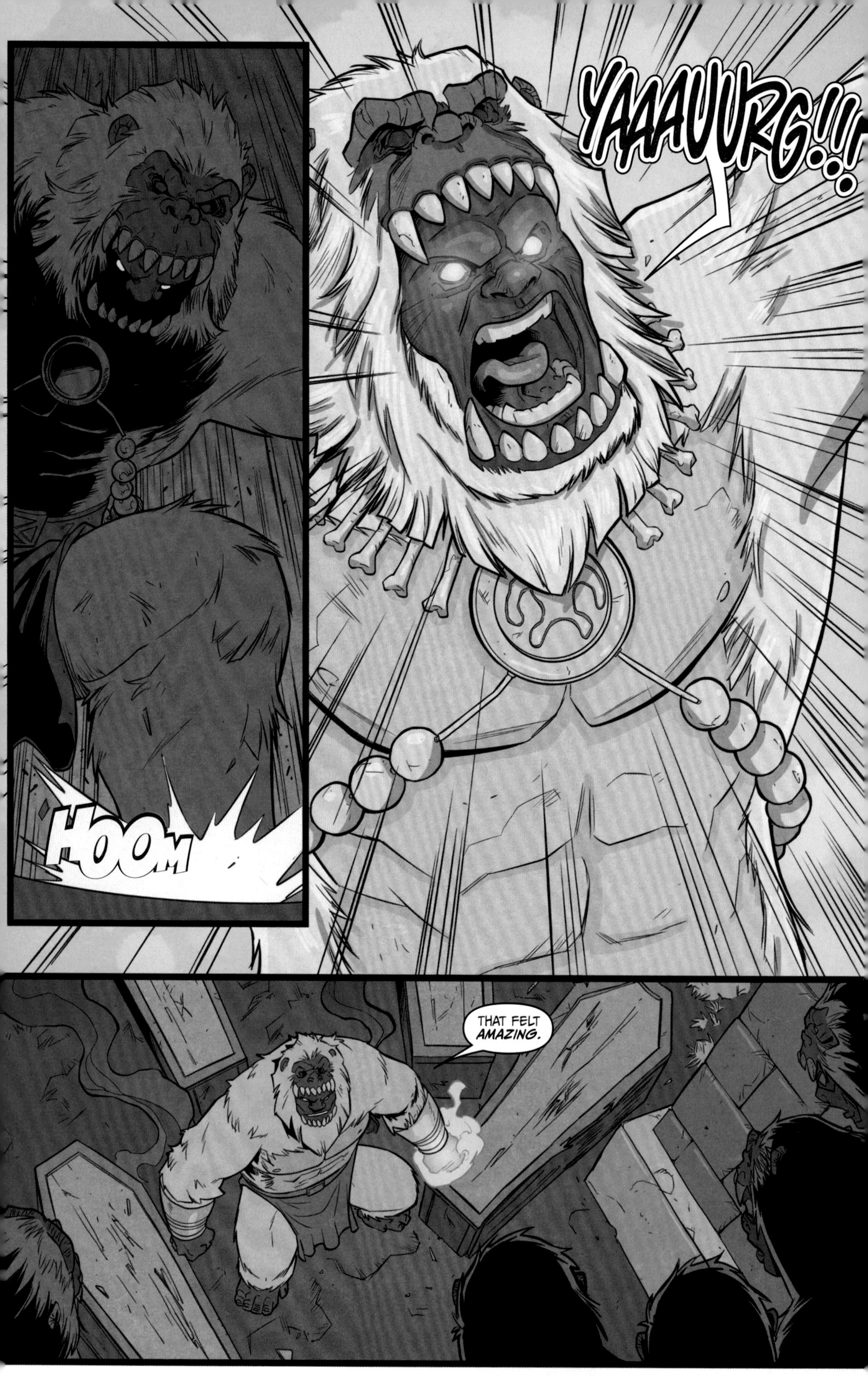
YAAAUURG!!!
HOOM
THAT FELT AMAZING.

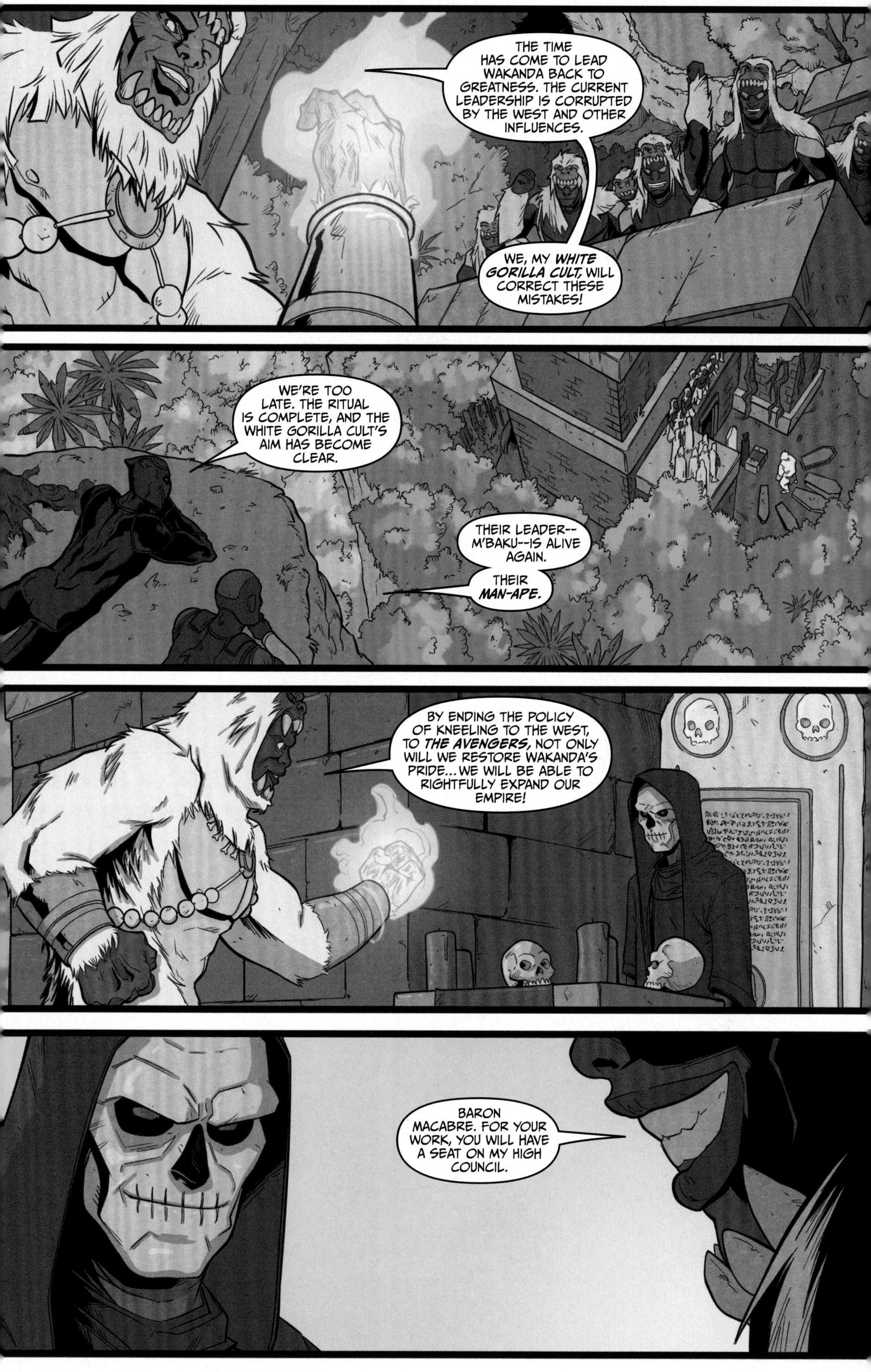
THE TIME HAS COME TO LEAD WAKANDA BACK TO GREATNESS. THE CURRENT LEADERSHIP IS CORRUPTED BY THE WEST AND OTHER INFLUENCES.
WE, MY WHITE GORILLA CULT, WILL CORRECT THESE MISTAKES!
WE'RE TOO LATE. THE RITUAL IS COMPLETE, AND THE WHITE GORILLA CULT'S AIM HAS BECOME CLEAR.
THEIR LEADER--M'BAKU--IS ALIVE AGAIN.
THEIR MAN-APE.
BY ENDING THE POLICY OF KNEELING TO THE WEST, TO THE AVENGERS, NOT ONLY WILL WE RESTORE WAKANDA'S PRIDE...WE WILL BE ABLE TO RIGHTFULLY EXPAND OUR EMPIRE!
BARON MACABRE. FOR YOUR WORK, YOU WILL HAVE A SEAT ON MY HIGH COUNCIL.

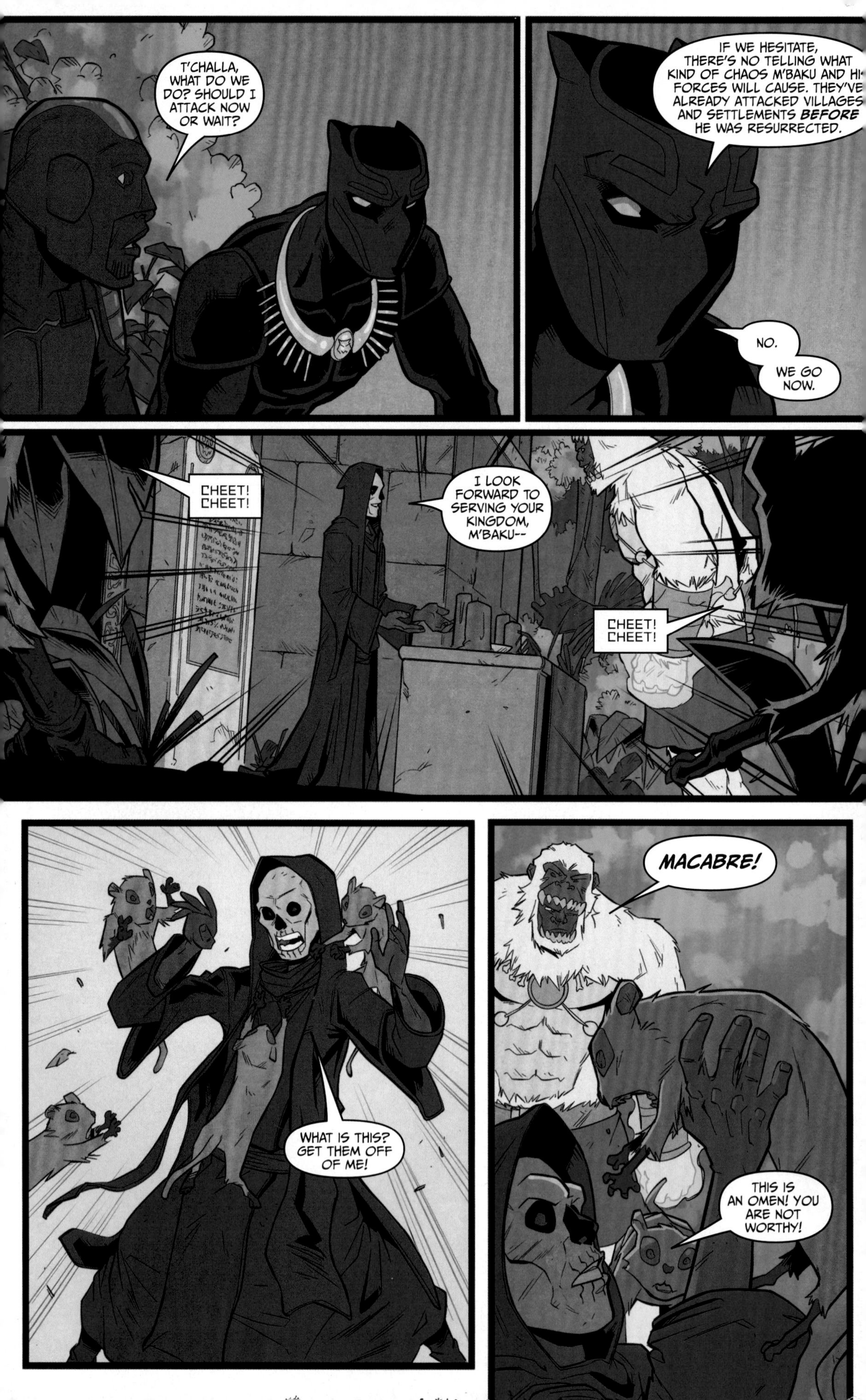
T'CHALLA, WHAT DO WE DO? SHOULD I ATTACK NOW OR WAIT?
IF WE HESITATE, THERE'S NO TELLING WHAT KIND OF CHAOS M'BAKU AND HI FORCES WILL CAUSE. THEY'VE ALREADY ATTACKED VILLAGES AND SETTLEMENTS BEFORE HE WAS RESURRECTED.
NO.
WE GO NOW.
CHEET! CHEET!
I LOOK FORWARD TO SERVING YOUR KINGDOM, M'BAKU--
CHEET! CHEET!
WHAT IS THIS? GET THEM OFF OF ME!
MACABRE!
THIS IS AN OMEN! YOU ARE NOT WORTHY!

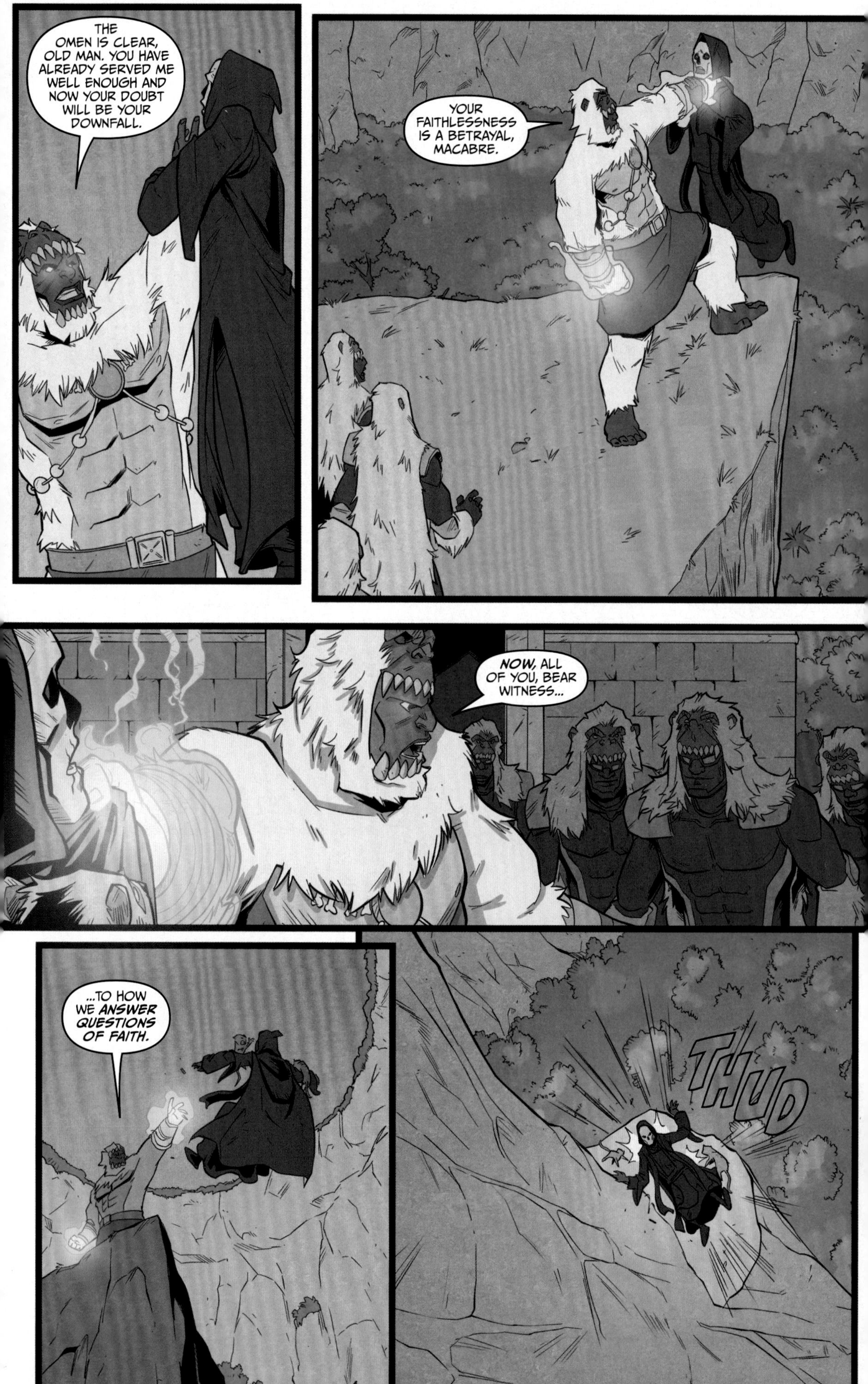
THE OMEN IS CLEAR, OLD MAN. YOU HAVE ALREADY SERVED ME WELL ENOUGH AND NOW YOUR DOUBT WILL BE YOUR DOWNFALL.
YOUR FAITHLESSNESS IS A BETRAYAL, MACABRE.
NOW, ALL OF YOU, BEAR WITNESS...
...TO HOW WE ANSWER QUESTIONS OF FAITH.
THUD

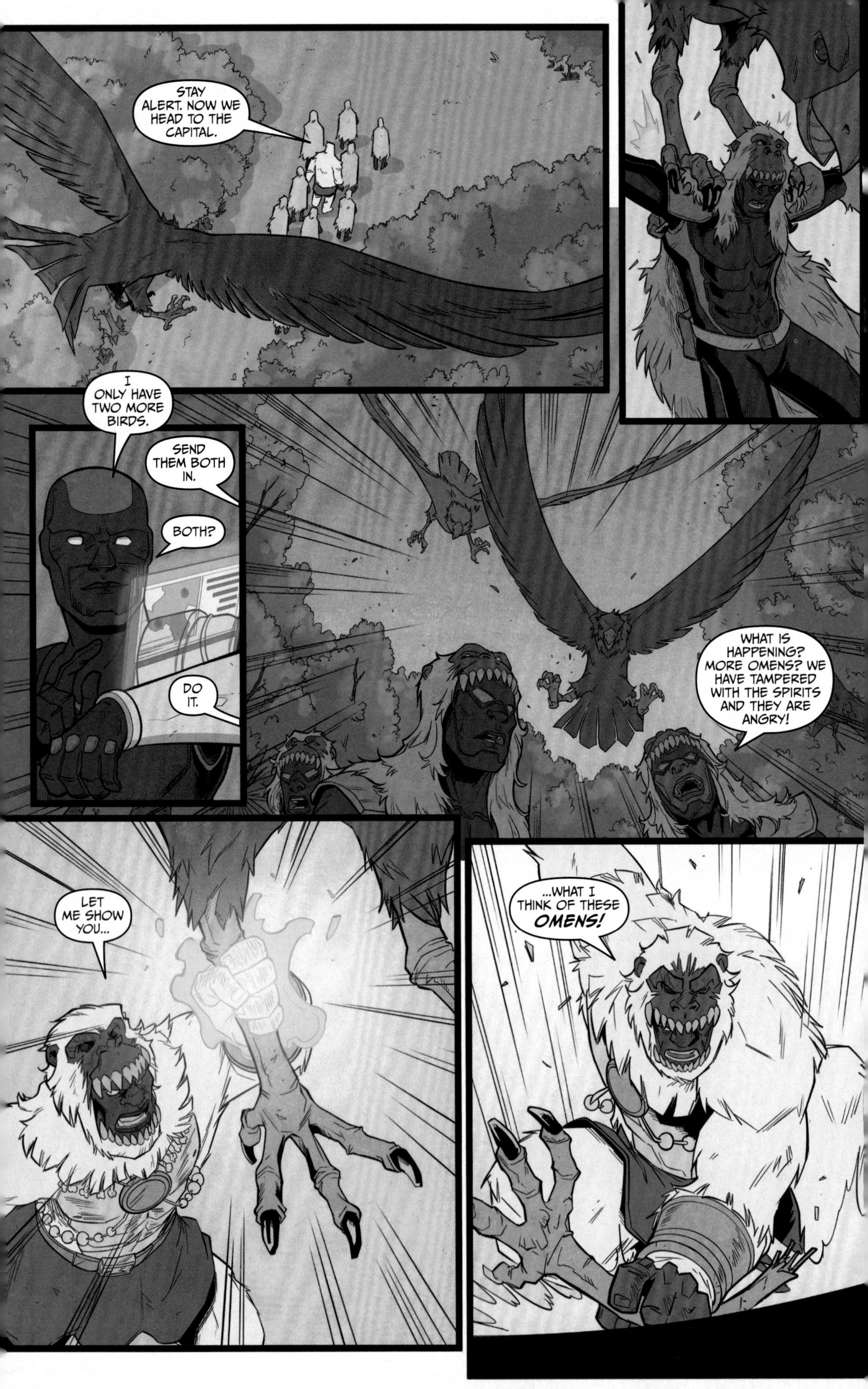
STAY ALERT. NOW WE HEAD TO THE CAPITAL.
I ONLY HAVE TWO MORE BIRDS.
SEND THEM BOTH IN.
BOTH?
DO IT.
WHAT IS HAPPENING? MORE OMENS? WE HAVE TAMPERED WITH THE SPIRITS AND THEY ARE ANGRY!
LET ME SHOW YOU...
...WHAT I THINK OF THESE *OMENS!*

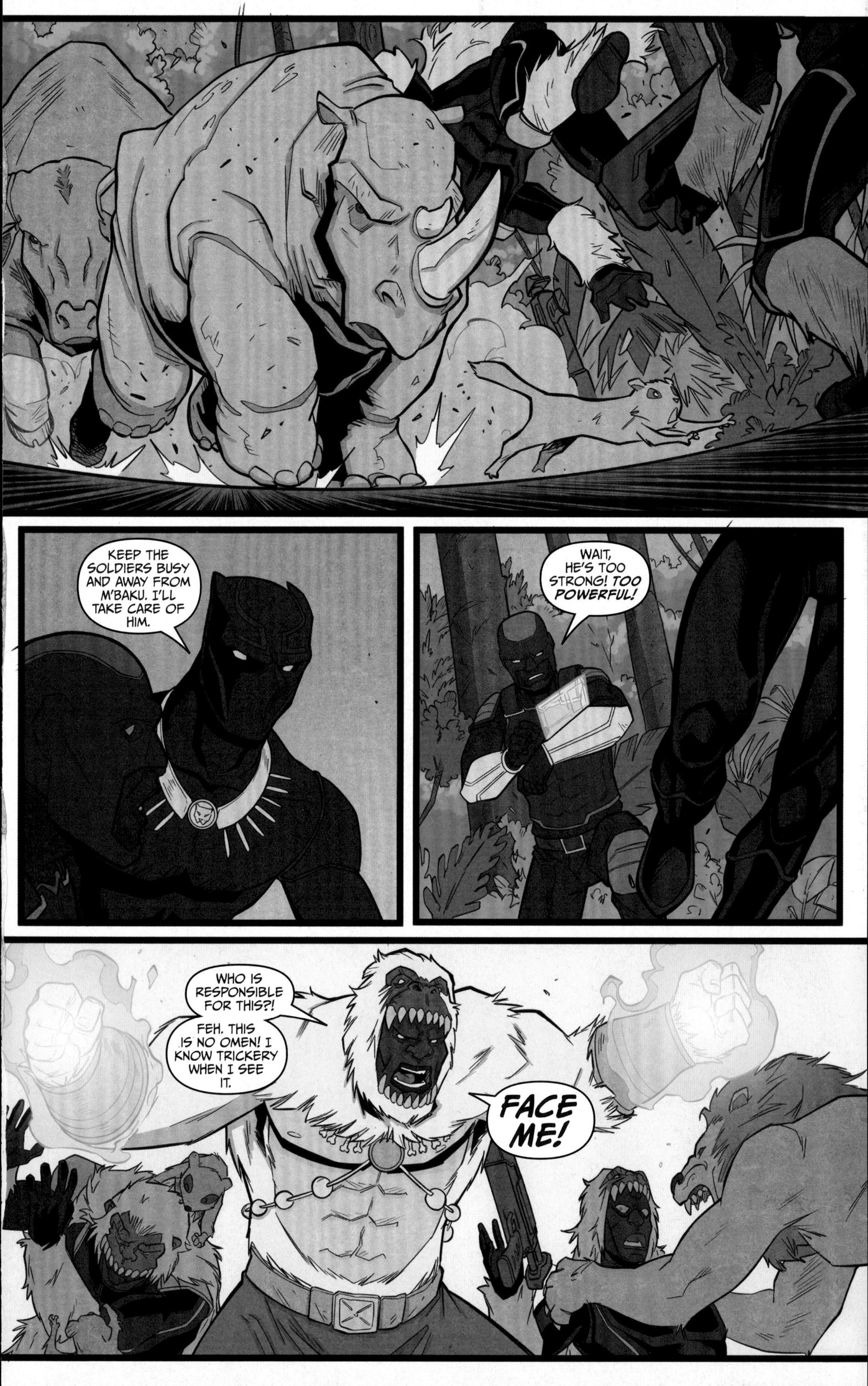
KEEP THE SOLDIERS BUSY AND AWAY FROM M'BAKU. I'LL TAKE CARE OF HIM.
WAIT, HE'S TOO STRONG! *TOO POWERFUL!*
WHO IS RESPONSIBLE FOR THIS?!
FEH. THIS IS NO OMEN! I KNOW TRICKERY WHEN I SEE IT.
FACE ME!

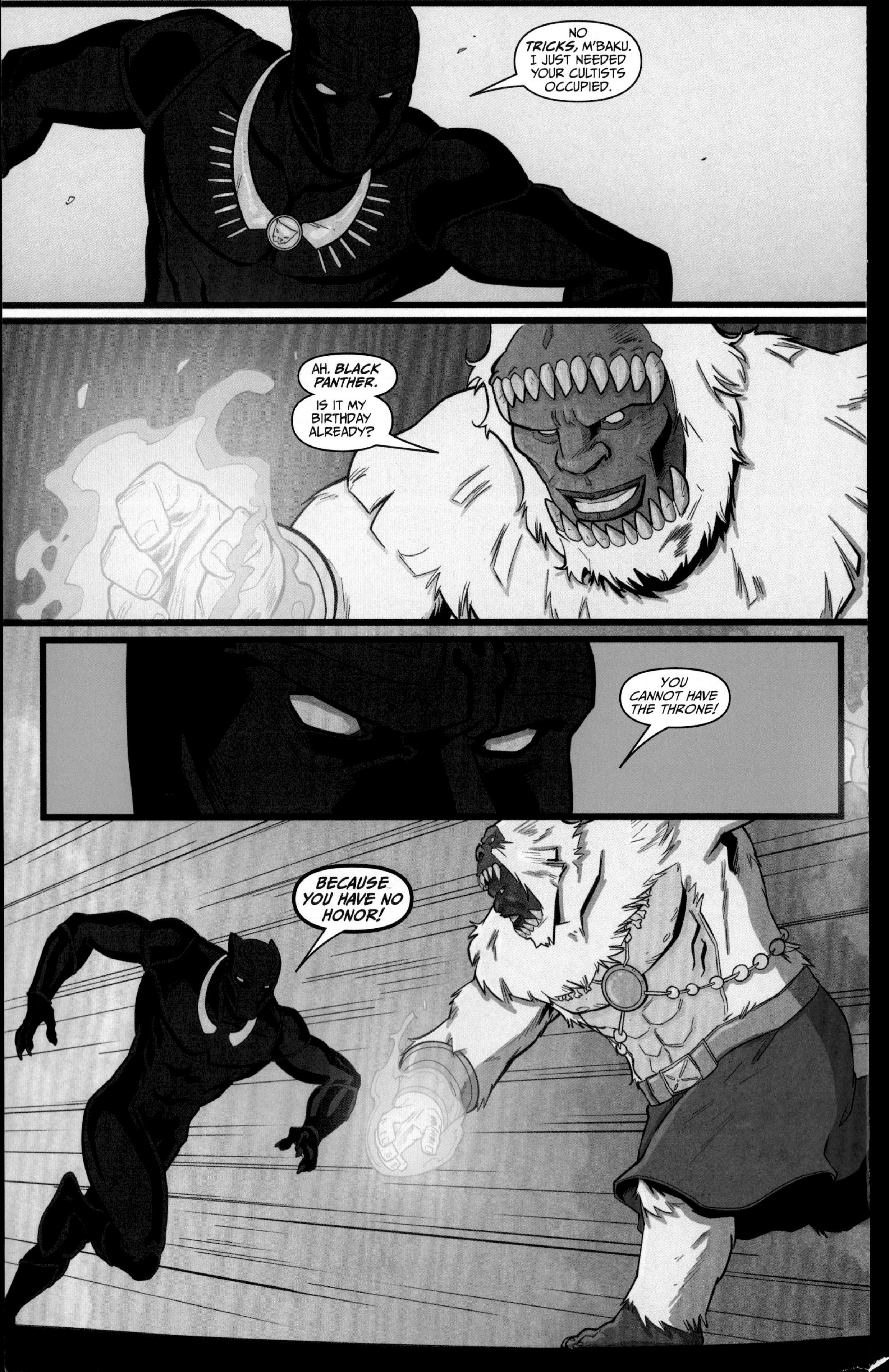
NO TRICKS, M'BAKU. I JUST NEEDED YOUR CULTISTS OCCUPIED.
AH. BLACK PANTHER.
IS IT MY BIRTHDAY ALREADY?
YOU CANNOT HAVE THE THRONE!
BECAUSE YOU HAVE NO HONOR!

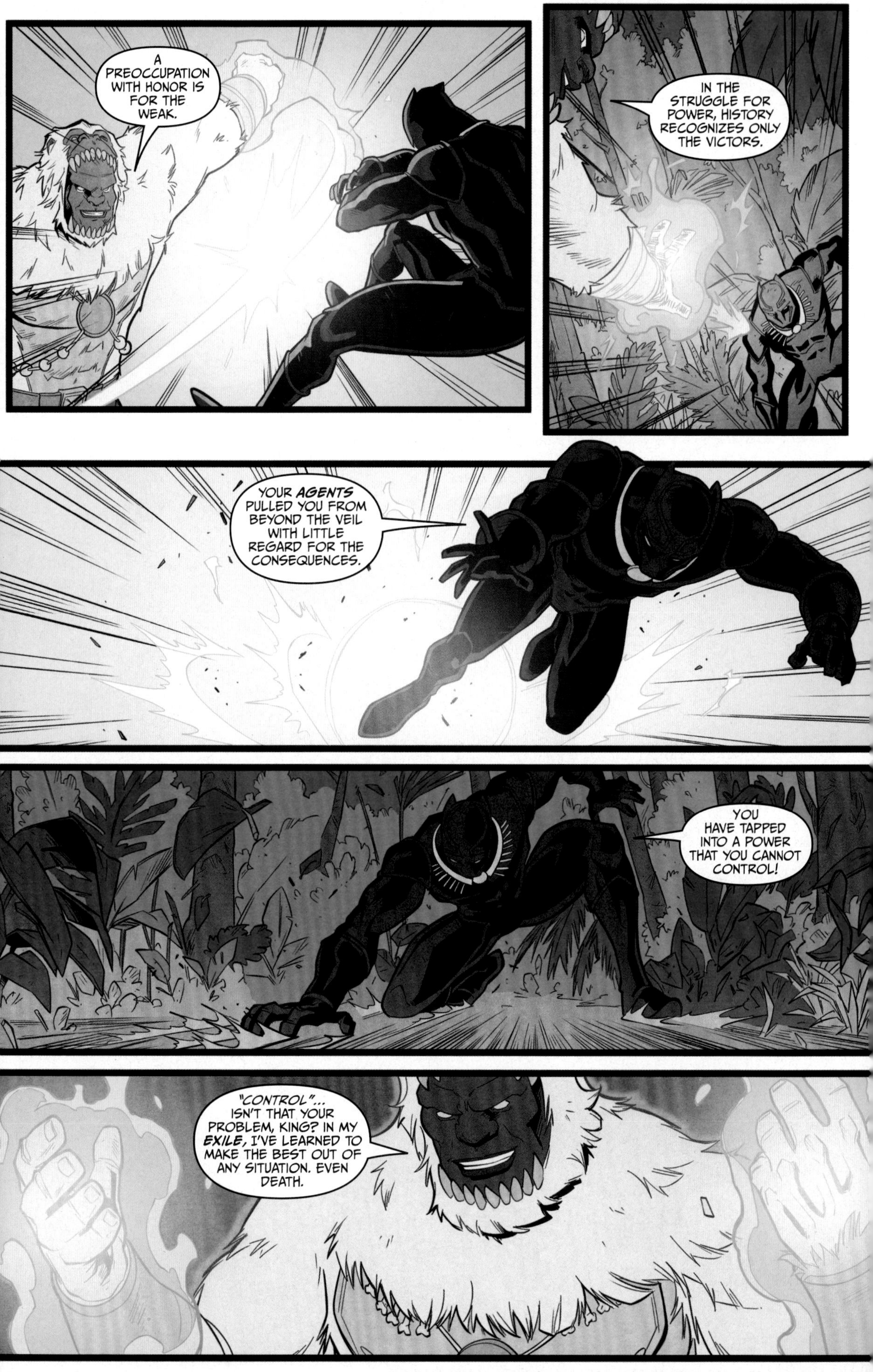
A PREOCCUPATION WITH HONOR IS FOR THE WEAK.
IN THE STRUGGLE FOR POWER, HISTORY RECOGNIZES ONLY THE VICTORS.
YOUR AGENTS PULLED YOU FROM BEYOND THE VEIL WITH LITTLE REGARD FOR THE CONSEQUENCES.
YOU HAVE TAPPED INTO A POWER THAT YOU CANNOT CONTROL!
"CONTROL"... ISN'T THAT YOUR PROBLEM, KING? IN MY EXILE, I'VE LEARNED TO MAKE THE BEST OUT OF ANY SITUATION. EVEN DEATH.

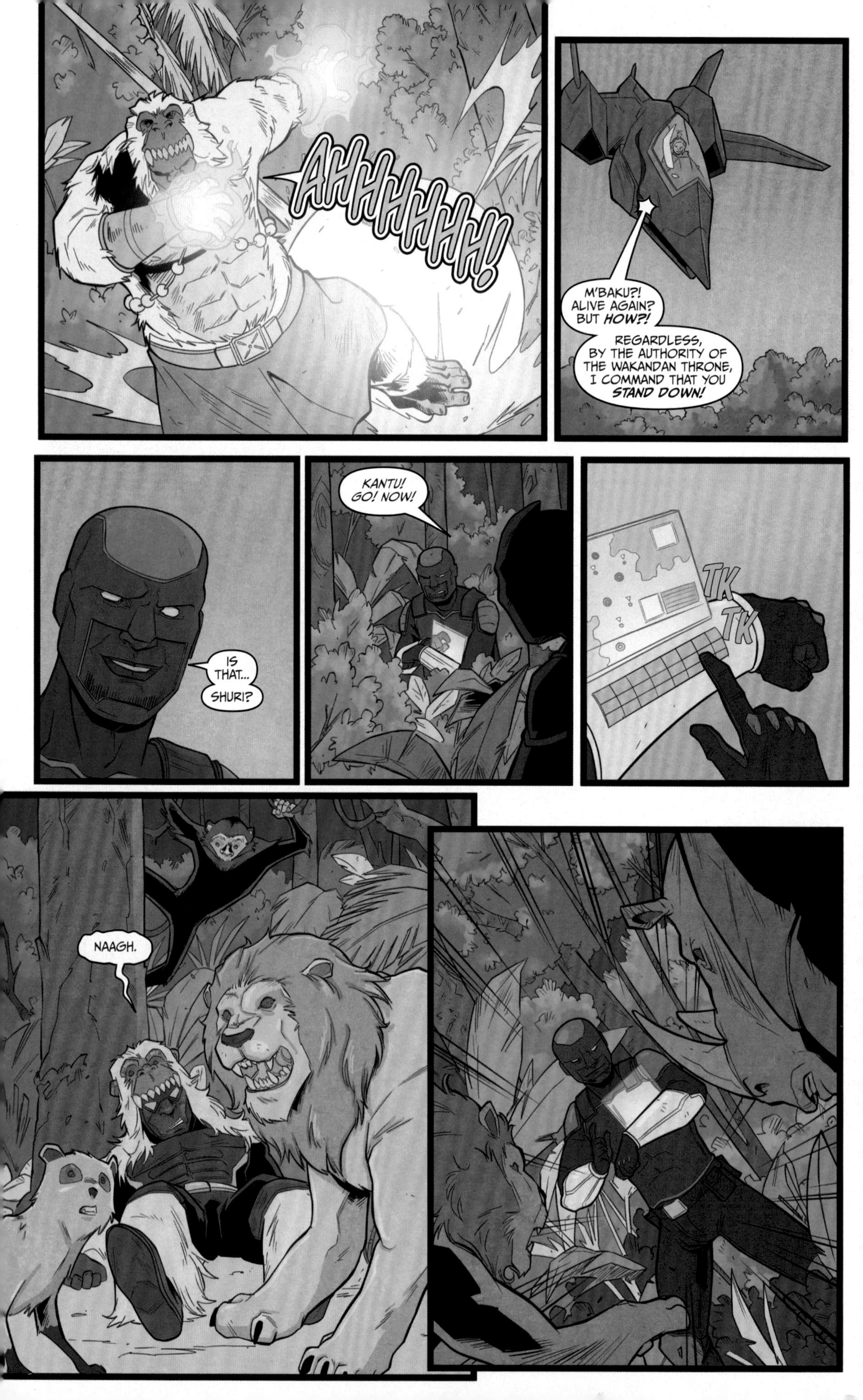
AHHHHHHH!
M'BAKU?! ALIVE AGAIN? BUT HOW?!
REGARDLESS, BY THE AUTHORITY OF THE WAKANDAN THRONE, I COMMAND THAT YOU STAND DOWN!
IS THAT... SHURI?
KANTU! GO! NOW!
TK
TK
NAAGH.

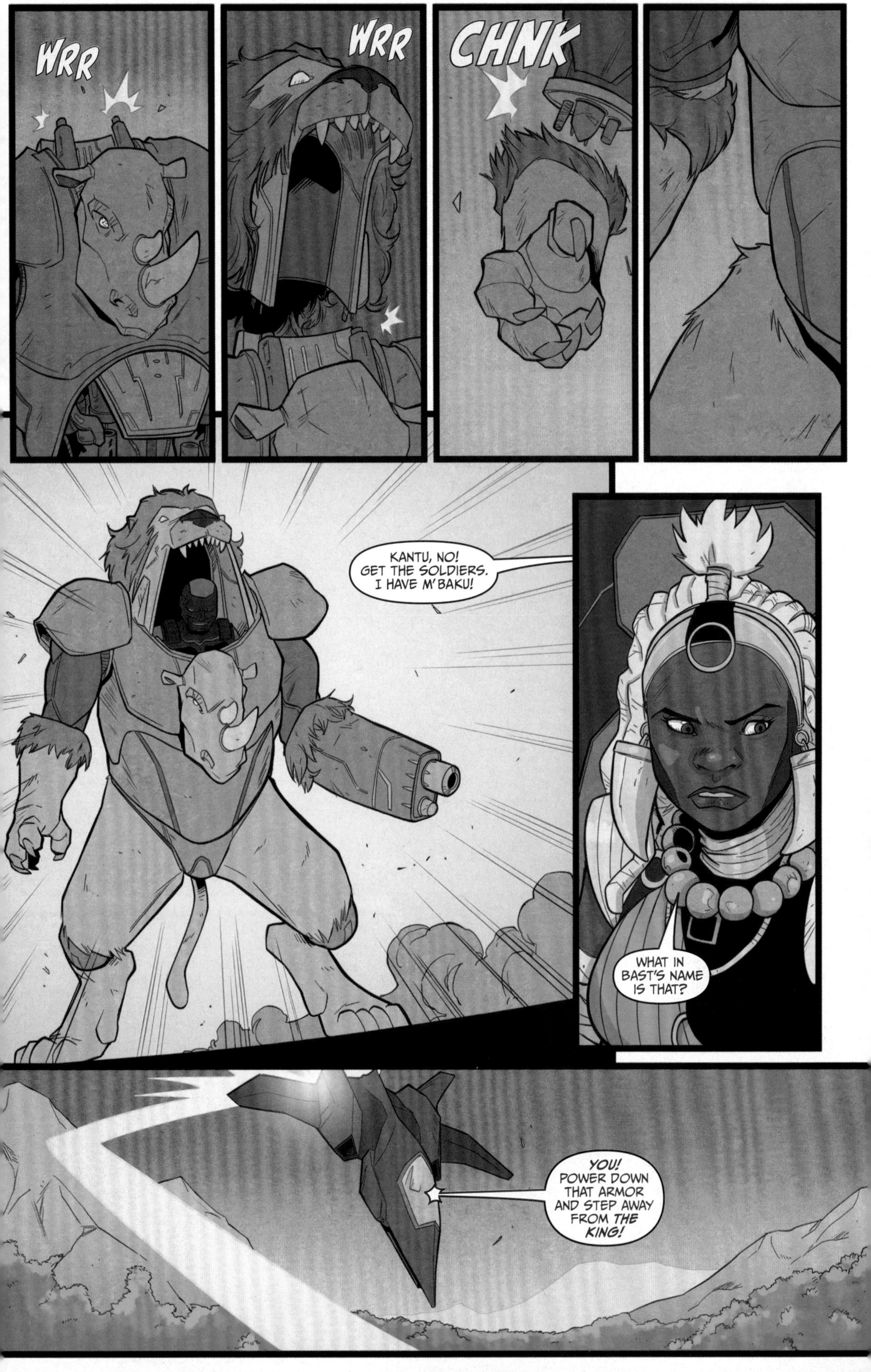
WRR
WRR
CHNK
KANTU, NO! GET THE SOLDIERS. I HAVE M'BAKU!
WHAT IN BAST'S NAME IS THAT?
YOU! POWER DOWN THAT ARMOR AND STEP AWAY FROM THE KING!

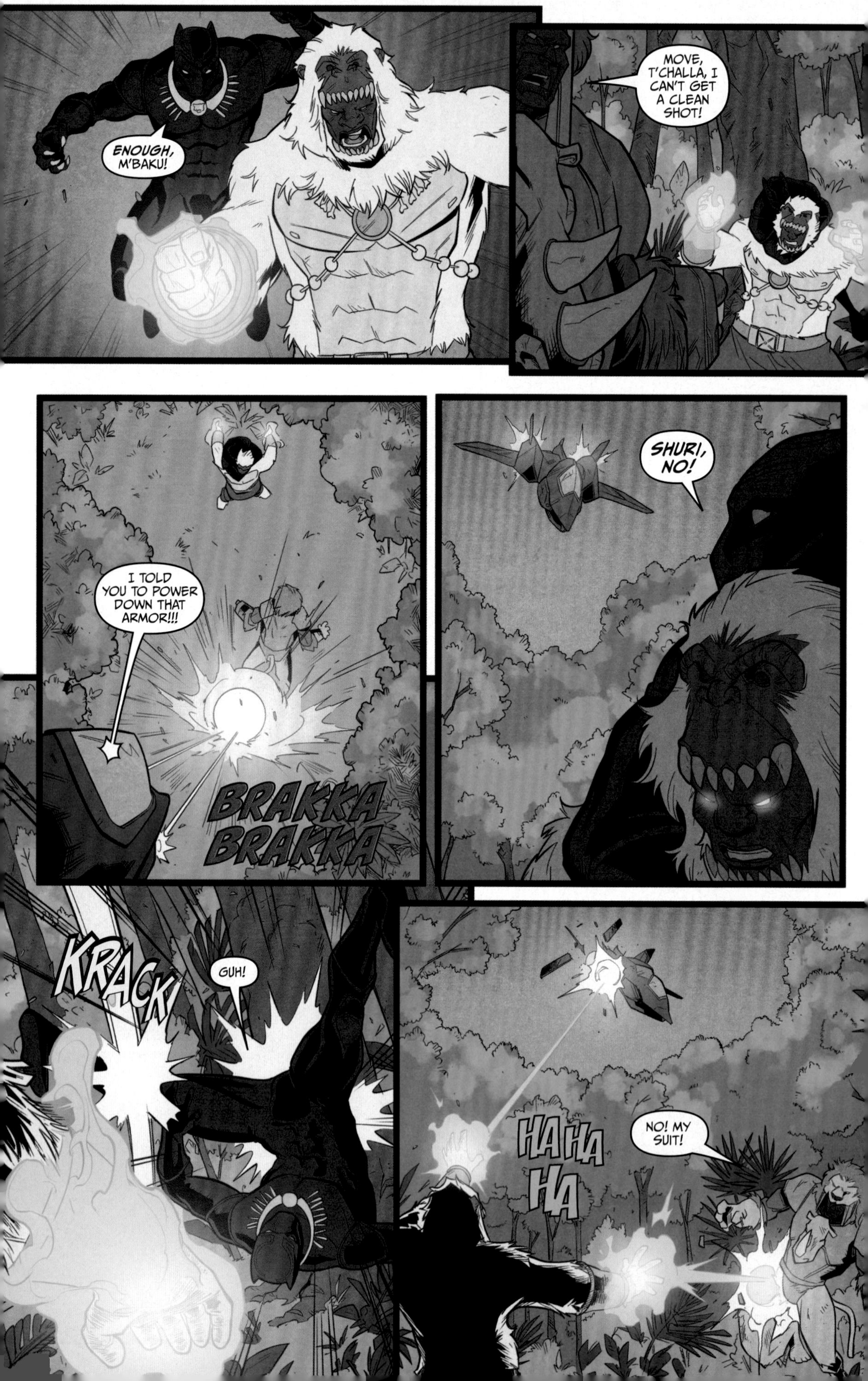
ENOUGH, M'BAKU!
MOVE, T'CHALLA, I CAN'T GET A CLEAN SHOT!
I TOLD YOU TO POWER DOWN THAT ARMOR!!!
BRAKKA BRAKKA
SHURI, NO!
KRACK!
GUH!
HA HA HA HA
NO! MY SUIT!

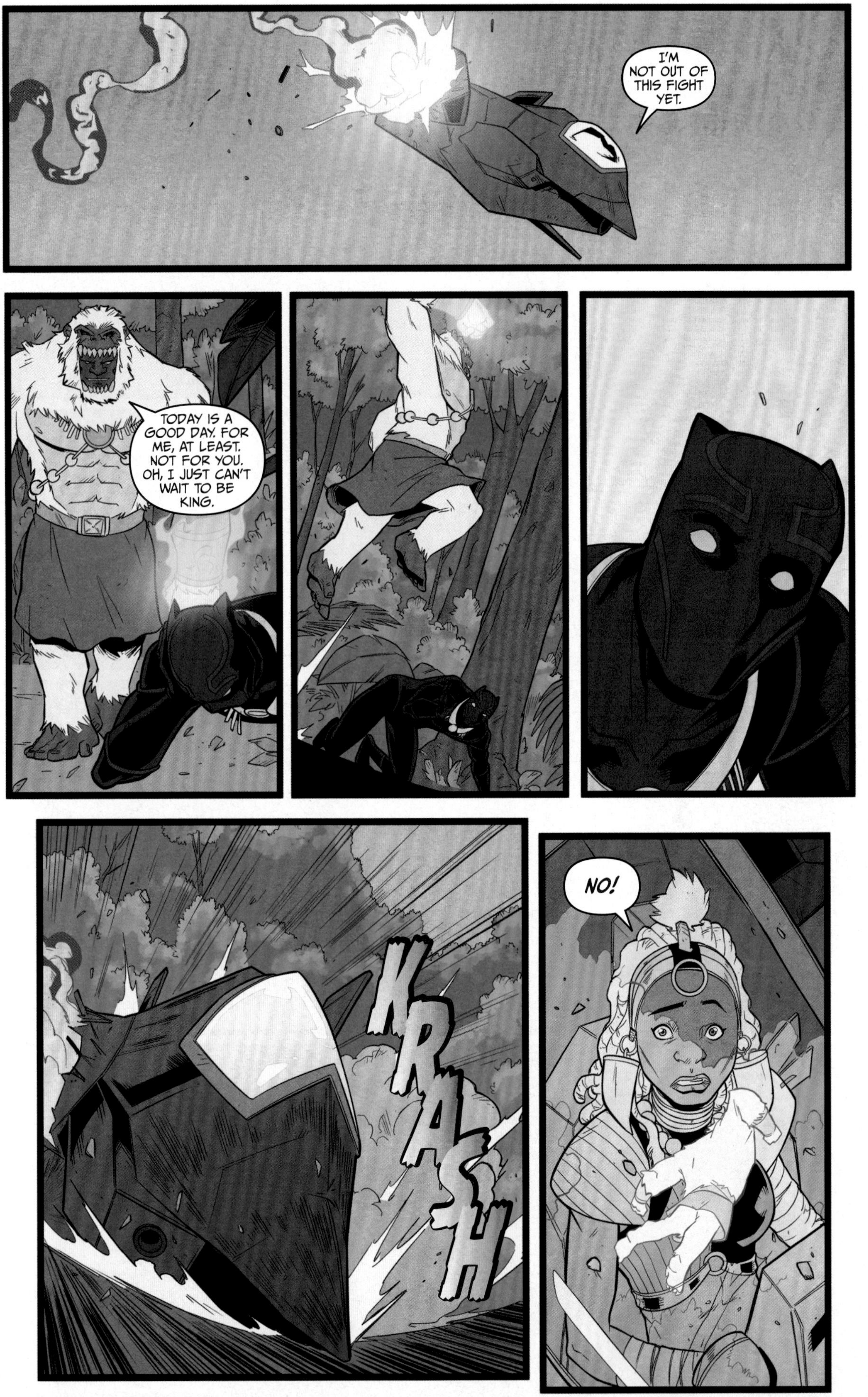
I'M NOT OUT OF THIS FIGHT YET.
TODAY IS A GOOD DAY. FOR ME, AT LEAST. NOT FOR YOU. OH, I JUST CAN'T WAIT TO BE KING.
KRASH
NO!

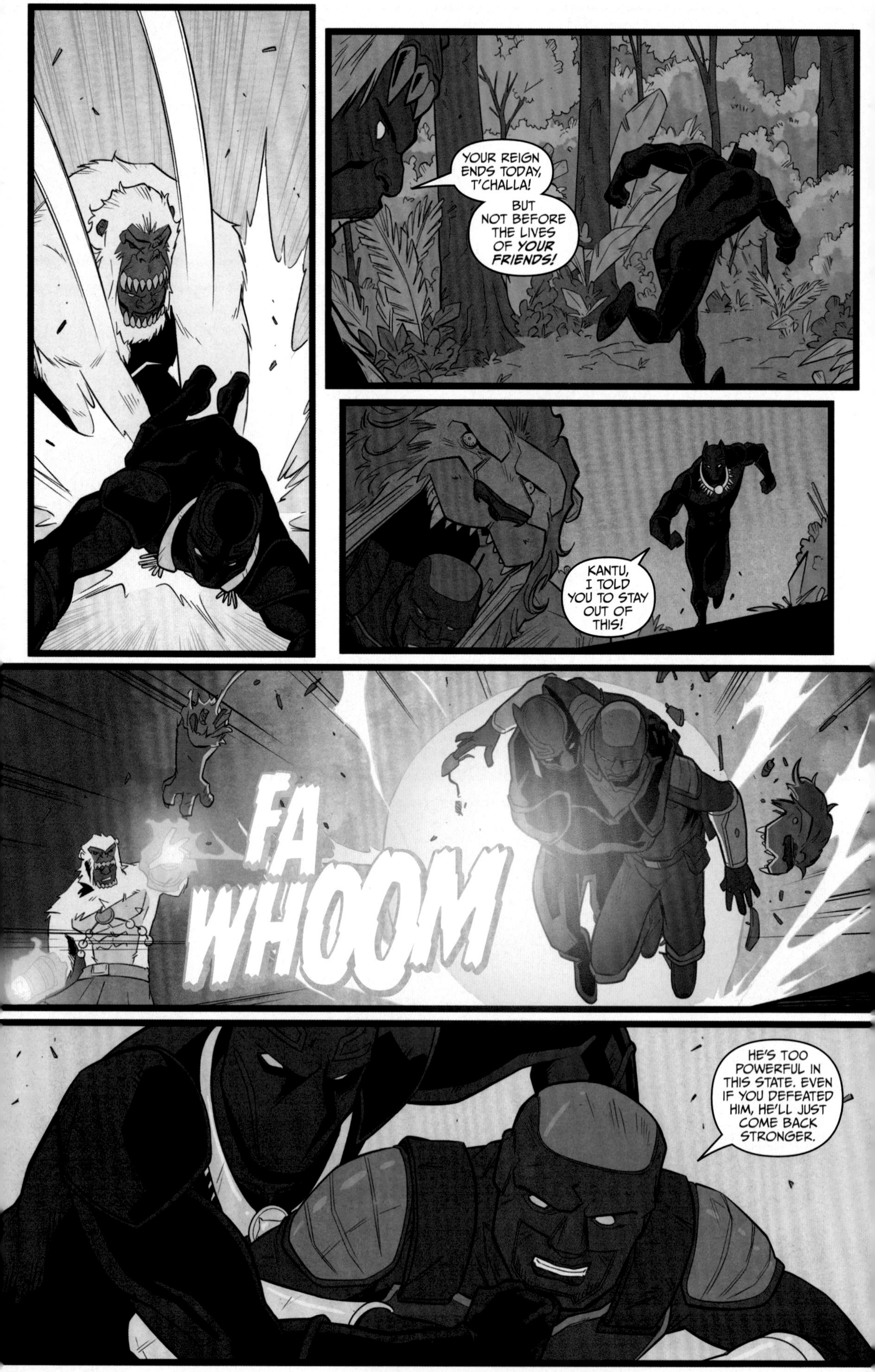
YOUR REIGN ENDS TODAY, T'CHALLA!
BUT NOT BEFORE THE LIVES OF YOUR FRIENDS!
KANTU, I TOLD YOU TO STAY OUT OF THIS!
FA WHOOM
HE'S TOO POWERFUL IN THIS STATE. EVEN IF YOU DEFEATED HIM, HE'LL JUST COME BACK STRONGER.

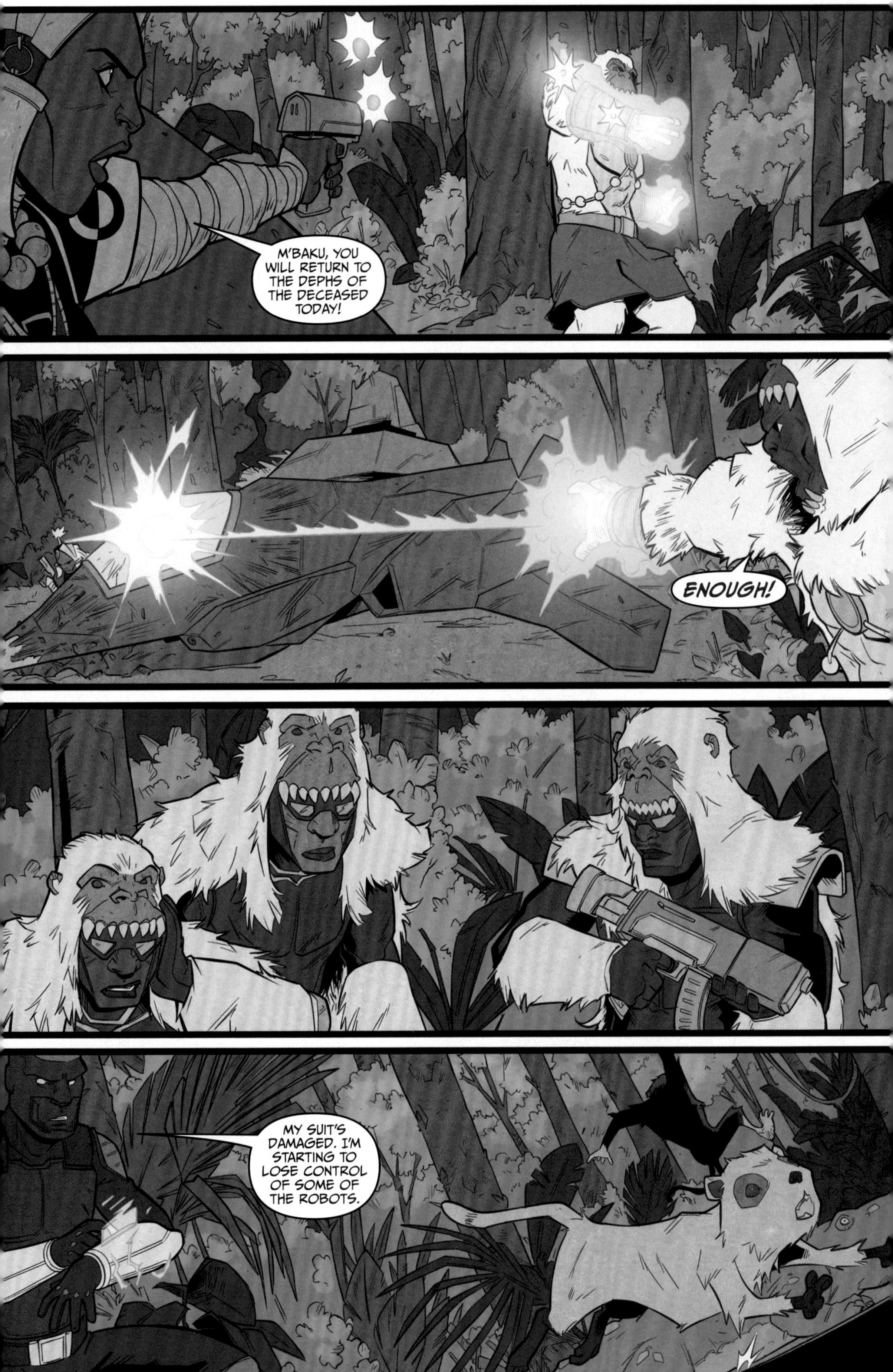
M'BAKU, YOU WILL RETURN TO THE DEPHS OF THE DECEASED TODAY!
ENOUGH!
MY SUIT'S DAMAGED. I'M STARTING TO LOSE CONTROL OF SOME OF THE ROBOTS.

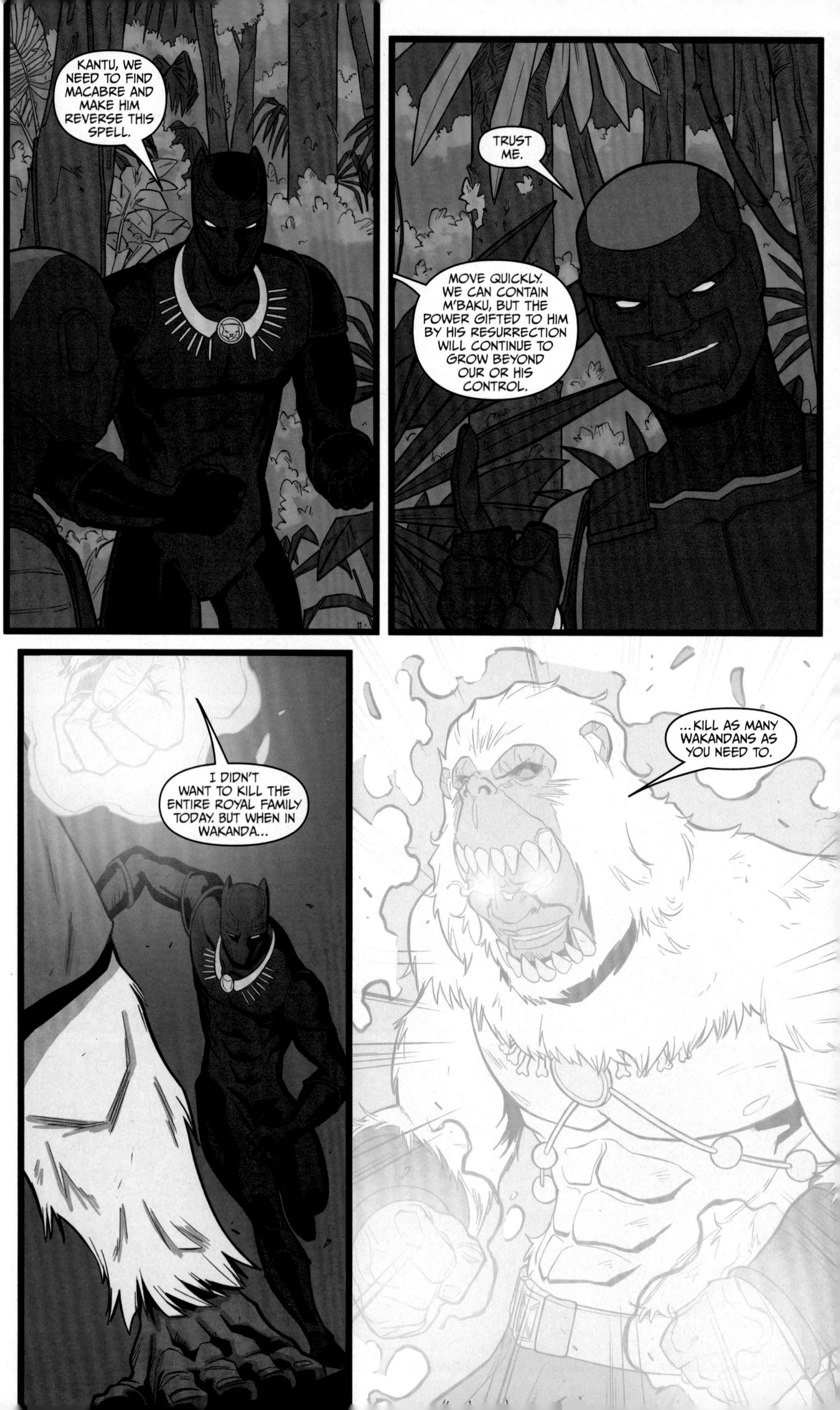
KANTU, WE NEED TO FIND MACABRE AND MAKE HIM REVERSE THIS SPELL.
TRUST ME.
MOVE QUICKLY. WE CAN CONTAIN M'BAKU, BUT THE POWER GIFTED TO HIM BY HIS RESURRECTION WILL CONTINUE TO GROW BEYOND OUR OR HIS CONTROL.
I DIDN'T WANT TO KILL THE ENTIRE ROYAL FAMILY TODAY. BUT WHEN IN WAKANDA...
...KILL AS MANY WAKANDANS AS YOU NEED TO.

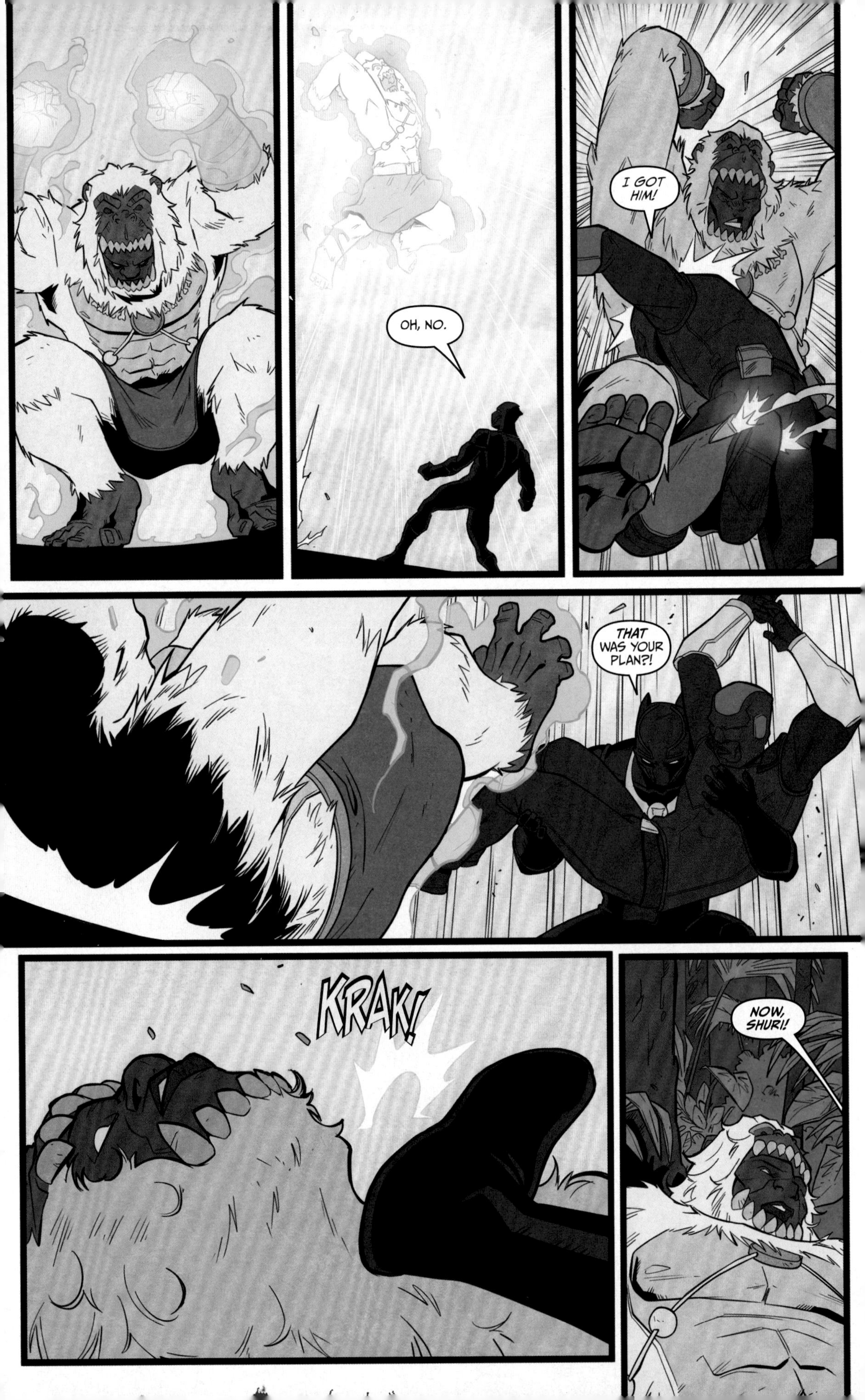

OH, NO.
I GOT HIM!
THAT WAS YOUR PLAN?!
KRAK!
NOW, SHURI!

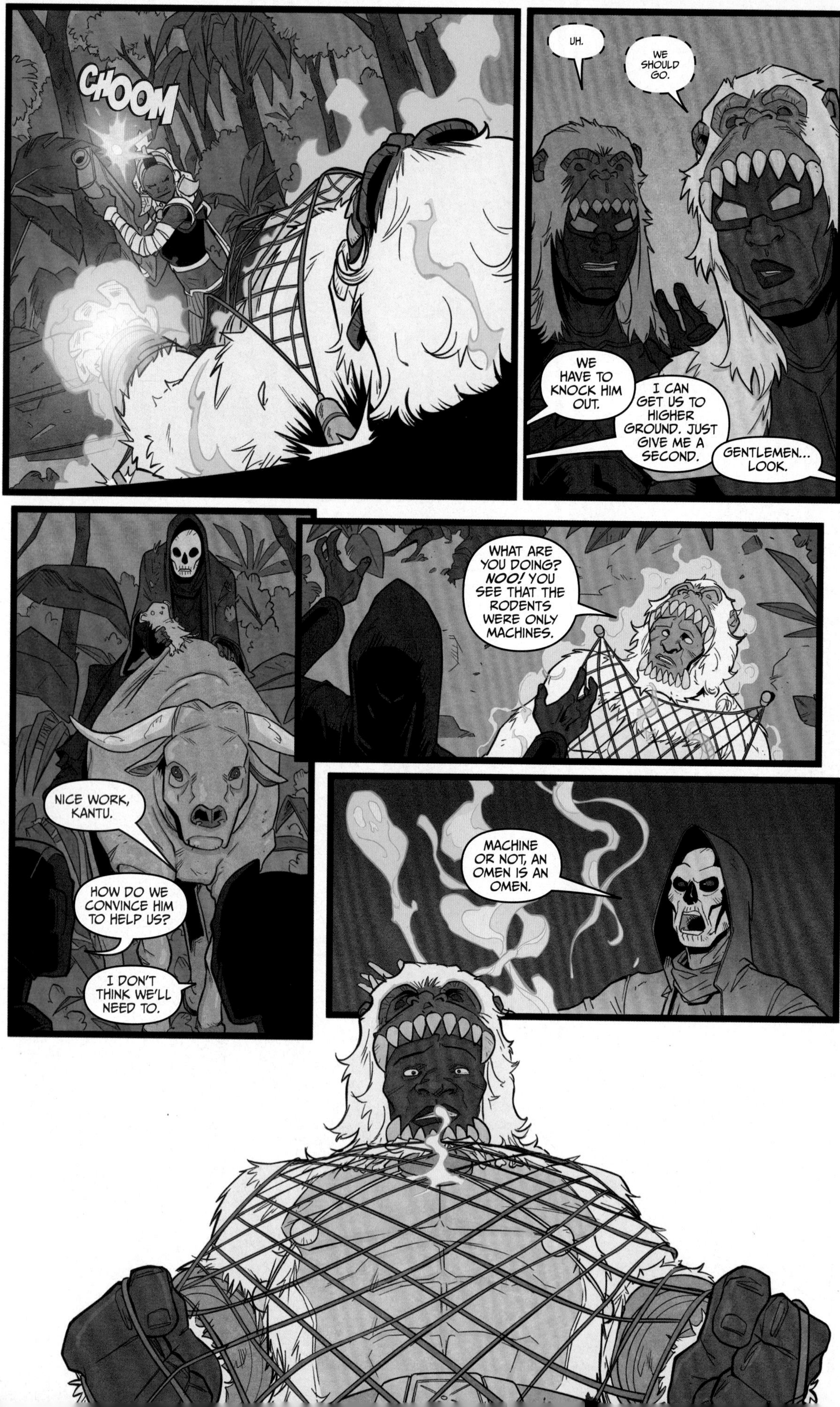
CHOOM
UH.
WE SHOULD GO.
WE HAVE TO KNOCK HIM OUT.
I CAN GET US TO HIGHER GROUND. JUST GIVE ME A SECOND.
GENTLEMEN... LOOK.
NICE WORK, KANTU.
HOW DO WE CONVINCE HIM TO HELP US?
I DON'T THINK WE'LL NEED TO.
WHAT ARE YOU DOING? NOO! YOU SEE THAT THE RODENTS WERE ONLY MACHINES.
MACHINE OR NOT, AN OMEN IS AN OMEN.

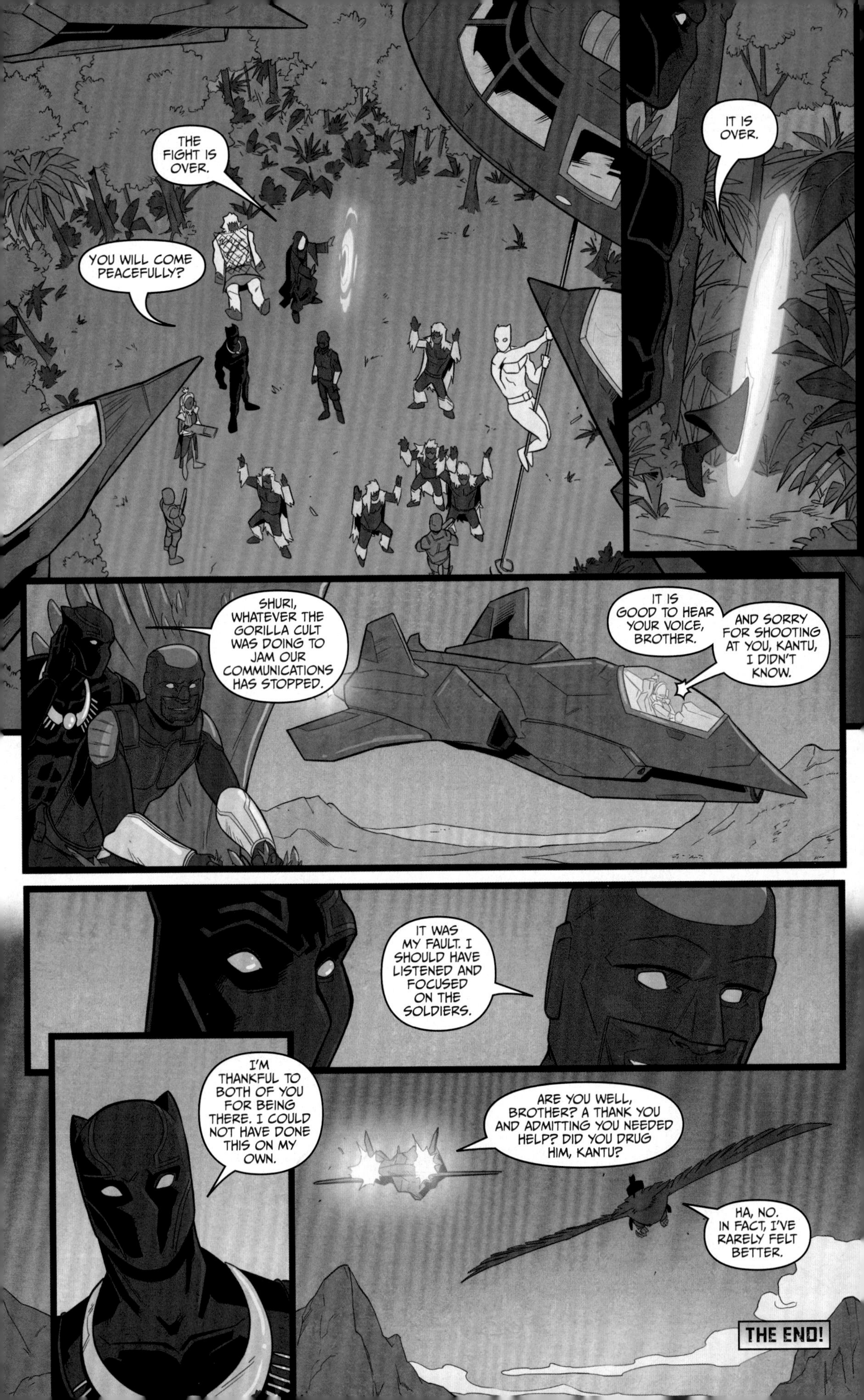
THE FIGHT IS OVER.
YOU WILL COME PEACEFULLY?
IT IS OVER.
SHURI, WHATEVER THE GORILLA CULT WAS DOING TO JAM OUR COMMUNICATIONS HAS STOPPED.
IT IS GOOD TO HEAR YOUR VOICE, BROTHER.
AND SORRY FOR SHOOTING AT YOU, KANTU, I DIDN'T KNOW.
IT WAS MY FAULT. I SHOULD HAVE LISTENED AND FOCUSED ON THE SOLDIERS.
I'M THANKFUL TO BOTH OF YOU FOR BEING THERE. I COULD NOT HAVE DONE THIS ON MY OWN.
ARE YOU WELL, BROTHER? A THANK YOU AND ADMITTING YOU NEEDED HELP? DID YOU DRUG HIM, KANTU?
HA, NO. IN FACT, I'VE RARELY FELT BETTER.
THE END!

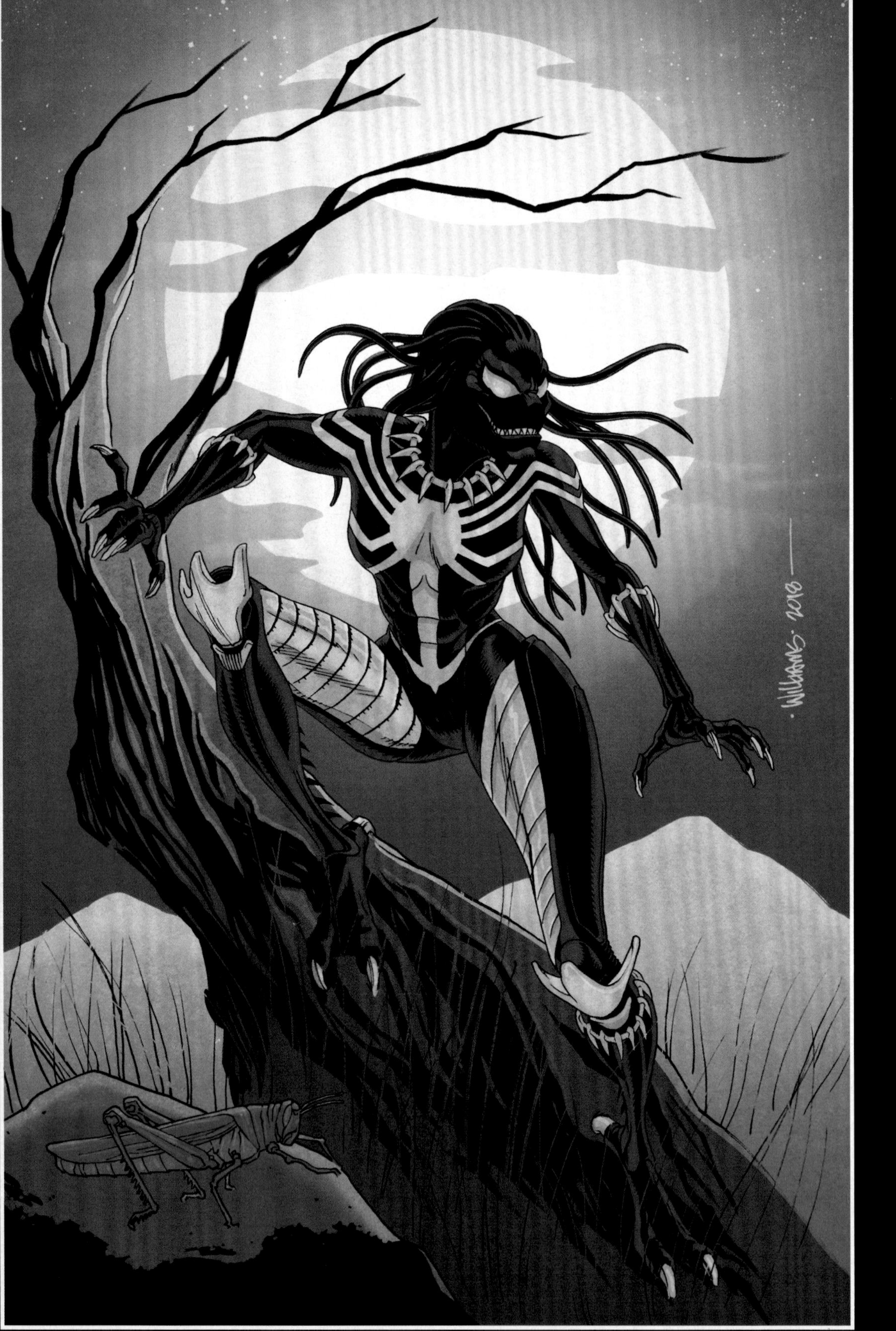
WILLIAMS · 2018

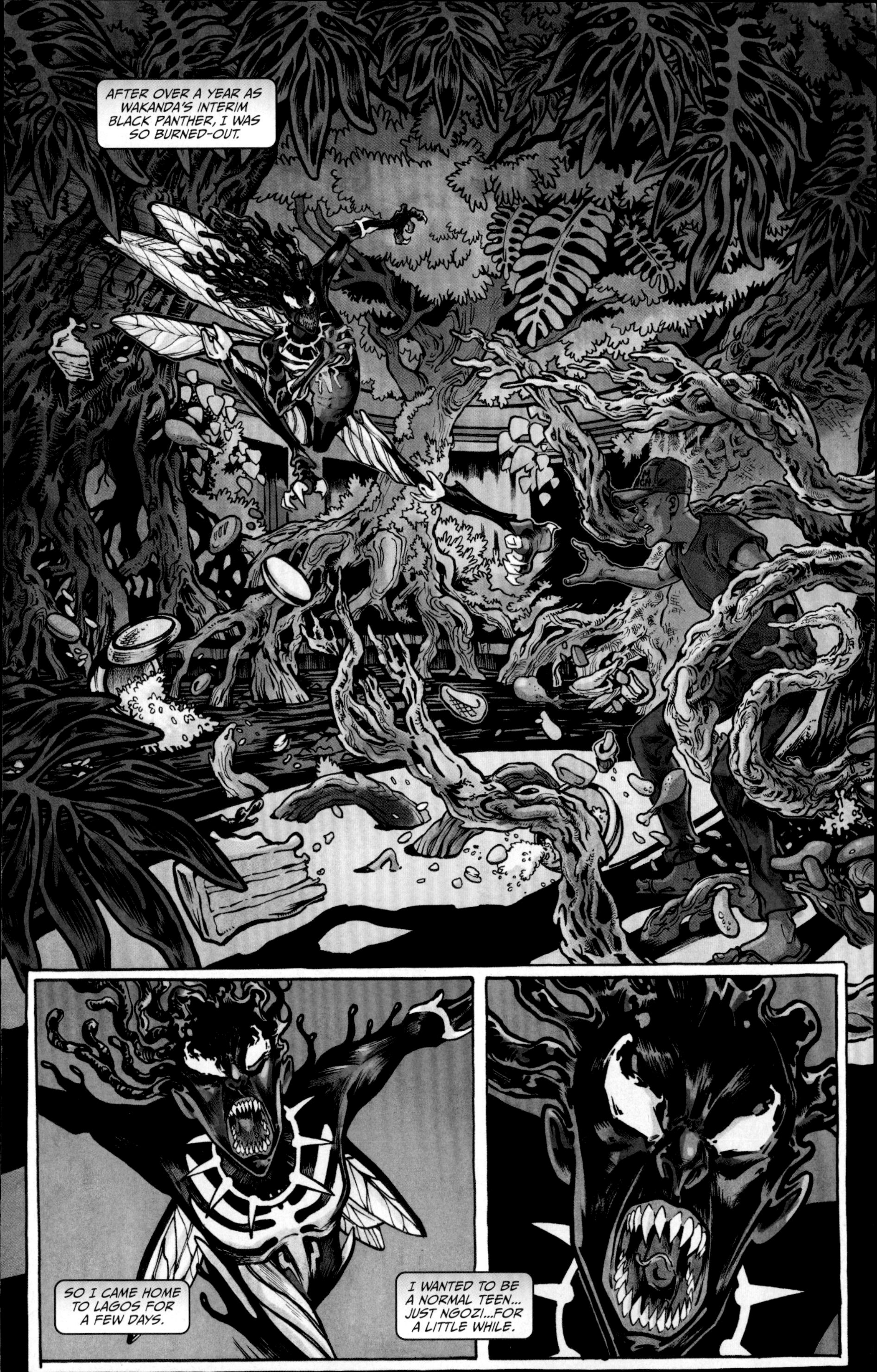
AFTER OVER A YEAR AS WAKANDA'S INTERIM BLACK PANTHER, I WAS SO BURNED-OUT.
SO I CAME HOME TO LAGOS FOR A FEW DAYS.
I WANTED TO BE A NORMAL TEEN... JUST NGOZI...FOR A LITTLE WHILE.

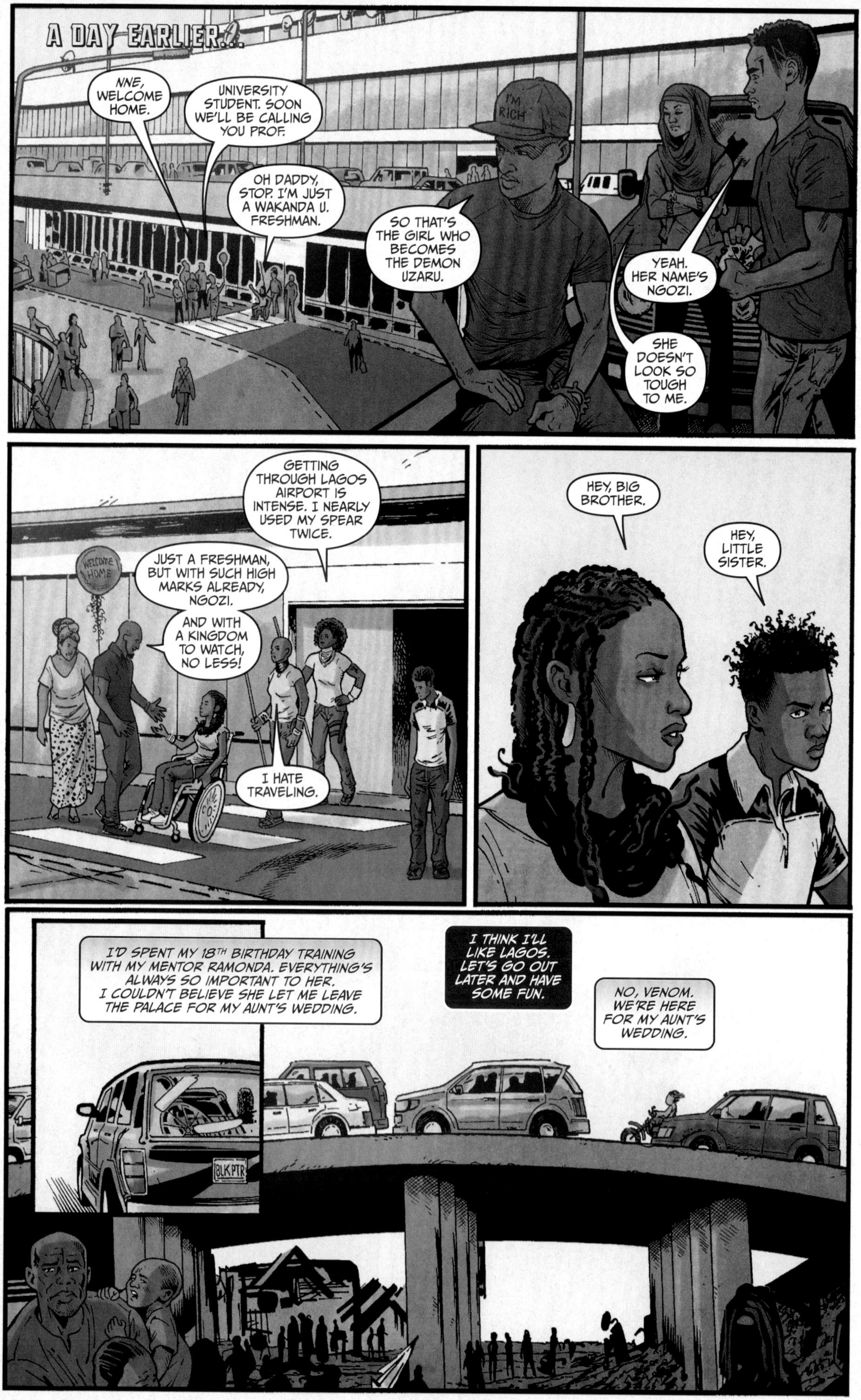
A DAY EARLIER...
NNE, WELCOME HOME.
UNIVERSITY STUDENT. SOON WE'LL BE CALLING YOU PROF.
OH DADDY, STOP. I'M JUST A WAKANDA U. FRESHMAN.
SO THAT'S THE GIRL WHO BECOMES THE DEMON UZARU.
YEAH. HER NAME'S NGOZI.
SHE DOESN'T LOOK SO TOUGH TO ME.
I'M RICH
GETTING THROUGH LAGOS AIRPORT IS INTENSE. I NEARLY USED MY SPEAR TWICE.
WELCOME HOME
JUST A FRESHMAN, BUT WITH SUCH HIGH MARKS ALREADY, NGOZI.
AND WITH A KINGDOM TO WATCH, NO LESS!
I HATE TRAVELING.
HEY, BIG BROTHER.
HEY, LITTLE SISTER.
I'D SPENT MY 18TH BIRTHDAY TRAINING WITH MY MENTOR RAMONDA. EVERYTHING'S ALWAYS SO IMPORTANT TO HER. I COULDN'T BELIEVE SHE LET ME LEAVE THE PALACE FOR MY AUNT'S WEDDING.
I THINK I'LL LIKE LAGOS. LET'S GO OUT LATER AND HAVE SOME FUN.
NO, VENOM. WE'RE HERE FOR MY AUNT'S WEDDING.
BLKPTR

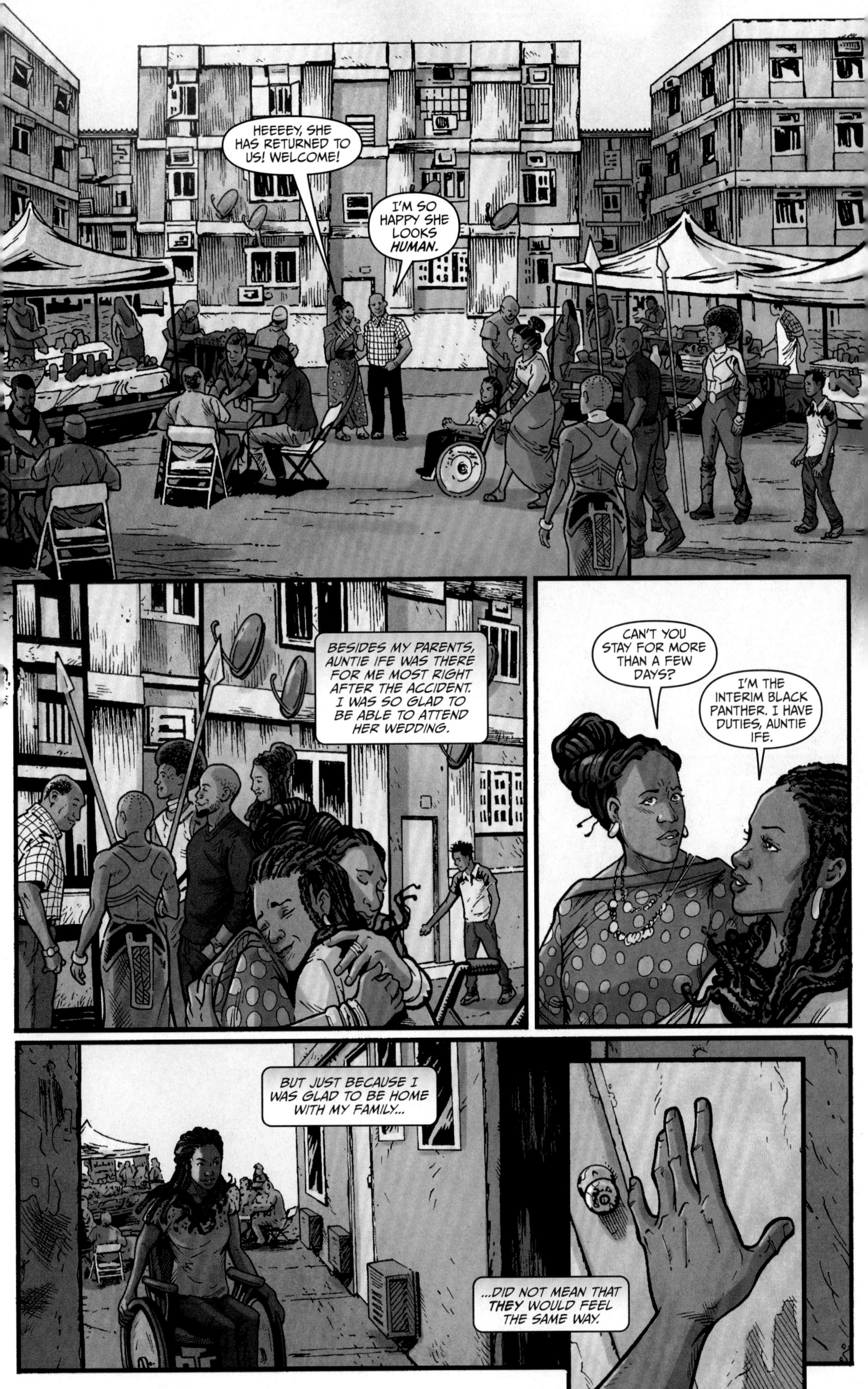
HEEEEY, SHE HAS RETURNED TO US! WELCOME!
I'M SO HAPPY SHE LOOKS *HUMAN.*
BESIDES MY PARENTS, AUNTIE IFE WAS THERE FOR ME MOST RIGHT AFTER THE ACCIDENT. I WAS SO GLAD TO BE ABLE TO ATTEND HER WEDDING.
CAN'T YOU STAY FOR MORE THAN A FEW DAYS?
I'M THE INTERIM BLACK PANTHER. I HAVE DUTIES, AUNTIE IFE.
BUT JUST BECAUSE I WAS GLAD TO BE HOME WITH MY FAMILY...
...DID NOT MEAN THAT *THEY* WOULD FEEL THE SAME WAY.

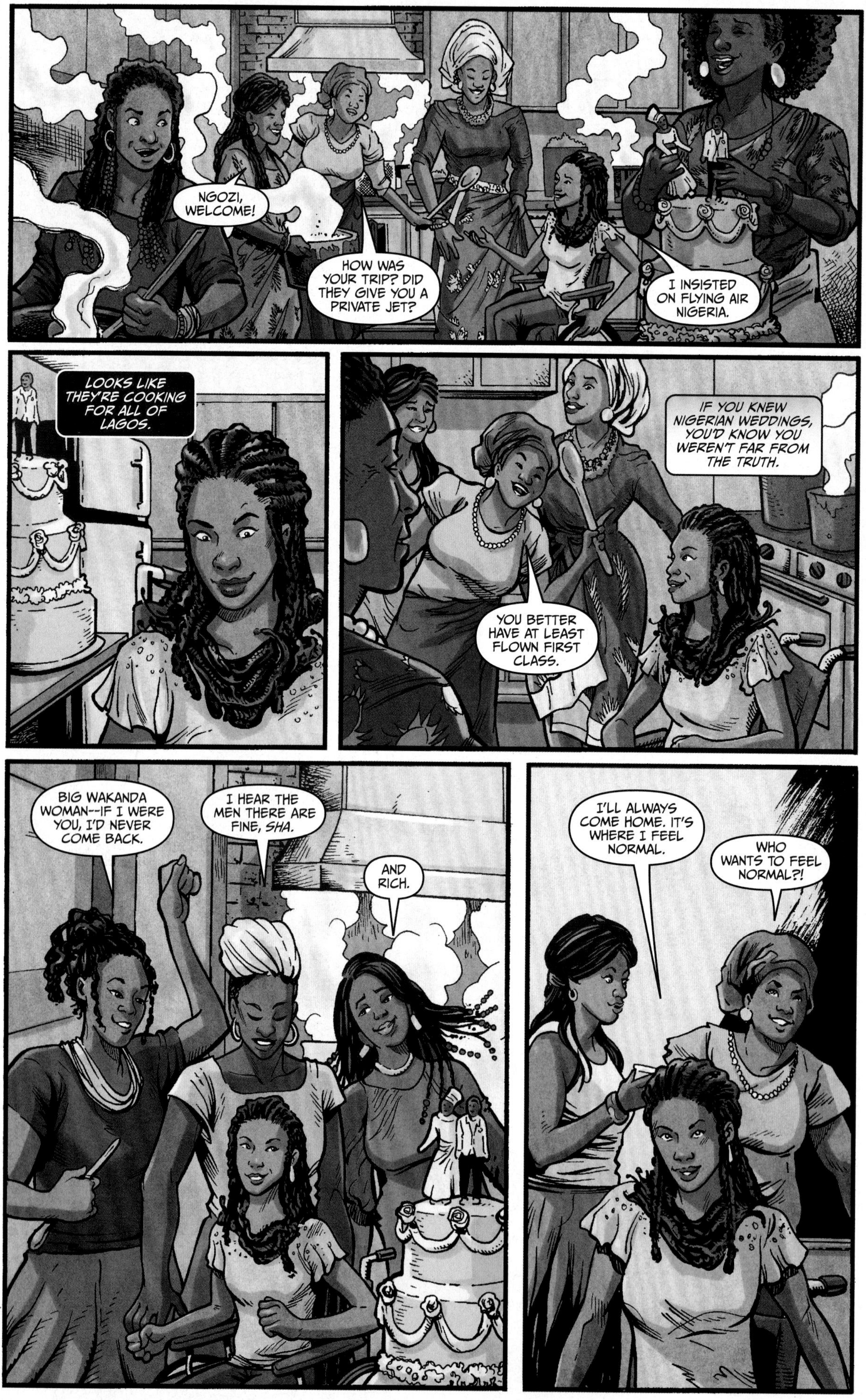
NGOZI, WELCOME!
HOW WAS YOUR TRIP? DID THEY GIVE YOU A PRIVATE JET?
I INSISTED ON FLYING AIR NIGERIA.
LOOKS LIKE THEY'RE COOKING FOR ALL OF LAGOS.
IF YOU KNEW NIGERIAN WEDDINGS, YOU'D KNOW YOU WEREN'T FAR FROM THE TRUTH.
YOU BETTER HAVE AT LEAST FLOWN FIRST CLASS.
BIG WAKANDA WOMAN--IF I WERE YOU, I'D NEVER COME BACK.
I HEAR THE MEN THERE ARE FINE, *SHA*.
AND RICH.
I'LL ALWAYS COME HOME. IT'S WHERE I FEEL NORMAL.
WHO WANTS TO FEEL NORMAL?!

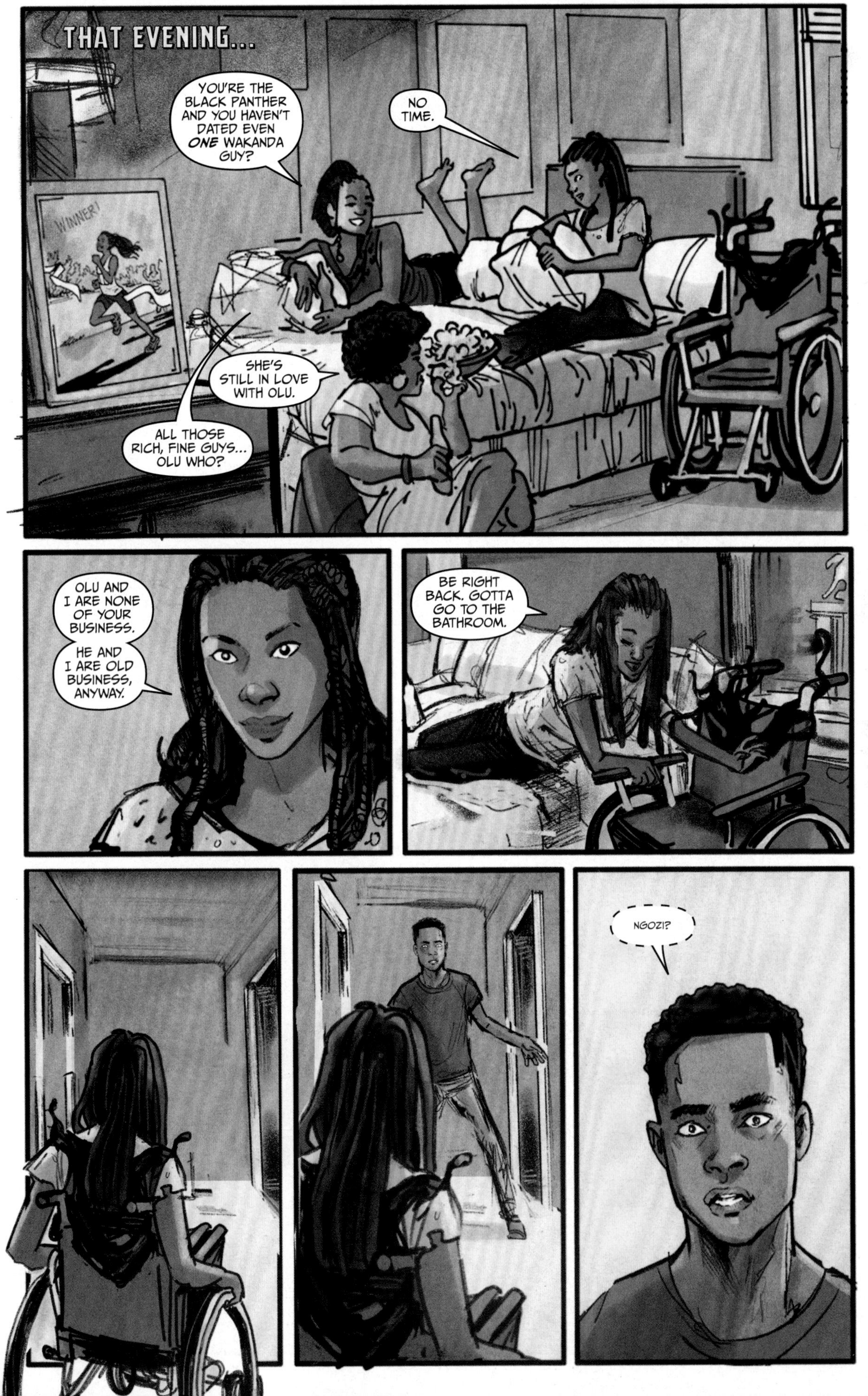
THAT EVENING...
YOU'RE THE BLACK PANTHER AND YOU HAVEN'T DATED EVEN ONE WAKANDA GUY?
NO TIME.
SHE'S STILL IN LOVE WITH OLU.
ALL THOSE RICH, FINE GUYS... OLU WHO?
OLU AND I ARE NONE OF YOUR BUSINESS.
HE AND I ARE OLD BUSINESS, ANYWAY.
BE RIGHT BACK. GOTTA GO TO THE BATHROOM.
NGOZI!?

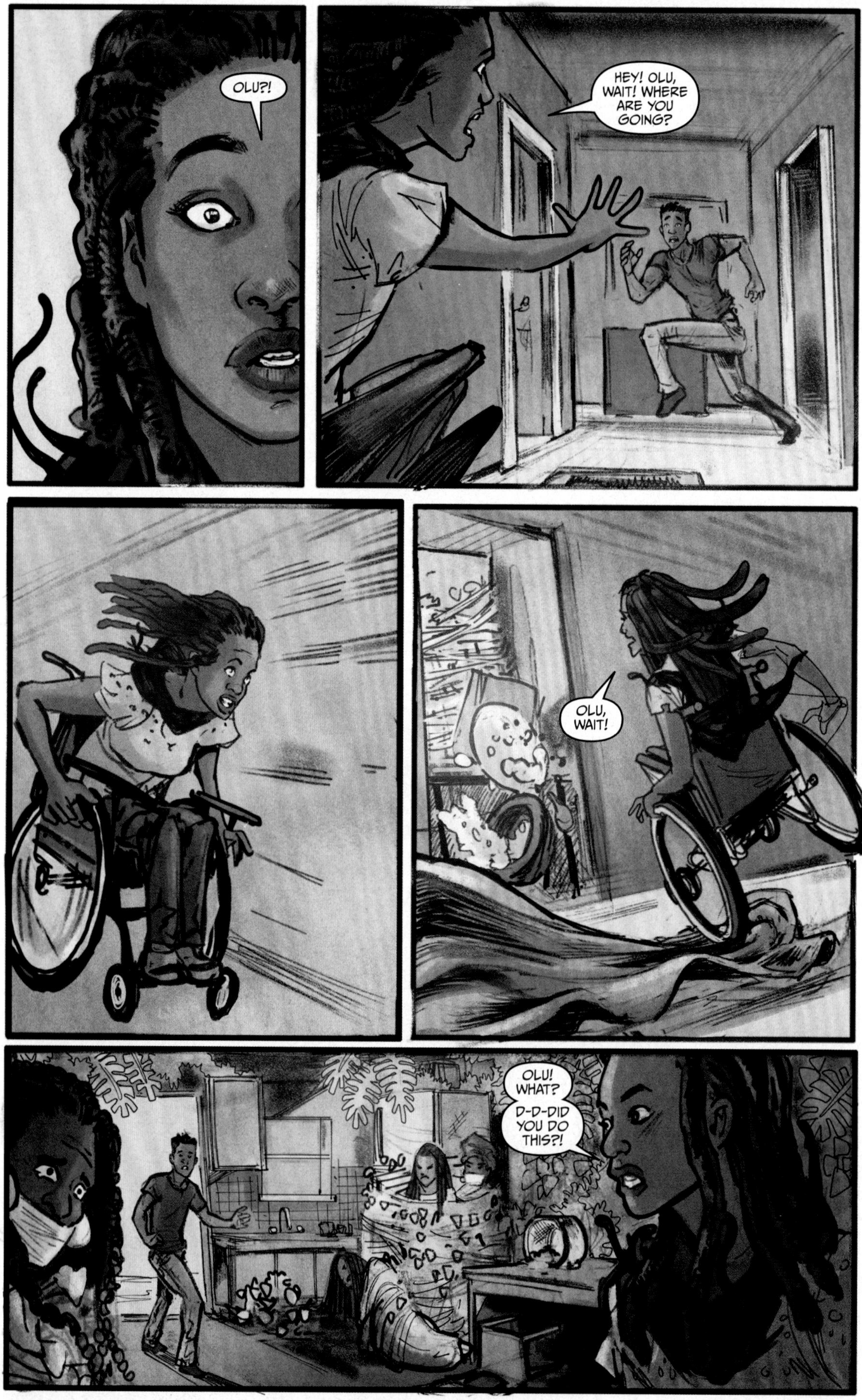
OLU?!
HEY! OLU, WAIT! WHERE ARE YOU GOING?
OLU, WAIT!
OLU! WHAT?
D-D-DID YOU DO THIS?!

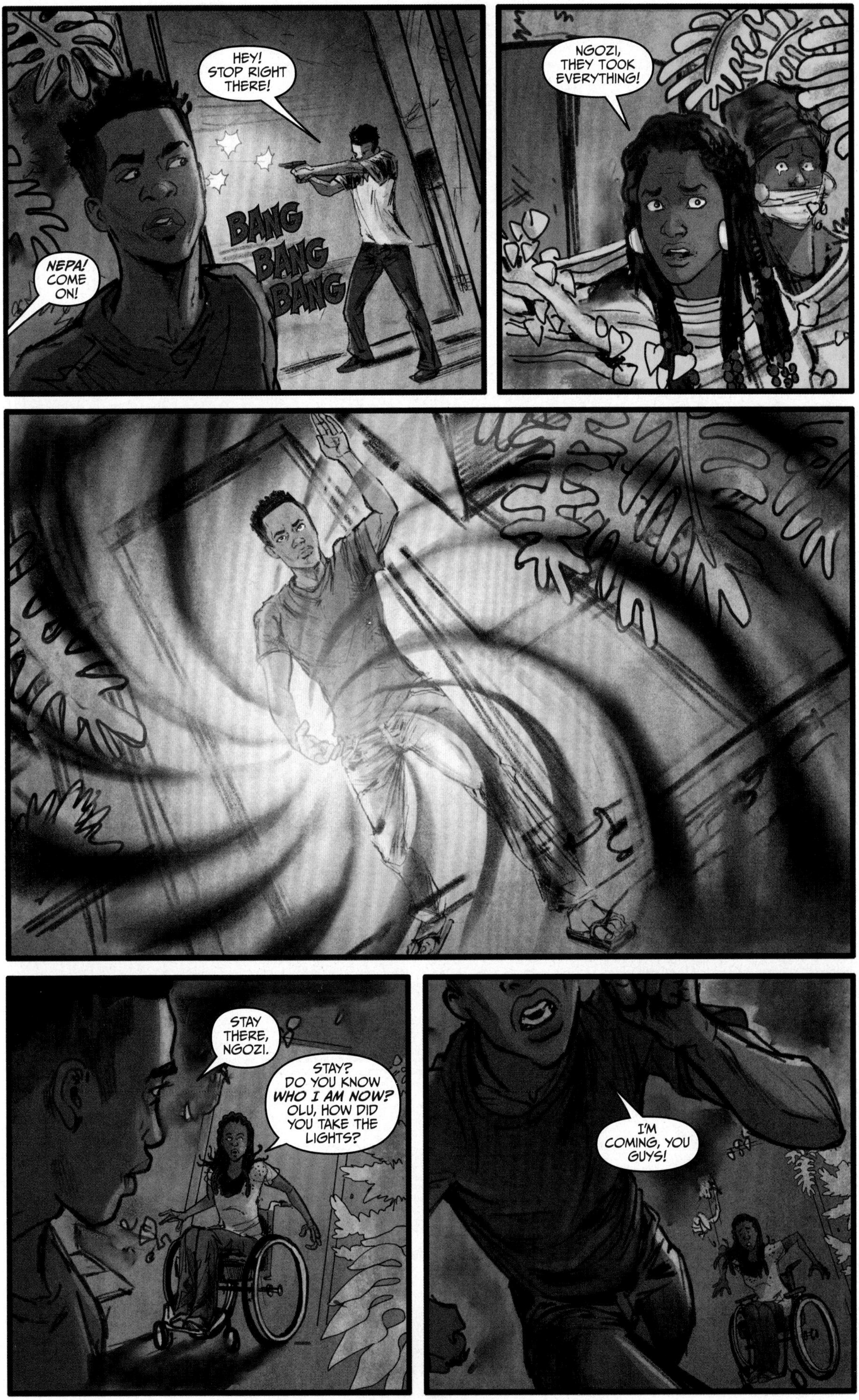
HEY! STOP RIGHT THERE!
BANG BANG BANG
NEPA! COME ON!
NGOZI, THEY TOOK EVERYTHING!
STAY THERE, NGOZI.
STAY? DO YOU KNOW WHO I AM NOW? OLU, HOW DID YOU TAKE THE LIGHTS?
I'M COMING, YOU GUYS!

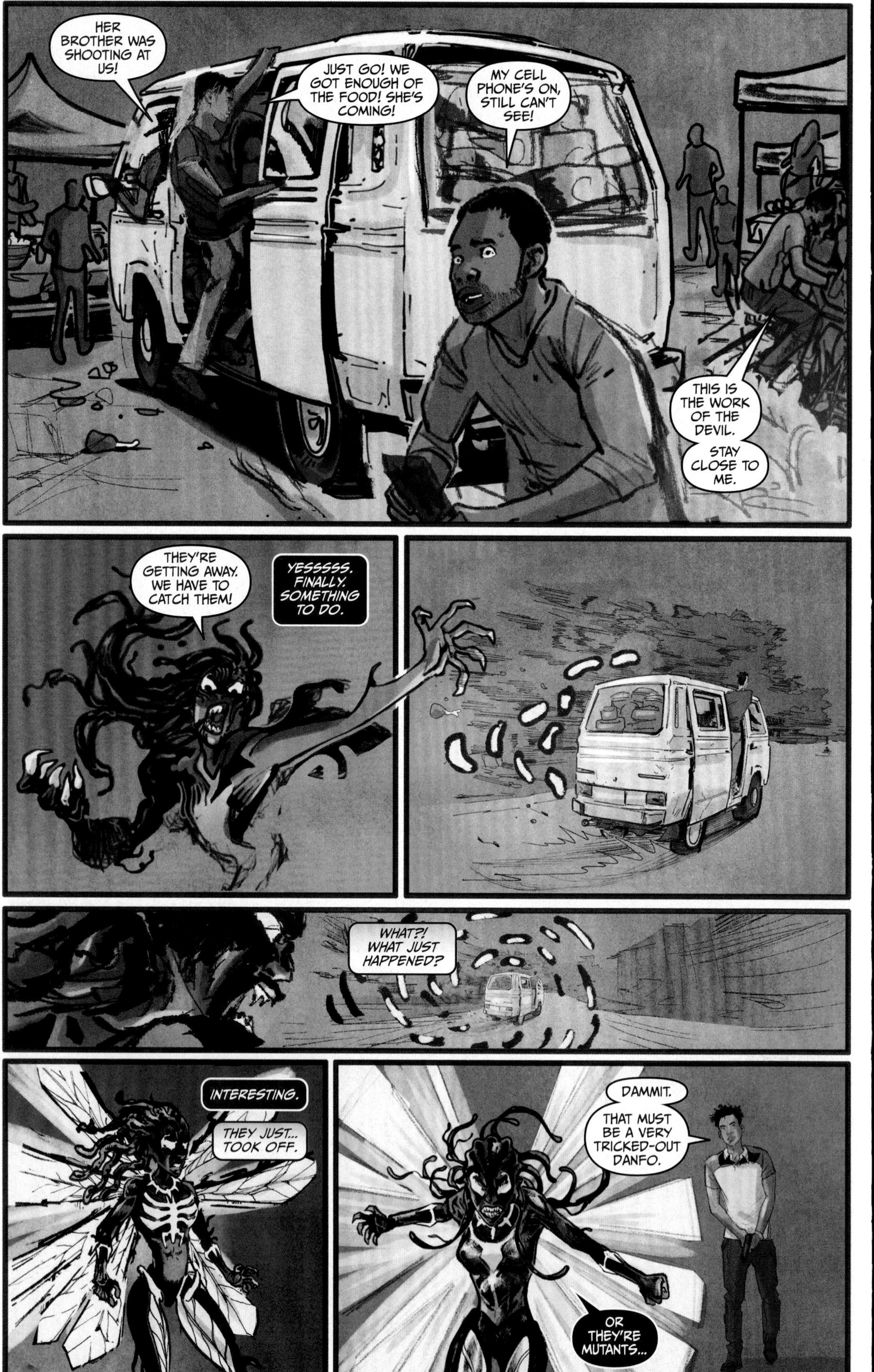

HER BROTHER WAS SHOOTING AT US!
JUST GO! WE GOT ENOUGH OF THE FOOD! SHE'S COMING!
MY CELL PHONE'S ON, STILL CAN'T SEE!
THIS IS THE WORK OF THE DEVIL.
STAY CLOSE TO ME.
THEY'RE GETTING AWAY. WE HAVE TO CATCH THEM!
YESSSSS. FINALLY. SOMETHING TO DO.
WHAT?! WHAT JUST HAPPENED?
INTERESTING.
THEY JUST... TOOK OFF.
DAMMIT.
THAT MUST BE A VERY TRICKED-OUT DANFO.
OR THEY'RE MUTANTS...

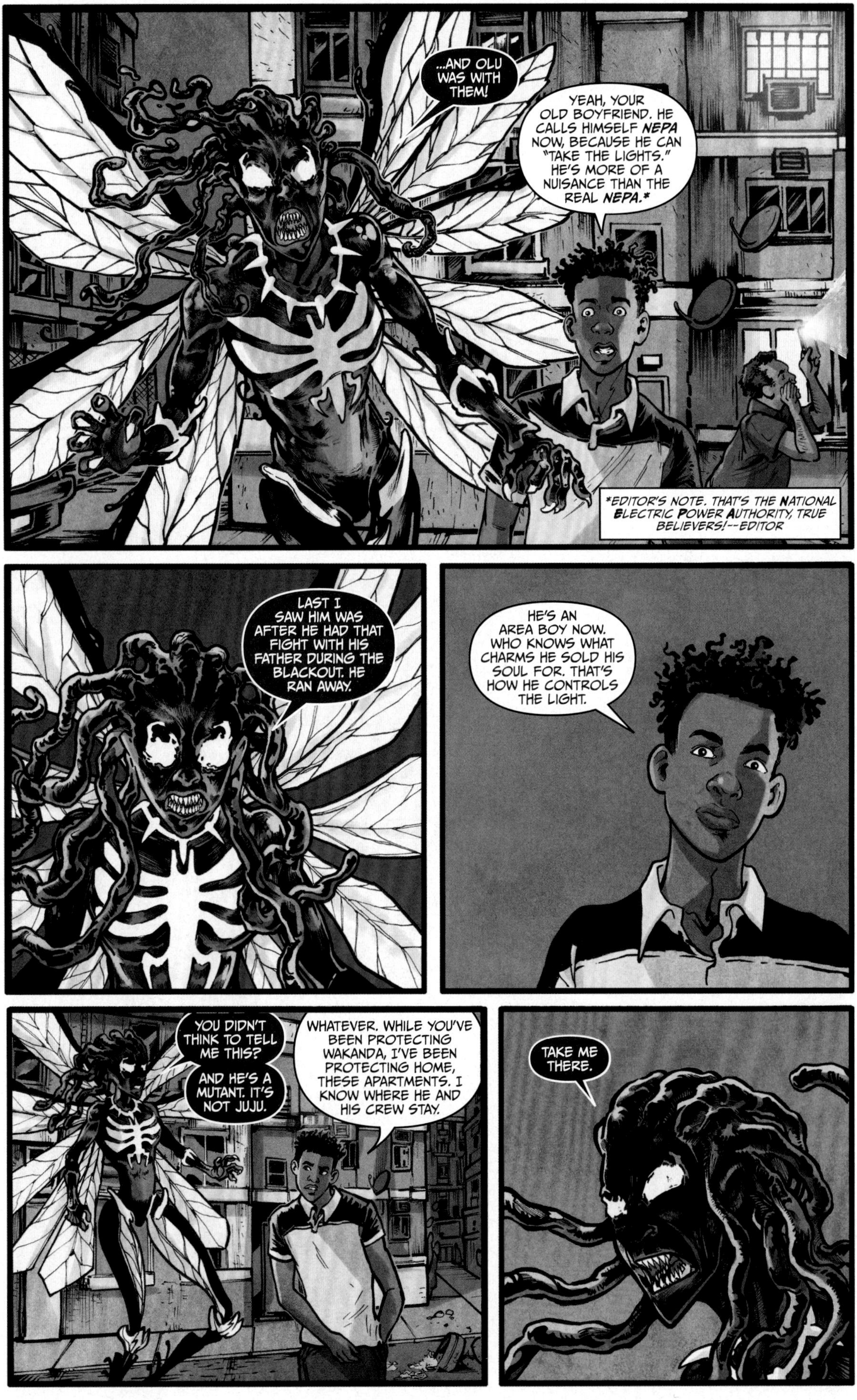
...AND OLU WAS WITH THEM!
YEAH, YOUR OLD BOYFRIEND. HE CALLS HIMSELF NEPA NOW, BECAUSE HE CAN "TAKE THE LIGHTS." HE'S MORE OF A NUISANCE THAN THE REAL NEPA.*
*EDITOR'S NOTE. THAT'S THE NATIONAL ELECTRIC POWER AUTHORITY, TRUE BELIEVERS!--EDITOR
LAST I SAW HIM WAS AFTER HE HAD THAT FIGHT WITH HIS FATHER DURING THE BLACKOUT. HE RAN AWAY.
HE'S AN AREA BOY NOW. WHO KNOWS WHAT CHARMS HE SOLD HIS SOUL FOR. THAT'S HOW HE CONTROLS THE LIGHT.
YOU DIDN'T THINK TO TELL ME THIS?
AND HE'S A MUTANT. IT'S NOT JUJU.
WHATEVER. WHILE YOU'VE BEEN PROTECTING WAKANDA, I'VE BEEN PROTECTING HOME, THESE APARTMENTS. I KNOW WHERE HE AND HIS CREW STAY.
TAKE ME THERE.

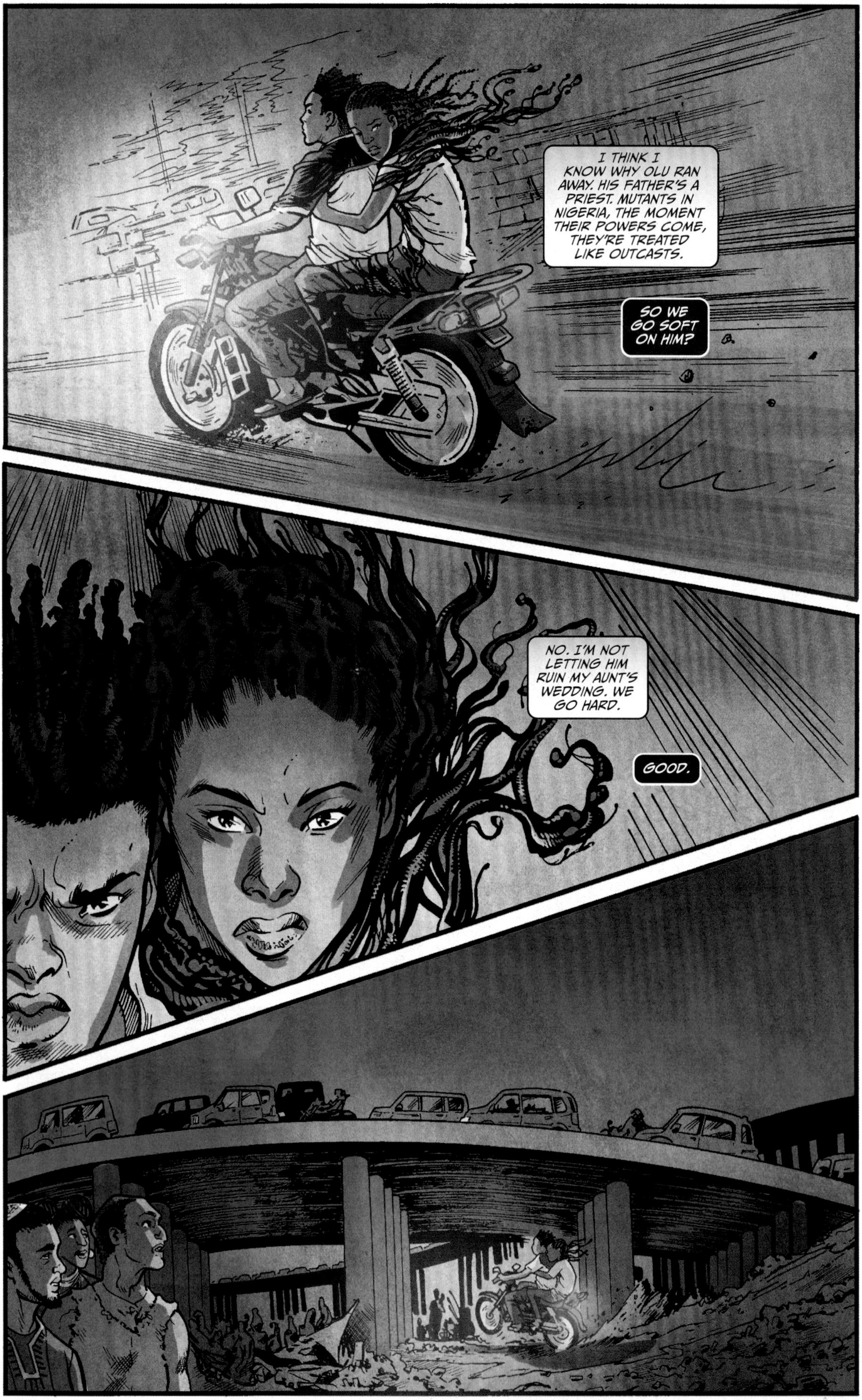
I THINK I KNOW WHY OLU RAN AWAY. HIS FATHER'S A PRIEST. MUTANTS IN NIGERIA, THE MOMENT THEIR POWERS COME, THEY'RE TREATED LIKE OUTCASTS.
SO WE GO SOFT ON HIM?
NO. I'M NOT LETTING HIM RUIN MY AUNT'S WEDDING. WE GO HARD.
GOOD.

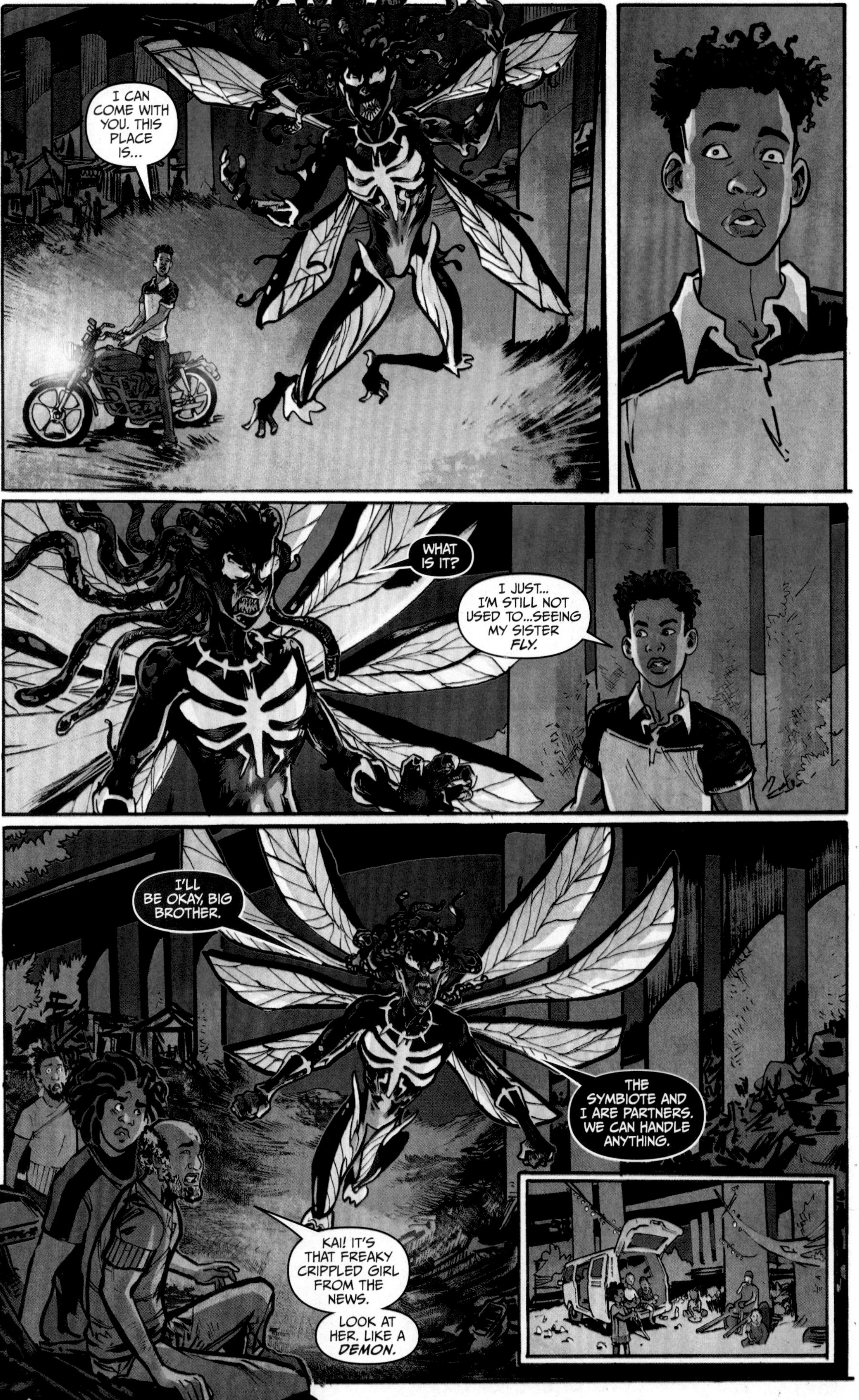
I CAN COME WITH YOU. THIS PLACE IS...
WHAT IS IT?
I JUST... I'M STILL NOT USED TO...SEEING MY SISTER *FLY.*
I'LL BE OKAY, BIG BROTHER.
THE SYMBIOTE AND I ARE PARTNERS. WE CAN HANDLE ANYTHING.
KAI! IT'S THAT FREAKY CRIPPLED GIRL FROM THE NEWS.
LOOK AT HER. LIKE A *DEMON.*

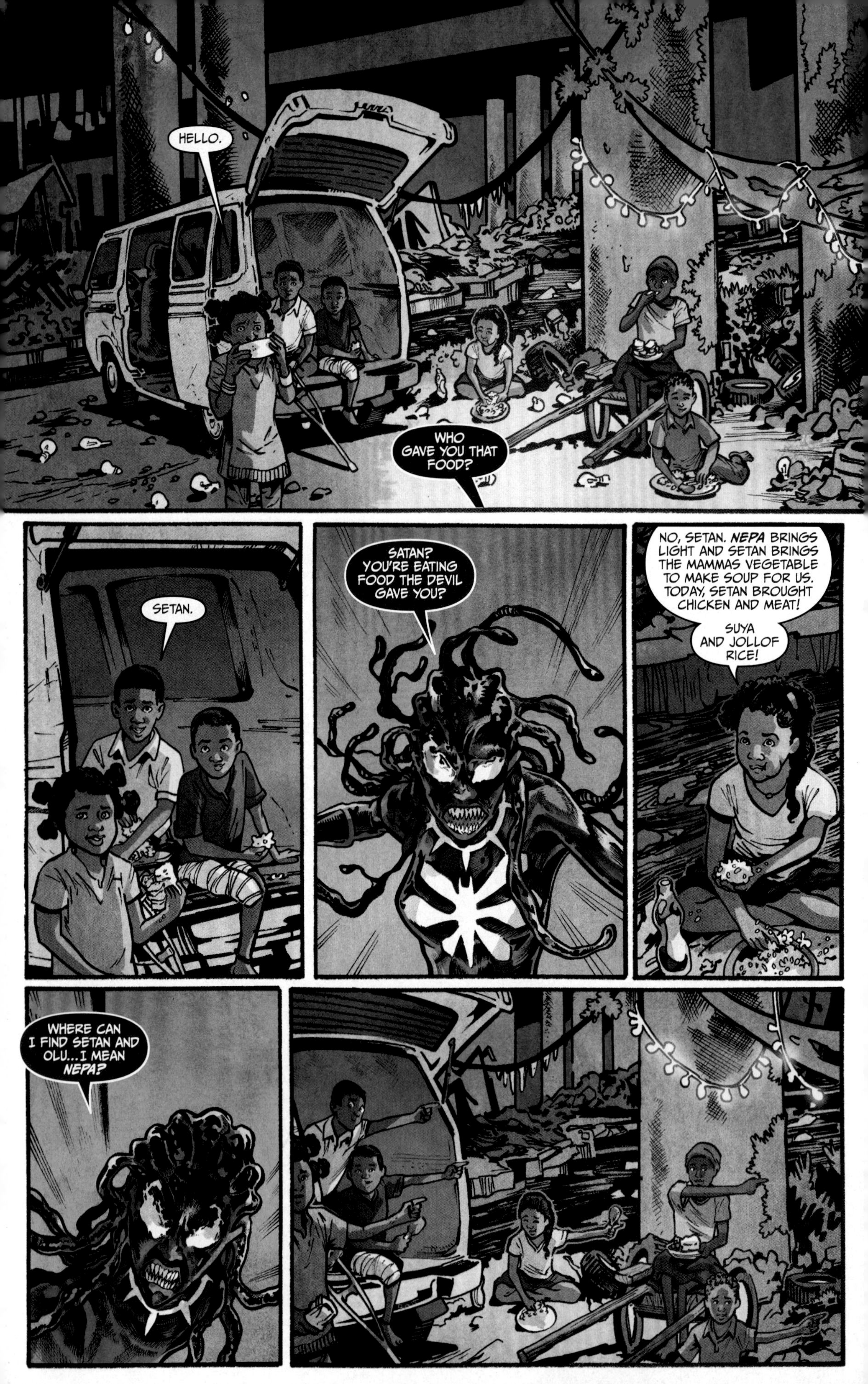
HELLO.
WHO GAVE YOU THAT FOOD?
SETAN.
SATAN? YOU'RE EATING FOOD THE DEVIL GAVE YOU?
NO, SETAN. NEPA BRINGS LIGHT AND SETAN BRINGS THE MAMMAS VEGETABLE TO MAKE SOUP FOR US. TODAY, SETAN BROUGHT CHICKEN AND MEAT!
SUYA AND JOLLOF RICE!
WHERE CAN I FIND SETAN AND OLU...I MEAN NEPA?

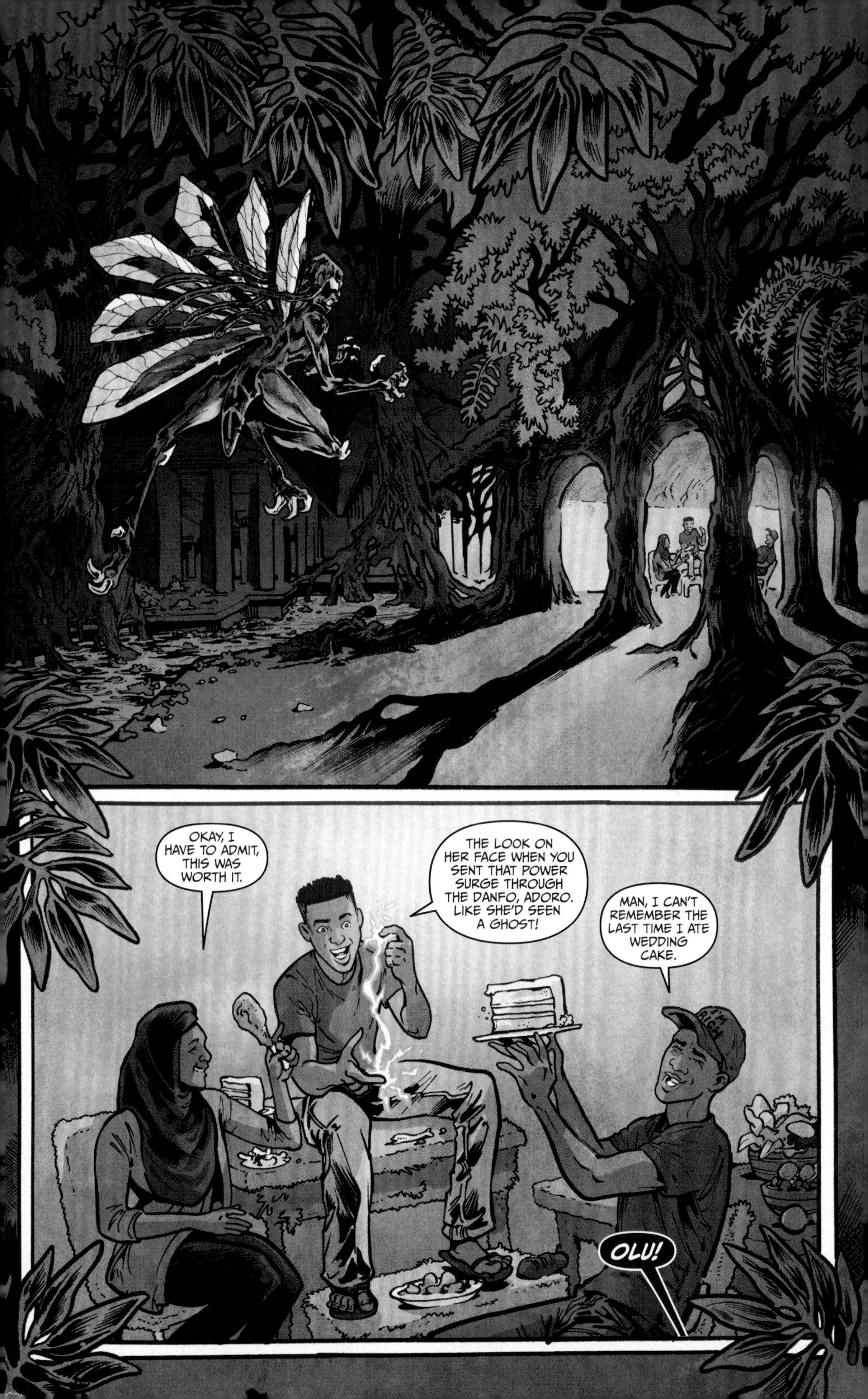

OKAY, I HAVE TO ADMIT, THIS WAS WORTH IT.
THE LOOK ON HER FACE WHEN YOU SENT THAT POWER SURGE THROUGH THE DANFO, ADORO. LIKE SHE'D SEEN A GHOST!
MAN, I CAN'T REMEMBER THE LAST TIME I ATE WEDDING CAKE.
OLU!

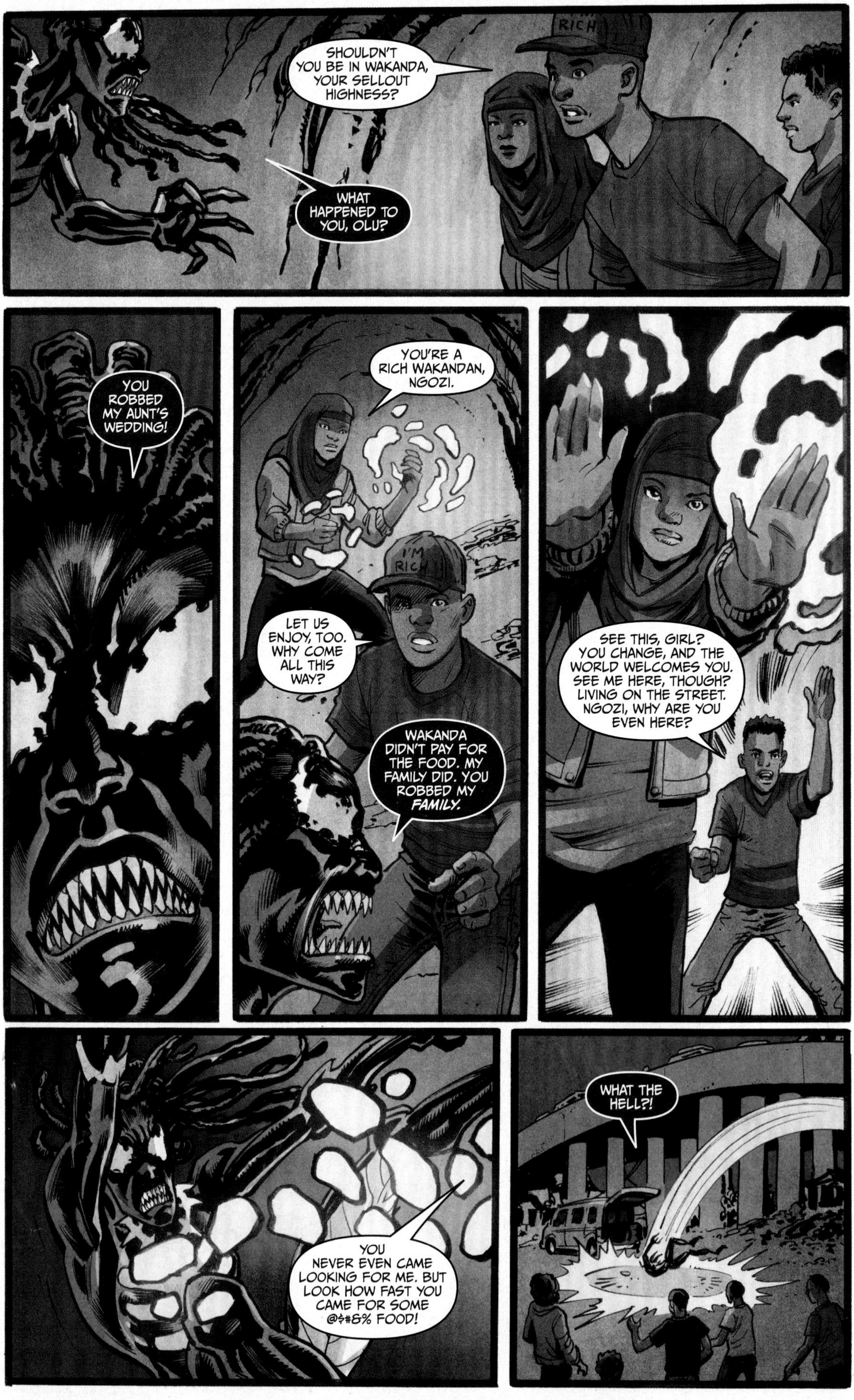
SHOULDN'T YOU BE IN WAKANDA, YOUR SELLOUT HIGHNESS?
WHAT HAPPENED TO YOU, OLU?
YOU ROBBED MY AUNT'S WEDDING!
YOU'RE A RICH WAKANDAN, NGOZI.
LET US ENJOY, TOO. WHY COME ALL THIS WAY?
WAKANDA DIDN'T PAY FOR THE FOOD. MY FAMILY DID. YOU ROBBED MY *FAMILY.*
SEE THIS, GIRL? YOU CHANGE, AND THE WORLD WELCOMES YOU. SEE ME HERE, THOUGH? LIVING ON THE STREET. NGOZI, WHY ARE YOU EVEN HERE?
YOU NEVER EVEN CAME LOOKING FOR ME. BUT LOOK HOW FAST YOU CAME FOR SOME @$#&% FOOD!
WHAT THE HELL?!

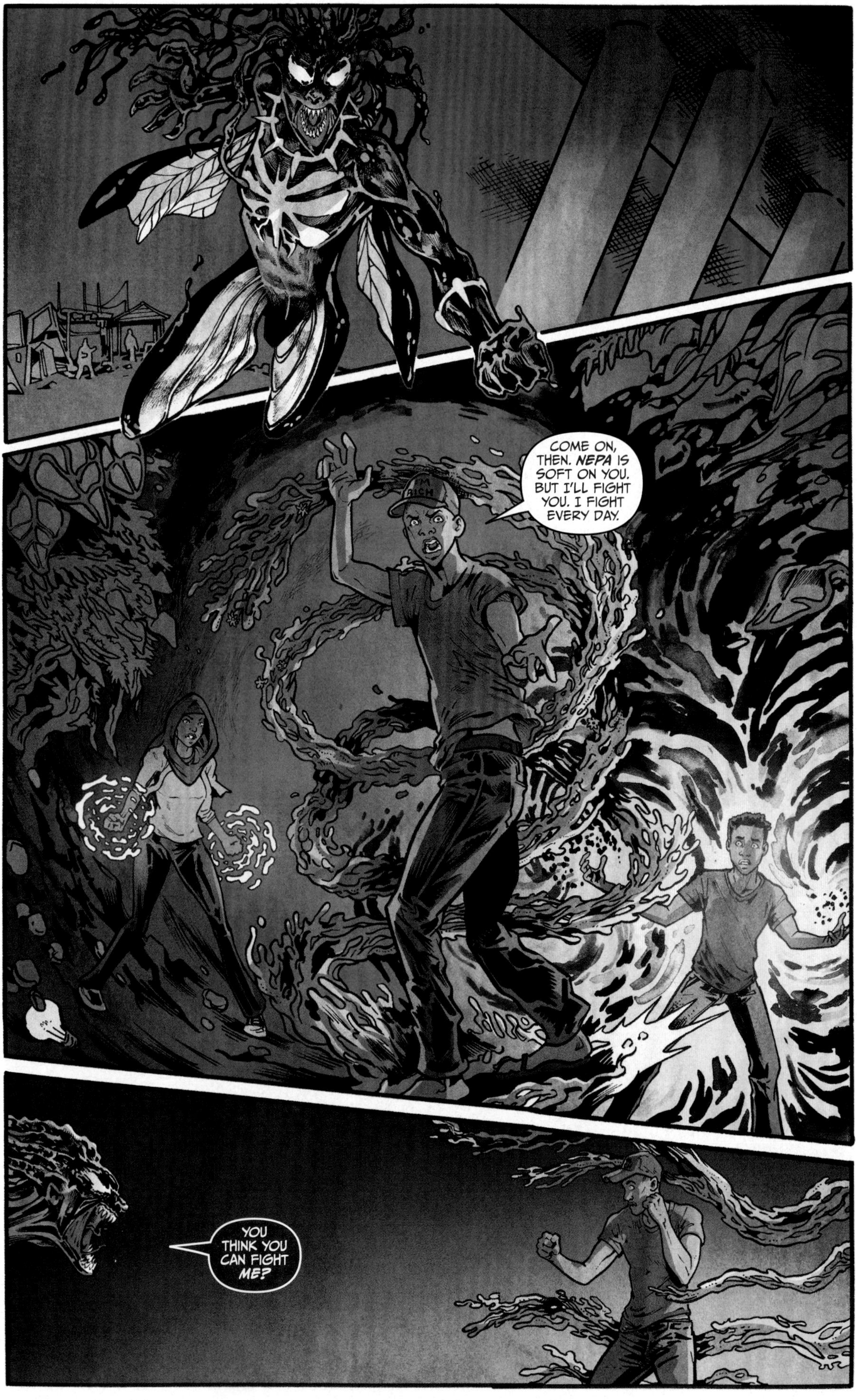
COME ON, THEN. NEPA IS SOFT ON YOU. BUT I'LL FIGHT YOU. I FIGHT EVERY DAY.
YOU THINK YOU CAN FIGHT ME?

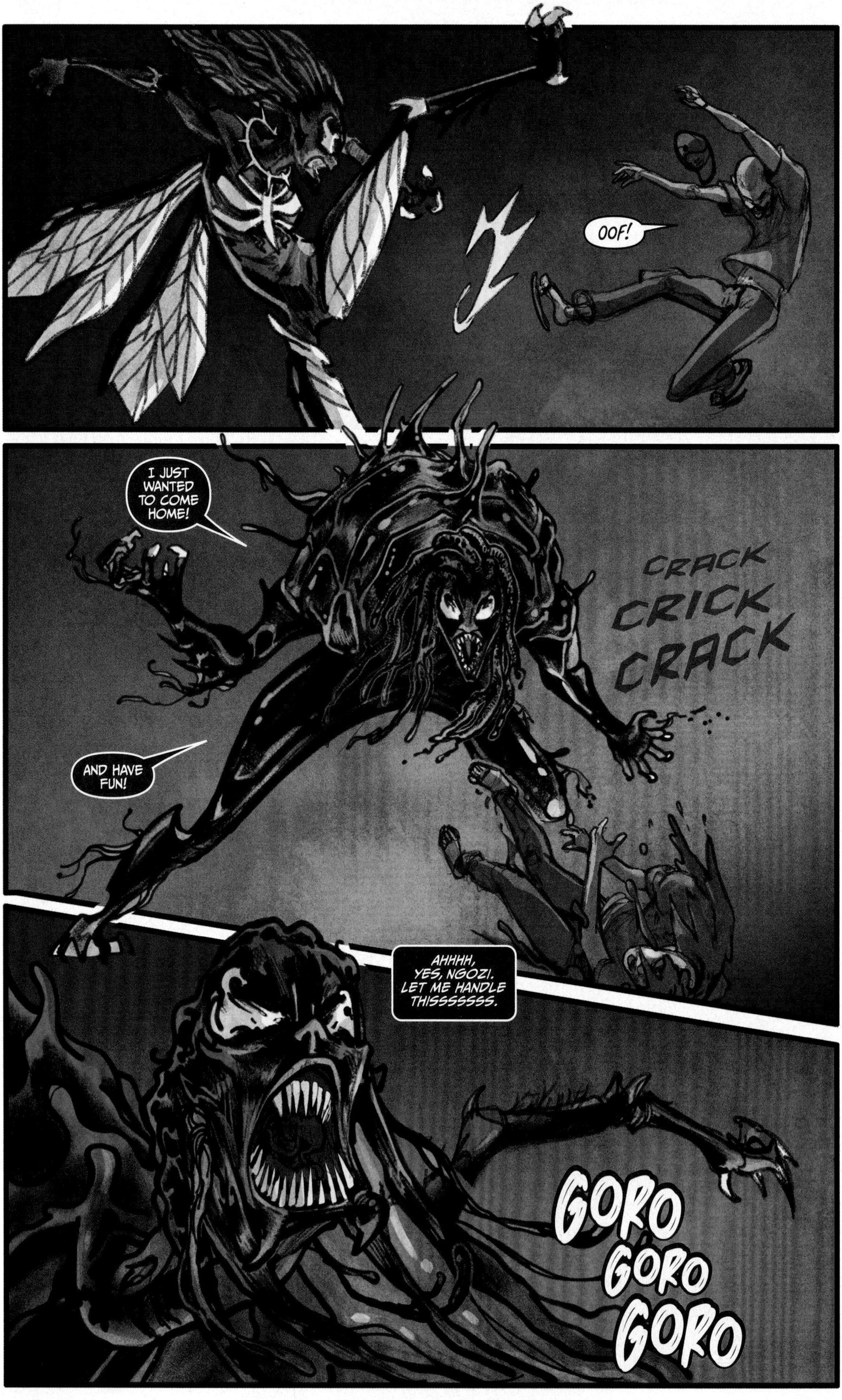
OOF!
I JUST WANTED TO COME HOME!
CRACK
CRICK
CRACK
AND HAVE FUN!
AHHHH, YES, NGOZI. LET ME HANDLE THISSSSSSS.
GORO
GORO
GORO

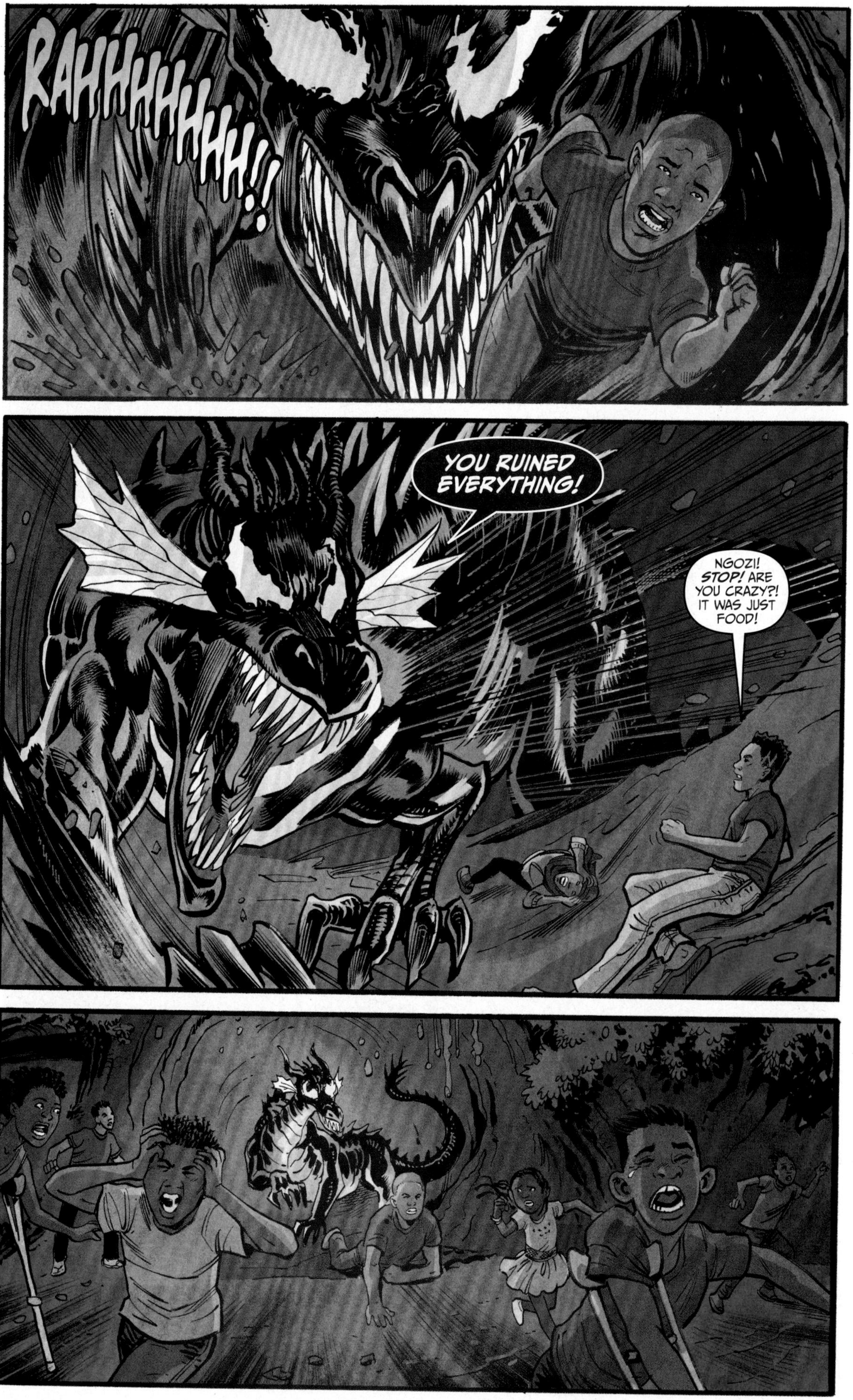
RAHHHHHHH!!
YOU RUINED EVERYTHING!
NGOZI! STOP! ARE YOU CRAZY?! IT WAS JUST FOOD!

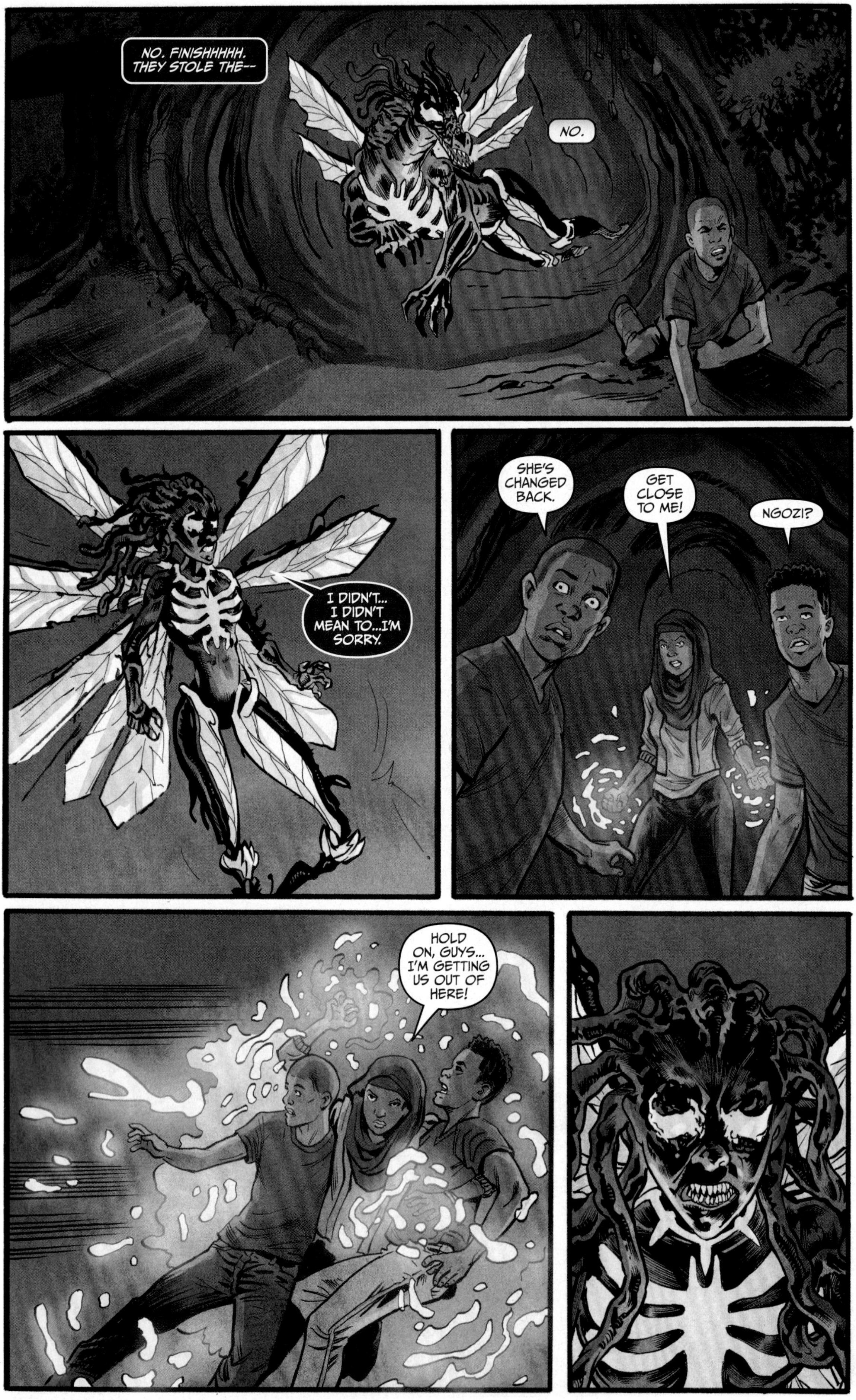
NO. FINISHHHHH. THEY STOLE THE--
NO.
I DIDN'T... I DIDN'T MEAN TO...I'M SORRY.
SHE'S CHANGED BACK.
GET CLOSE TO ME!
NGOZI?
HOLD ON, GUYS... I'M GETTING US OUT OF HERE!

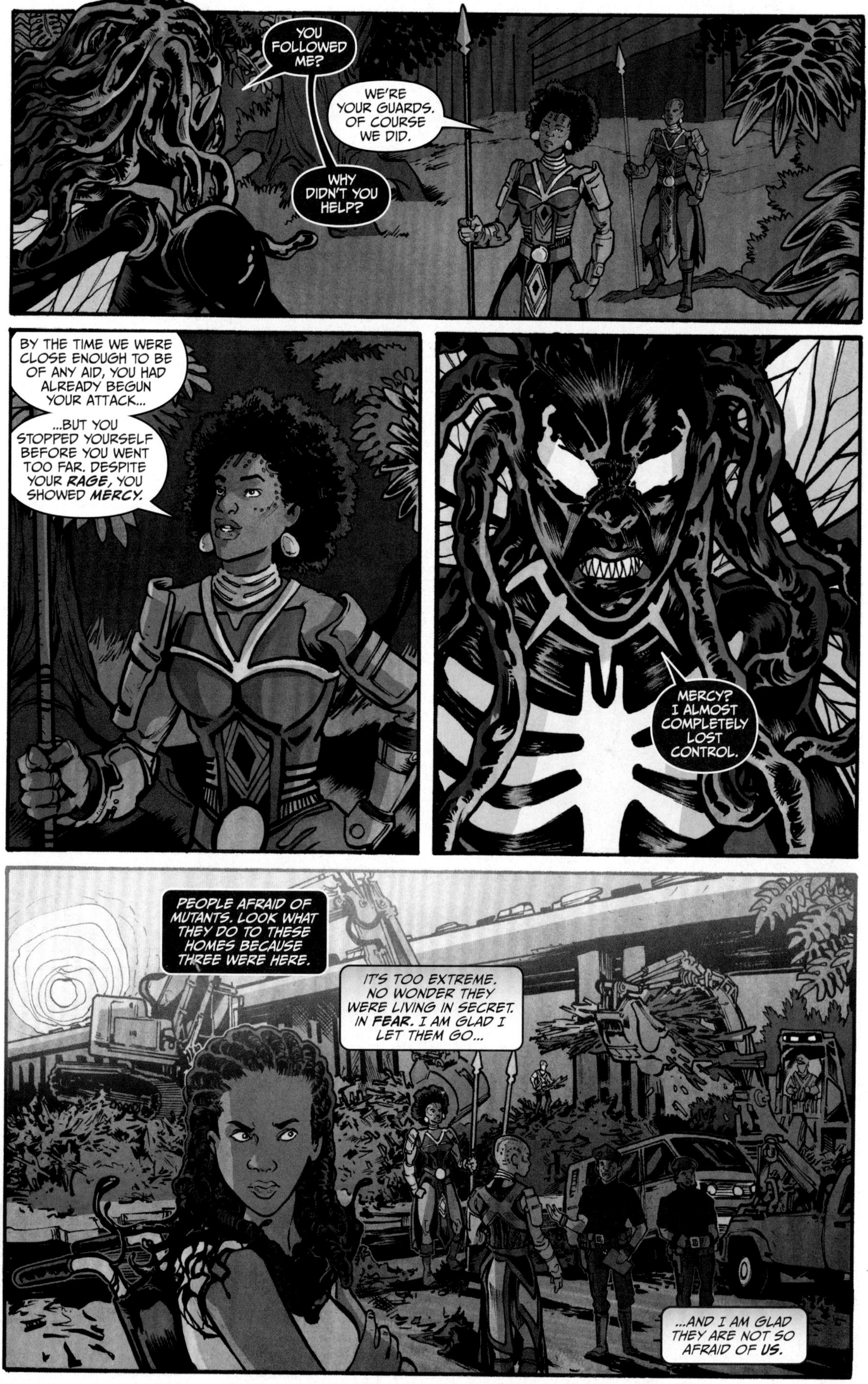
YOU FOLLOWED ME?
WE'RE YOUR GUARDS. OF COURSE WE DID.
WHY DIDN'T YOU HELP?
BY THE TIME WE WERE CLOSE ENOUGH TO BE OF ANY AID, YOU HAD ALREADY BEGUN YOUR ATTACK...
...BUT YOU STOPPED YOURSELF BEFORE YOU WENT TOO FAR. DESPITE YOUR RAGE, YOU SHOWED MERCY.
MERCY? I ALMOST COMPLETELY LOST CONTROL.
PEOPLE AFRAID OF MUTANTS. LOOK WHAT THEY DO TO THESE HOMES BECAUSE THREE WERE HERE.
IT'S TOO EXTREME. NO WONDER THEY WERE LIVING IN SECRET. IN FEAR. I AM GLAD I LET THEM GO...
...AND I AM GLAD THEY ARE NOT SO AFRAID OF US.

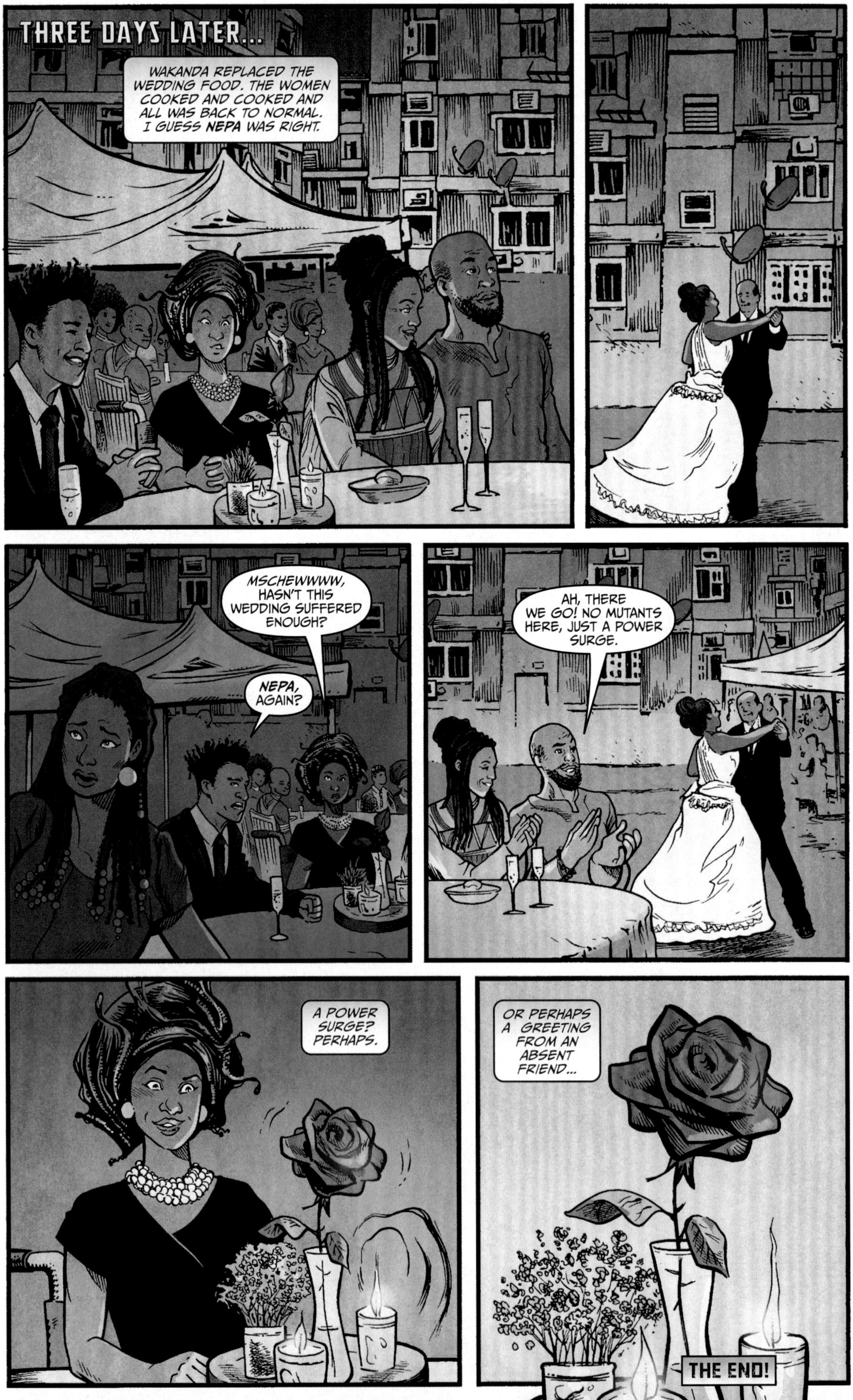
THREE DAYS LATER...
WAKANDA REPLACED THE WEDDING FOOD. THE WOMEN COOKED AND COOKED AND ALL WAS BACK TO NORMAL. I GUESS NEPA WAS RIGHT.
MSCHEWWWW, HASN'T THIS WEDDING SUFFERED ENOUGH?
NEPA, AGAIN?
AH, THERE WE GO! NO MUTANTS HERE, JUST A POWER SURGE.
A POWER SURGE? PERHAPS.
OR PERHAPS A GREETING FROM AN ABSENT FRIEND...
THE END!

Hello, Black Panther fans!

We hope you enjoyed reading LONG LIVE THE KING. We had a blast exploring the world of Wakanda with our talented team over the last few months. A very special thanks to our in-house team at Marvel as well as Nnedi, Andrē, Aaron, Mario, Chris, Jimmy and the entire creative crew who made this book a worthy addition to the BLACK PANTHER annals. Before you go, here's a couple of notes from writer Nnedi Okorafor and artist Andrē Lima Araūjo! Read on, True Believers!

Writing BLACK PANTHER has been a marvelous experience. I came into this looking at King T'Challa and the country of Wakanda out of the side of my eye. I'm Igbo (a Nigerian ethnic group) and amongst the Igbo there's a popular saying, "Igbo enwe eze," which means, "The Igbo have no king." Being a more democratic society consisting of many small independent communities, historically, Igbos never had a centralized government or royalty. I've grown up hearing this phrase and between this and also being an American, any type of monarchy gets my side-eye of disapproval...even a mythical one.

Writing BLACK PANTHER felt like visiting a country for the first time, and not as a tourist, but as a diplomat. I couldn't be passive during my visit and that made my visit even more interesting. I wanted to get to know T'Challa and the people and land of Wakanda. I wanted T'Challa to speak to me, I wanted to see the adventures he took me on and I wanted to see him kick some butt.

When LONG LIVE THE KING was announced, I heard from plenty of Black Panther fans, especially on Twitter. They expressed excitement (and suspicion) about what I'd bring to the narrative. And many also adamantly told me what they hoped to see me do. I had my own ideas, but I listened and considered, too. Thankfully, what many wanted and what I was interested in tended to be in the same vein. Several wanted to see T'Challa in action, others wanted answers about Wakanda from the ground level, still others wanted to see more of how technology operates in Wakanda. I was a bit nervous, a good kind of nervous. Then I plunged in. And it definitely helped that I got to partner up with Andrē Araūjo, an experienced sorcerer of illustration obsessed with detail, motion and space, and a really stellar Marvel team.

I feel like I know T'Challa now. Heck, I've gotten to see what he does when he's just chilling. I've seen him fight a black panther without the help of his suit, using only his bare hands. I've seen that he has a sense of humor. I've seen him fail and humbly learn from that failure. I've seen him face his privilege, and get checked about it. All in just three issues.

What I feel I was able to give to T'Challa and Wakanda, I think I also took from it. I'll always have a strained relationship with any type of monarchy, but I've learned that this one is struggling with its own success, structure and evolution. And I've also learned that there are many different types of freedom in the country of Wakanda.

--Nnedimma Nkemdili Okorafor
1/31/18

The most interesting part for me about drawing BLACK PANTHER was drawing Wakanda. It's a different place, with different people on it, different heroes, different stories. It could and should look different, vastly different from other places in the Marvel Universe. So that's where I focused my efforts--in making sure the book looked unique because of its setting and its landscapes, because I wanted Wakanda to feel real. And for that I was fortunate that Nnedi made my life easy, by supplying me with a steady flow of reference pictures of African art, sculptures, people, patterns, clothing, cityscapes, forests and much more.

Hopefully I did it justice, because I loved my time with Nnedi and Chris, with T'Challa and Wakanda. Dear reader, enjoy.

--Andrē Lima Araūjo
1/31/18

And I'd like to extend a very special thanks to everyone who worked hard on this series. That does it for us and BLACK PANTHER: LONG LIVE THE KING. Keep those tweets and letters coming, especially if you want to see more of T'Challa, Ngozi and the world of Wakanda. Until next time, friends!

--Tom
1/31/18

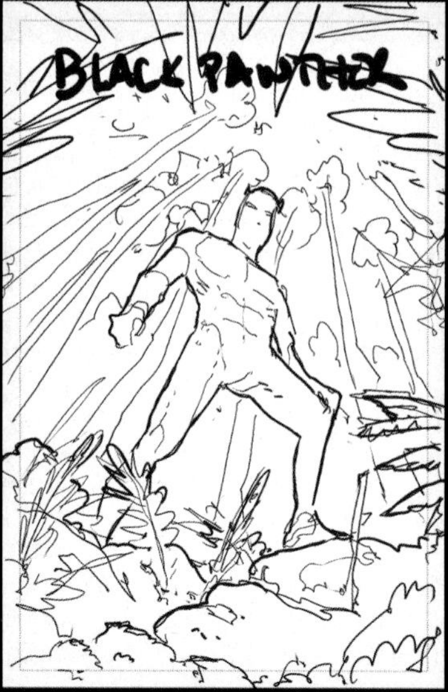
BLACK PANTHER

#1 COVER SKETCH BY **ANDRÉ LIMA ARAÚJO**

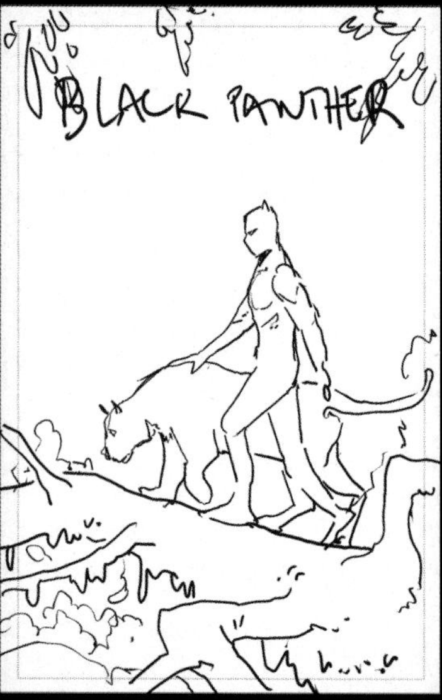
BLACK PANTHER

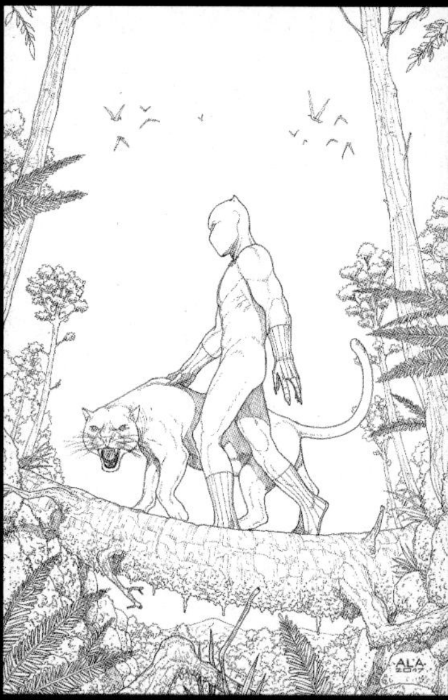

#2 COVER SKETCH AND INKS BY **ANDRÉ LIMA ARAÚJO**

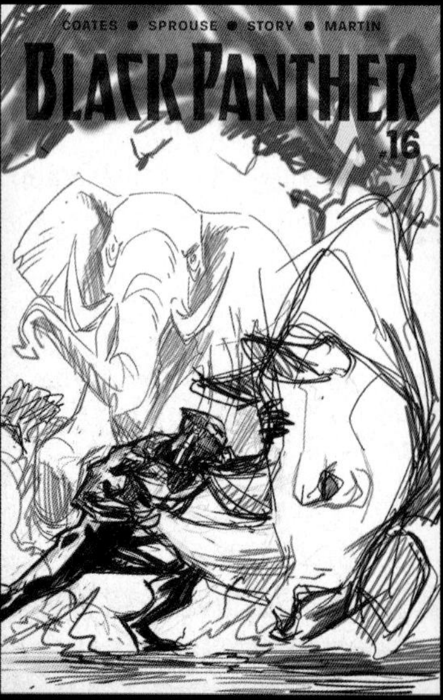
COATES • SPROUSE • STORY • MARTIN
BLACK PANTHER
#16

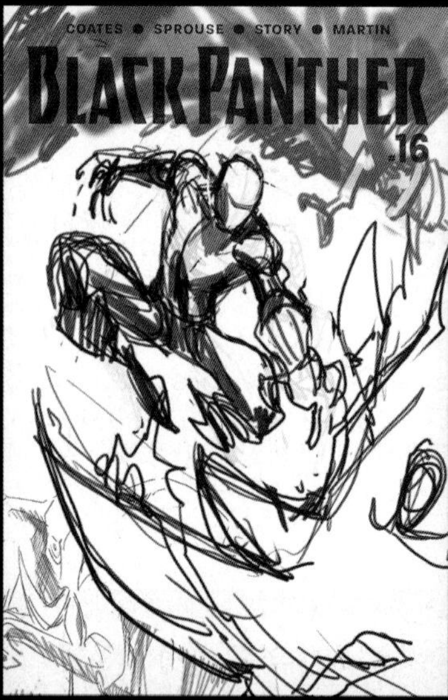
COATES • SPROUSE • STORY • MARTIN
BLACK PANTHER
#16

#3 COVER SKETCHES BY **KHARY RANDOLPH**

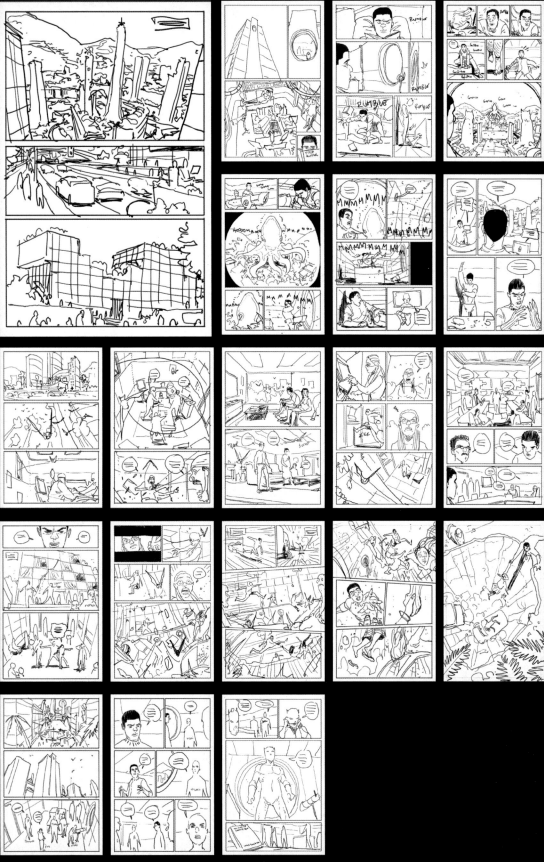

#1, PAGE LAYOUTS BY **ANDRÉ LIMA ARAÚJO**

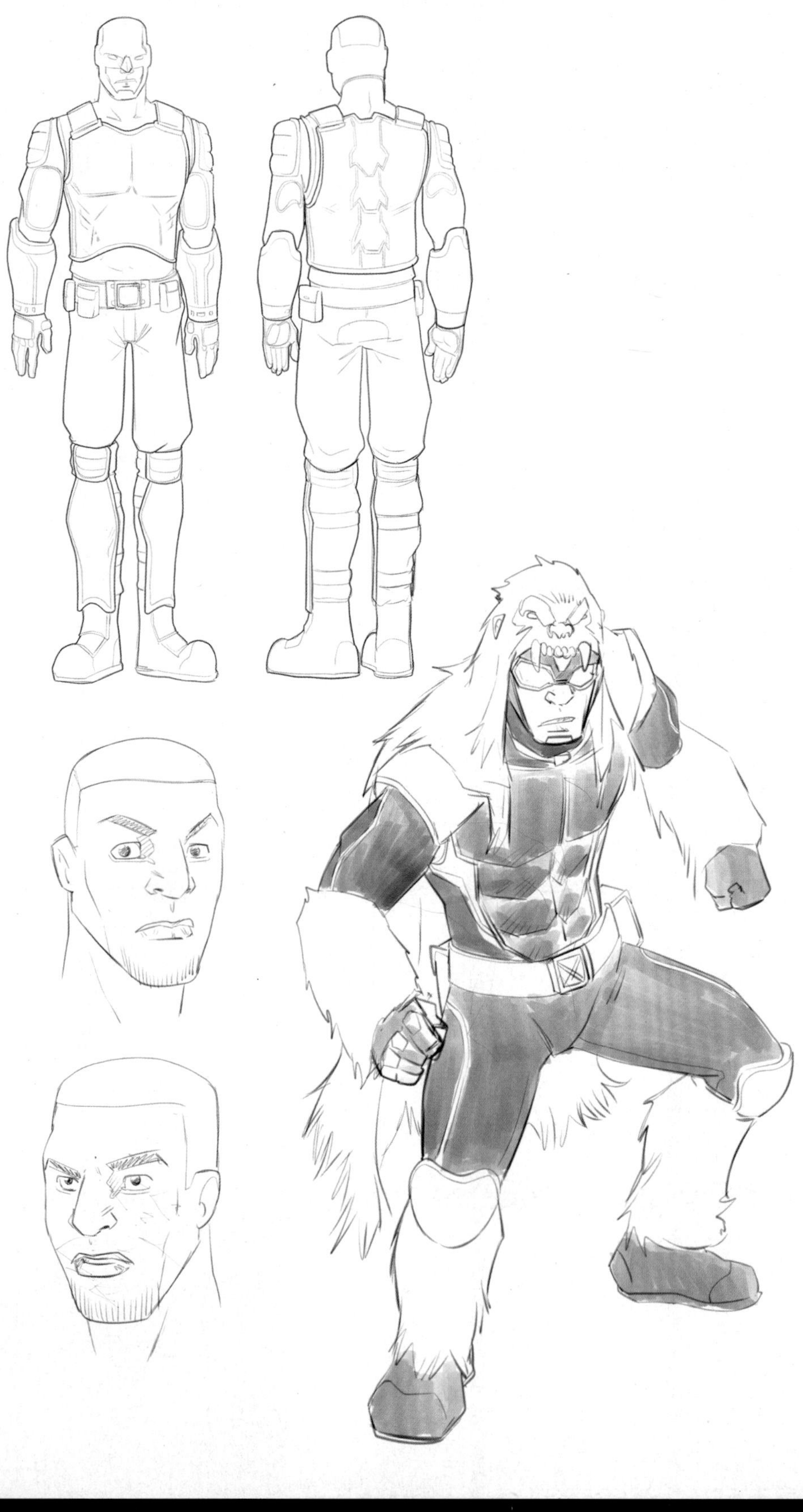

KANTU & WHITE GORILLA CHARACTER SKETCHES BY **MARIO DEL PENNINO**

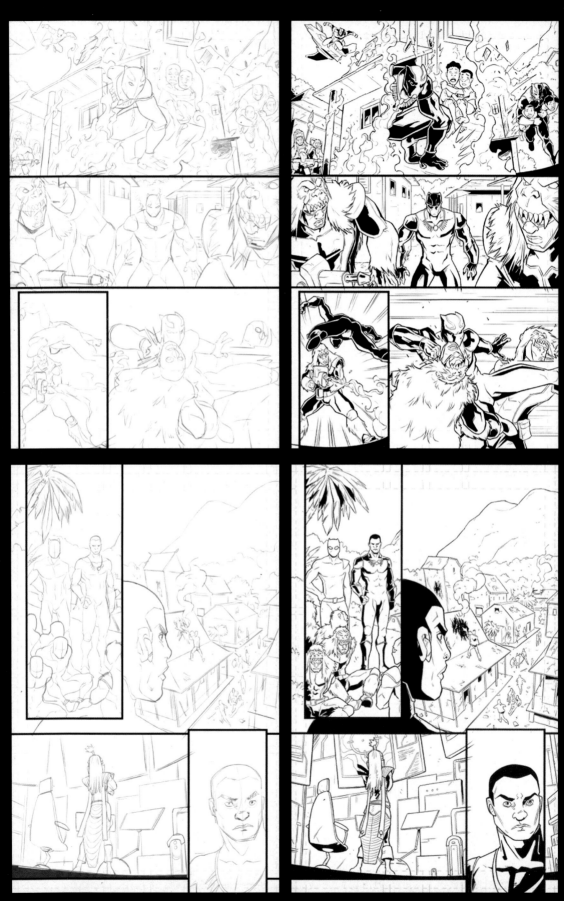

#3, PAGES 2-3 PENCILS AND INKS BY **MARIO DEL PENNINO**

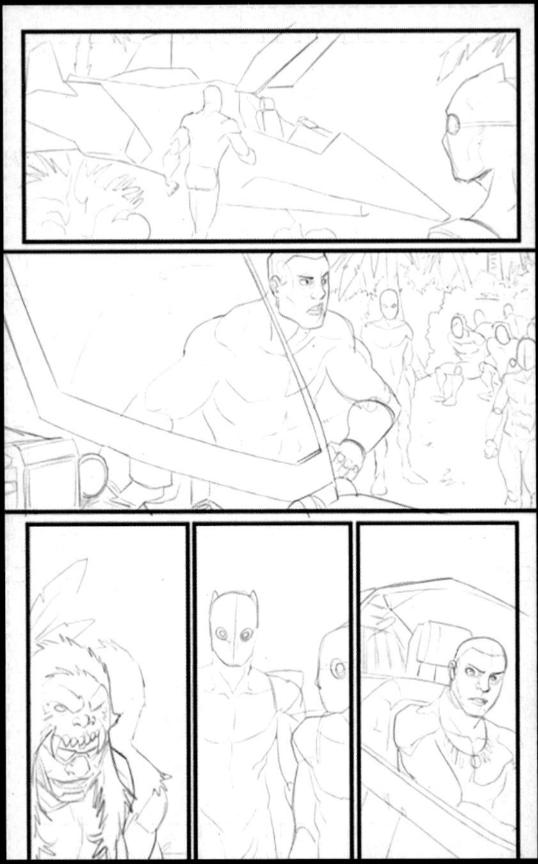

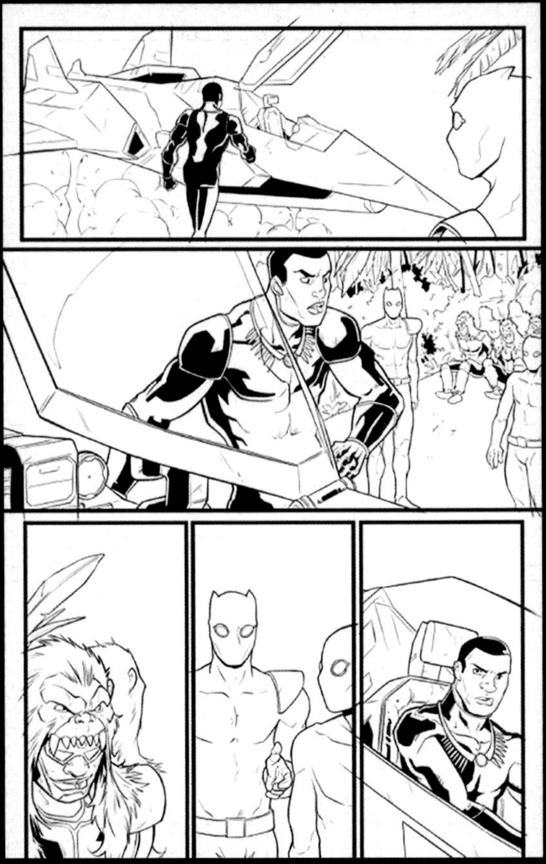

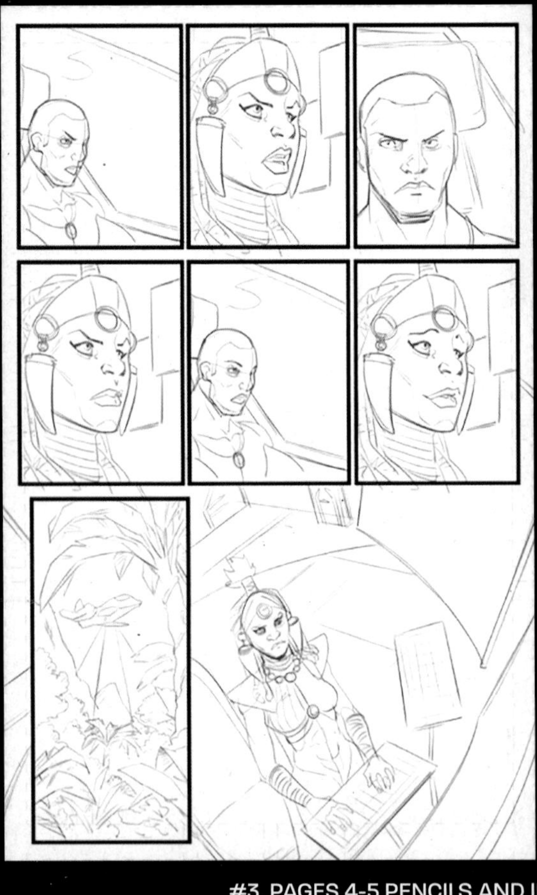

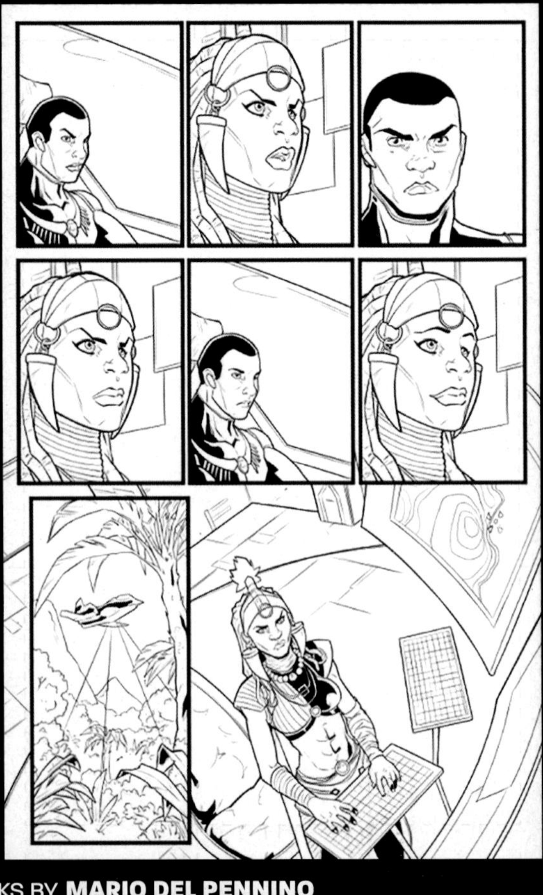

#3, PAGES 4-5 PENCILS AND INKS BY **MARIO DEL PENNINO**